FLAME WARS

THE DISCOURSE OF CYBERCULTURE

EDITED BY MARK DERY

DUKE UNIVERSITY PRESS

DURHAM AND LONDON 1994

© 1994 Duke University Press
Second printing, 1997
All rights reserved
Printed in the United States of America on acid-free paper ∞
"Flame Wars" and "Back to the Future: Interviews with Samuel R. Delany, Greg Tate, and Tricia Rose" both by Mark Dery; chapter 14 of *Synners*, by Pat Cadigan; "A Rape in Cyberspace," by Julian Dibbell; and the graphics in Mark Pauline's article, "Survival Research Laboratories Performs in Austria" are all reprinted by permission of the authors. With the exception of "A Rape in Cyberspace," by Julian Dibbell, and the index, this work appeared originally as volume 92, number 4 of the *South Atlantic Quarterly*.
Library of Congress Cataloging-in-Publication Data
Flame wars: the discourse of cyberculture / edited by Mark Dery.
p.   cm.
Includes bibliographical references and index.
ISBN 0-8223-1531-9 (acid-free paper) : $39.95
— ISBN 0-8223-1540-8 (acid-free paper) : $13.95
1. Computers and civilization.   2. Artificial intelligence.
3. Internet (Computer network).   I. Dery, Mark.
QA76.9.c66F55   1994
306.1—dc20   94-24517

CONTENTS

MARK DERY

FLAME WARS

Flame wars, in compu-slang, are vitriolic on-line exchanges. Often, they are conducted publicly, in discussion groups clustered under thematic headings on electronic bulletin boards, or—less frequently—in the form of poison pen letters sent via E-mail to private mailboxes. John A. Barry's definition of "flame" (n., v.) as "a (usually) electronic diatribe" suggests that such exchanges occasionally take place off-line, although denizens of computer networks are putatively PC junkies and hence likely to prefer virtual invective to FTF (on-line shorthand for "face-to-face") tongue-lashings.[1]

Then, too, the wraithlike nature of electronic communication—the flesh become word, the sender reincarnated as letters floating on a terminal screen—accelerates the escalation of hostilities when tempers flare; disembodied, sometimes pseudonymous combatants tend to feel that they can hurl insults with impunity (or at least without fear of bodily harm). Moreover, E-mail missives or "posts" seem to encourage misinterpretation in the same way that written correspondence sometimes does. Like "snailmail" (compu-slang for conventional letters), electronic messages must be interpreted without the aid of nonverbal cues or what sociolinguist Peter Farb calls "paralanguage"—expressive vocal phenomena such as pitch, intensity, stress, tempo, and volume. The importance of body language is universally conceded, of course; books on the subject are staples of the supermarket check-out stand. Paralanguage, Farb writes, is no less essential to accurate reading: "No protestation by a speaker that he is uttering the truth is equal to the nonverbal confirmation of his credibility contained in the way he says it."[2] Both, significantly, are missing from on-line, text-based interaction, which may account for the umbrage frequently taken at innocently intended remarks. It accounts, too, for the cute use of punctuation to telegraph facial expressions. Here is a key for some commonly used "emoticons," defined in *The New Hacker's Dictionary* as "glyph[s] . . . used to indicate an emotional state" (read them sideways):

> :−) = smiley face; used to underscore a user's good intentions.
>
> :) or, less frequently, :} = variations on the same theme.
>
> ;−) = wink; used to indicate sardonic humor or a tongue-in-cheek quip ("nudge, nudge; wink, wink").
>
> :(= sadness, sometimes used facetiously.

Of course, no signaling system, as one "net surfer" observes, is foolproof:

> Shit happens, especially on the Net, where everyone speaks with flattened affect. I think the attempt to signal authorial intent with little smileys is interesting but futile. They're subject to slippage like any other kind of sign. The bottom line is, anyone who plans to spend time on-line has to grow a few psychic calluses.[3]

Electronic notes, posted in group discussions, differ from hand- or typewritten letters in several significant ways. Like public bathroom graffiti, their authors are sometimes anonymous, often pseudonymous, and almost always strangers. Which is the upside of incorporeal interaction: a technologically enabled, postmulticultural vision of identity disengaged from gender, ethnicity, and other problematic constructions. On line, users can float free of biological and sociocultural determinants, at least to the degree that their idiosyncratic language usage does not mark them as white, black, college-educated, a high-school dropout, and so on. "There is no visual contact, no hearing of accents," says Wayne Gregori, a thirty-five-year-old computer consultant who runs SFNet. "People are judged on the content of what they say."[4]

Posts are read and responded to by computer users scattered across the Internet, the global meta-network that comprises information services such as Bitnet; the private, academic, and government laboratories interwoven by NSFNET (the National Science Foundation Network); mainstream networks such as America On-line and CompuServe; and smaller, more esoteric bulletin boards like San Francisco's WELL (Whole Earth 'Lectronic Link) and New York's MindVOX. (Mitch Kapor, founder of the Lotus Development Corporation, once compared the Internet to a "library where all of the books are dumped on the floor in no particular order."[5]) But unlike profundities scrawled on rest-room stalls (which always seem, somehow, as if they belong on the walls of Pompeian ruins), on-line conversations exhibit a curious half-life; as the reader scrolls downscreen, scanning the lively back-and-forth of a discussion that may go back weeks, months, or even years, he experiences the puns, philippics, true confessions, rambling dissertations, and Generation X-er one-liners as if they were taking place in real time—which, for the reader watching them flow past on his screen, they are.

On occasion, one might stumble onto a flame war, although verbal brawling lowers the tone of colloquia and is therefore frowned upon. In the WELL's *Mondo 2000* conference, users take their disputes outside the topic, into the virtual version of the back alley— a topic-cum-boxing ring called "Flame Box," where they may roll up their sleeves and pummel each other witless. Witlessness, in fact, was the order of the day in the flame war I witnessed, where squabblers seemed to specialize in a baroque slackerbabble related to the mock-Shakespearean put-downs used by Alex on his droogies in *A*

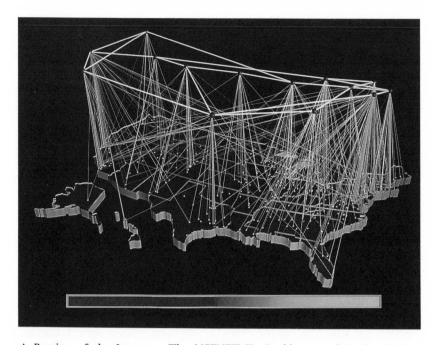

A Portion of the Internet: The NSFNET T1 Backbone and Regional Networks. This image is a visualization study of inbound traffic measured in
billions of bytes on the NSFNET T1 backbone for September 1991. Image
created by Donna Cox and Robert Patterson, National Center for Supercom-
puting Applications, University of Illinois at Urbana-Champaign. Reprinted
with permission.

Clockwork Orange: "Look, you syphilitic bovine harpy," "You heav-
ing purulent mammoth," "Get thine swampy effluvia away from me,
you twitching gelatinous yolk of rancid smegma," and on, and on.
"This standoff will probably end in Koreshian glory," predicted one
user, with thinly disguised relish.

In some ways, flame wars are a less ritualized, cybercultural
counterpart to the African-American phenomenon known as "the
dozens," in which duelists one-up each other with elaborate, sometimes rhyming gibes involving the sexual exploits of each other's
mothers. At their best, flame wars give way to tour-de-force jeremiads

called "rants"—demented soliloquies that elevate soapbox demagoguery to a guerrilla art form. Characterized by fist-banging punctuation, emphatic capitals, and the kill-'em-all-and-let-God-sort-'em-out rhetoric patented by Hunter S. Thompson, rants are spiritual kin to Antonin Artaud's blasphemous screeds and the Vorticist harangues in Wyndham Lewis's *Blast*. Here is a classic, written by a female user who calls herself "outrider":

> Never give in, never submit. Or just never go out of your house anymore. In twenty years this will be Life: stay home all the time because it's too dangerous to go out/you can't eat red meat in public/or sugar either/or grease/and you damn sure can't smoke; get all stimuli, info, human contact, groceries, money, etc. on your computer. All materials will be delivered by heavily armed people in tanks: they must cross the moat filled with piranha, crocodiles, and weird water-borne disease organisms, and also pass the security check that keeps them from getting Swiss-cheesed by the remote control firepower in the gun turrets at the razorwire perimeter, then they have to pass the DNA identity scanner at the last portal—and they absolutely refuse ALL TIPS AND GRATUITIES. After a pleasant meal of micronuked frozen blah, you can jump onto the Net and read the Daily Horros in the form of movingpicto-news; go to the library and download the original French version of *Madame Bovary* and a decent French dictionary. Read in the comfort of your cozy warm bed, safe behind triple-wall steel constructed building. Pet your cat/dog. Clean your arsenal. Sleep. Dream of a more lifelike life . . . remember the olden days when you could walk outside in the Night and go places, when you could drive safely from here to there . . . go back to sleep.[6]

This special issue's title is intentionally ironic. The tone, as in most intellectual discourse, is decorous; there are no flame wars here, and no rants in the proper sense (although Tricia Rose's inspired peroration on feminist mothers as "the most dangerous muthafuckahs out there," with its call for "feminist women to have as much power and as many babies as they want to, creating universes of feminist children," comes close). Even so, the compu-slang title reminds us that our interaction with the world around us is increasingly mediated by computer technology, and that, bit by digital bit, we are being "Borged," as devotees of *Star Trek: The Next Generation* would have it—transformed into cyborgian hybrids of technology and biology through our ever-more-frequent interactions with machines, or with one another *through* technological interfaces.

(According to Clark Fife, who works at New York's Forbidden Planet sci-fi bookstore and memorabilia shop, a cap-and-T-shirt set produced by a merchandiser to capitalize on the inexplicable appeal of the Borg—implacable *Star Trek* villains who function as a "hive mind," or collective entity, and whose bleached flesh is interpenetrated by fetishistic high-tech prostheses—have proven wildly popular. According to Fife, the Borg are popular because they resonate with the cyberpunk sensibility and because "they're symbols of technological victimization that appeal to people." Simultaneously, their cultish following bespeaks a pervasive desire among sci-fi readers, *Star Trek* fans, and other members of fringe technoculture to sheathe the body in an impenetrable carapace, render it invincible through mechatronic augmentation[7]—a hypostatization, perhaps, of a creeping body-loathing congruent with the growing awareness that wires are twined through all of our lives, that our collective future is written on confetti-sized flakes of silicon.)

Jejune though they may seem, flame wars merit serious consideration; offering ample evidence of the subtle ways in which on-line group psychology is shaped by the medium itself, these subcultural practices offer a precognitive glimpse of mainstream culture a few years from now, when ever-greater numbers of Americans will be part-time residents in virtual communities. As Gareth Branwyn notes in "Compu-Sex: Erotica for Cybernauts," the "rate of growth for new computer networks joining the Internet is 25 percent *every three months*," an astonishing statistic that attests to the explosion of interest in electronic interconnectedness. Approximately 10 million people frequent electronic bulletin boards, and their ranks are growing by the score.[8] A WELL employee told me, shortly after the appearance of *Time* magazine's 8 February 1993 cover story on cyberpunk, that the bulletin board's population—already 3,000 strong—had swollen by several thousand more. "People call and ask, 'Is this the cyberspace?'" he said.

Indeed, it is—"the desert of the real," where the shreds of the territory, to invoke Baudrillard, "are slowly rotting across the map."[9] Those who spend an inordinate amount of time connected by modem via telephone lines to virtual spaces often report a peculiar sensation of "thereness"; prowling from one conference to another, eavesdropping on discussions in progress, bears an uncanny resemblance to wandering the hallways of some labyrinthine mansion, poking one's head into room after room. "One of the most striking features of the WELL," observed a user named Ioca, "is that it actually creates a feeling of 'place.' I'm staring at a computer screen. But the feeling really is that I'm 'in' something; I'm some 'where.'"[10]

Virtual-reality interfaces, facilitated by high-bandwidth information highways of the sort proposed by the Clinton administration, will concretize Ioca's "feeling of 'place'"; at last, there *will* be a "there" there. Using current developments as a springboard, one might imagine users in head-tracking 3-D goggles, a quadriphonic sound system embedded in the goggles' earpieces. As the user looks up, down, or from side to side, the computer's high-speed program animates the world—and its soundscape—accordingly, creating the illusion of a 360-degree, real-time hyperreality. Howard Rheingold completes the sensorium with the sense of touch, imagining high-tech body stockings that "know" where their wearer's limbs are in space. The inner surfaces of these suits would be covered with

> an array of intelligent sensor-effectors—a mesh of tiny tactile detectors coupled to vibrators of varying degrees of hardness, hundreds of them per square inch, that can receive and transmit a realistic sense of tactile presence.[11]

Plugging into the global telephone network, the user connects with similarly equipped individuals or groups. All appear to each other as believable fictions: lifelike characters inhabiting a three-dimensional environment. (Reality, here, is mutable, evoking Greg Tate's mock-serious vision of the defaced, re-faced Michael Jackson as "harbinger of a transracial tomorrow where genetic deconstruction has become the norm and Narcissism wears the face of all human Desire"; gender, ethnicity, age, and other variables can be altered with a keystroke or two.[12]) "You run your hand over your partner's clavicle," imagines Rheingold, "and 6,000 miles away, an array of effectors [is] triggered, in just the right sequence, at just the right frequency, to convey the touch exactly the way you wish it to be conveyed."[13]

It must be noted, however, that virtual embodiment of the Rheingoldian sort is an early to mid-twenty-first-century technology. It would require a global fiber-optic network in concert with massively parallel supercomputers capable of monitoring and controlling the numberless sensors and effectors fitted to every hill and dale, plane and protuberance of the body's topography. Then, too, a reticulated fabric of safe, high-speed micro-vibrators is only a mirage, given the state of the art in current technologies.

Nonetheless, there is more to cyberculture than cyberspace. Cyberculture, as I defined it in an earlier essay, is

> a far-flung, loosely knit complex of sublegitimate, alternative, and oppositional subcultures [whose common project is the subversive use of technocommodities, often framed by radical body politics]. . . . [Cyberculture] is divisible into several major territories: visionary technology, fringe science, avant-garde art, and pop culture.[14]

Fredric Jameson has noted the correspondence between cyberpunk novelist William Gibson's cyberspace and "the world space of multinational capital," where vast sums are blipped through fiber-optic bundles, and has called for a cognitive cartography, "a pedagogical political culture which seeks to endow the individual subject with some new heightened sense of its place in the global system."[15] A map of the increasingly virtual geography in which we find ourselves, suggests Jameson, is essential in "grasp[ing] our positioning as individual and collective subjects and regain[ing] a capacity to act and struggle which is at present neutralized by our spatial as well as our social confusion."[16] Compasses and sextants in hand, the writers in this collection embark on Jameson's project, mindful (if intuitively) of one WELL-dweller's corrective:

This medium gives us the possibility (illusory as it may be) that we can build a world unmediated by authorities and experts. The roles of reader, writer, and critic are so quickly interchangeable that they become increasingly irrelevant in a community of co-creation such as the WELL (cf. Benjamin's "revolutionary literature"; on-line far supersedes the newspaper as a medium in which the reader is likely to also be the writer). I really have no objection to someone who has come into our community, lived here and participated, analyzing [his] experience and trying to put it into perspective. I think the objection to the "critics" who are now fawning over cyberthis and cyberthat is that they are perceived as intellectual carpetbaggers who don't bother to learn the terrain before they create the map.[17]

Notes

I am greatly indebted to Gareth Branwyn, a longtime resident of virtual communities and serious thinker about cyberculture. His many insights, articulated in lengthy conversations on- and off-line, proved invaluable in the writing of this essay, as did his willingness to fact-check the finished work, sparing me the fate of the "intellectual carpetbagger."

1 John A. Barry, *Technobabble* (Cambridge, MA, 1991), 243.

2 Peter Farb, *Word Play* (New York, 1975), 69.

3 Anonymous correspondent, in a private E-mail letter to the author, 17 April 1993.

4 Katherine Bishop, "The Electronic Coffeehouse," *New York Times*, 2 August 1992, V3.

5 Robert E. Calem, "The Network of All Networks," *New York Times*, 6 December 1992, F12.

6 WELL-user known as "outrider," in the topic "Flame Box," in the *Mondo 2000* conference, 29 March 1993.

7 The mirror image of "electromechanical," "mechatronic" is a Japanese coinage; meaning "the fusion of machinery and electronics," it stresses the importance of the former in the equation. See Frederik L. Schodt, *Inside the Robot Kingdom: Japan, Mechatronics, and the Coming Robotopia* (New York, 1988), 42–43, 49.

8 Judith Berck, "All About Electronic Bulletin Boards," *New York Times*, 19 July 1992, F12.

9 Jean Baudrillard, "The Precession of Simulacra," in *Simulations*, trans. Paul Foss, Paul Patton, and Philip Beitchman (New York, 1983), 2.

10 Judith Moore, "The Way of the WELL," in *The Monthly*, 1990.

11 Howard Rheingold, *Virtual Reality* (New York, 1991), 346.

12   Greg Tate, "I'm White!: What's Wrong with Michael Jackson?" in *Flyboy in the Buttermilk: Essays on Contemporary America* (New York, 1992), 95.

13   Rheingold, *Virtual Reality*, 346.

14   Mark Dery, "Cyberculture," *SAQ* 91 (Summer 1992): 509.

15   Cited in *Storming the Reality Studio: A Casebook of Cyberpunk and Postmodern Fiction*, ed. Larry McCaffery (Durham, NC, 1991), 228.

16   Ibid.

17   William Rolf Knutson, a computer programmer, fiction writer, and occasional *Mondo 2000* contributor, in a private E-mail letter to the author, 25 March 1993.

VIVIAN SOBCHACK

NEW AGE MUTANT NINJA HACKERS:

READING *MONDO 2000*

In early 1991, *Artforum International* asked me to write a short essay that would "make sense" of *Mondo 2000*—a strange but "hot" new magazine that had happened their way from Berkeley, California.[1] At first read, *M2* seemed, somehow, important in its utopian plunge into the user-friendly future of better living not only through a chemistry left over from the 1960s, but also through personal computing, bio—and nano—technologies, virtual realities, and an unabashed commitment to consumerism. Cofounded in 1989 by "domineditrix" Queen Mu (a.k.a. Alison Kennedy) and editor-in-chief R. U. Sirius (a.k.a. Ken Goffman), *M2* had evolved from two previous "underground" publications—*High Frontiers* (a "space age newspaper of psychedelic science, human potential, irreverence, and modern art") and *Reality Hackers* (more of the same)—and, at the time, had published only three issues.[2]

≡≡≡≡

Surfing the Edge: Early Life on the New Frontier. Proclaiming its own position as "surfing" the "New Edge" of a novel and electronically configured social formation called "cyberculture," *M2* dubbed its (mostly male) readers "mondoids" and invited them to cruise the datascape, ride the electronic range, hip-hop their laptop, vacation in virtual reality, dine on designer foods, jack in to synchroenergizers and off with smart drugs guaranteed to enhance their brains and sex lives. Here, it is crucial to point out that *M2* provokes the kind of prose I've written and you've just read, and poses a real dilemma for the scholar who would dare to analyze and/or criticize it. On the one hand, academic style would be ridiculous and ironically at odds with the technofrenzy it claimed to comprehend; on the other, a more vernacular style keeps veering toward the mimetic use of alliteration, hyperbole, "hipness," and, worst of all, what must be called "prose bites"—in sum, ironically aping *M2*'s own easy indulgences at the same time it would call them into account. Constructing this "double bind," *M2* sits squarely, and safely, on the postmodern fence, covering its postmodern ass, using irony not only to back off from a too-serious commitment to its own stance, but also to unsettle the grounds from which it might be criticized.

Indeed, *M2*'s prose is almost always self-consciously ironic, often coy or frenzied, and even sometimes witty. Articles and interviews in the first three issues bore such titles as "Hyperwebs: 21st Century Media," "High Tech High Life—William Gibson & Timothy Leary in Conversation," "A Man & His Dog: Cryonics Today," "Cyberspace 1999: The Shell, the Image and Now the Meat," "Some Good Things to Say about Computer Viruses," "Hip Hop as Cyber Apocalypse," "ATM's & the Rise of the Hacker Leisure Class," "Teledildonics: Reach Out and Touch Someone," "Covert Design & Holographic Clothing: A Look at 21st Century Fashion," and "Designer Beings: In Conversation with Durk Pearson & Sandy Shaw" (regular contributors who sell "designer foods" and, as the magazine puts it, talk about "saving one's skin" and the latest in "intelligence increase agents"). Joining William Gibson (author of *Neuromancer*, the seminal cyberpunk SF novel) and the ever-mutable Timothy Leary as gurus of *M2*'s New Edge were Jaron Lanier (promoter of virtual reality systems), SF writers Bruce Sterling, John Shirley, Rudy Rucker, and Vernor Vinge, the singular William Burroughs, John Perry Barlow (a former lyricist for the Grateful Dead, "electronic frontier" advocate, and major supporter of the Republican party), and a variety of assorted heroes and (fewer) heroines who had—supposedly in the cause of democratic populism—hacked, cracked, and phone-phreaked their way into the corporate-controlled datascape and found it good to set (and get) information free.

Surrounding the editorials, articles, columns, interviews, and illustrations were an extraordinary collection of advertisements, both New Age and New Edge. For sale were assorted books (mostly by Leary and John Lilly), cassette tapes ("Fractal Music," which lets you "experience the elusive mysteries of fractal geometry with your ears!" and the "DNA Suite: Music of the Double Helix," which answers the question, "What is the sound of the genetic code?"), and videos (the "Thinking Allowed" collection of "in-depth, intimate conversations with writers, teachers and explorers on the leading edge of knowledge & discovery, hosted by Dr. Jeffrey Mishlove"). One could also buy computer programs and CD-ROMs (one containing the *Whole Earth Catalog*), a Danish-modern looking Flogiston chair ("for flying in cyberspace"), *Mondo 2000* T-shirts, and the aforementioned "Synchro-ENERGIZER" (a "high-tech computer-driven brain balancer" whose headphones and goggles provide "a salutary alternative to drugs in the 90's for dealing with stress, pain, dependencies, and burnout"). There were ads for orgone energy blankets, UFO detectors, OxyHigh, OxyVital, and OxyBliss ("Get High on Oxygen!"), Odwalla "juice for humans" (touting "Fresh Juice Kinetics"), and, surprisingly not out of place despite its hookup with the scholarly academy, Avital Ronell's *The Telephone Book* (advertised by the University of Nebraska Press with the boldface slogan: "It's for you"). And, finally, although the covers of the first three issues I was given were less glossy than they were later to become, from the beginning they tended to feature women's heads floating somewhere in the ether of an erotic wet(ware) dream.

What was being enacted here? What was really being sold? And an equally significant question, unasked at the time and to which I shall eventually return: Why were *Artforum* and I so fascinated by this *Mad* magazine for technophiles? Indeed, written by Queen Mu and R. U. Sirius and worth quoting in its entirety, the first editorial was an embarrassingly adolescent rallying cry, almost poignant in its impossibly generalized, but utopian yearnings:

> *Mondo 2000* is here to cover the leading edge in hyperculture. We'll bring you the latest in human/technological interactive mutational forms *as* they happen.
>
> We're talking Cyber-Chautauqua: bringing cyberculture to the people! Artificial awareness modules. Visual music. Vidscan magazines. Brain-boosting technologies. William Gibson's Cyberspace Matrix—fully realized!
>
> Our scouts are out there on the frontier sniffing the breeze and guess what? All the old war horses are dead. Eco-fundamentalism is out, conspiracy theory is démodé, drugs are obsolete. There's a new whiff of apocalypticism across the land. A general sense that we are living at a very special juncture in the evolution of the species.
>
> Back in the sixties, Carly Simon's brother wrote a book called *What to Do Until the Apocalypse Comes*. It was about going back to the land, growing tubers and soybeans, reading by oil lamps. Finite possibilities and small is beautiful. It was *boring*!
>
> Yet the pagan innocence and idealism that was the sixties remains and continues to exert its fascination on today's kids. Look at old footage of *Woodstock* and you wonder: where have all those wide-eyed, ecstatic, orgasm-slurping kids gone? They're all across the land, dormant like deeply buried perennials. But their mutated nucleotides have given us a whole new generation of sharpies, mutants and superbrights and in them we must put our faith—and power.
>
> The cybernet is in place. If fusion *is* real, we'll find out about it fast. The old information élites are crumbling. The kids are at the controls.
>
> This magazine is about what to do until the *millennium* comes. We're talking about Total Possibilities. Radical assaults on the limits of biology, gravity and time. The end of Artificial Scarcity. The dawn of a new humanism. High-jacking technology for personal empowerment, fun and games. Flexing those synapses!

Stoking those neuropeptides! Making Bliss States our normal waking consciousness. *Becoming* the Bionic Angel.

But things are going to get weirder before they get better. The Rupture before the Rapture. Social and economic dislocation that will make the Cracked 80's look like summer camp. So, in the words of the immortal Rudy Rucker, "Hang ten on the edge" because the 90's are going to be quite a ride!

Consistent with its vagaries of commitment, however, by the next issue pathos had given way to ironic self-awareness and a supposedly tougher line of virtual (political) commitment. *M2*'s second editorial aligned itself not only with the fight against AIDS and neo-Luddite eco-fundamentalists (while announcing plans for a future "Earth Also" issue), it also celebrated the seduction of the Soviets by "free-wheelin' consumer hypercapitalism" and promoted saving both "ourselves and our comrades to the East from a 21st Century legalistic, megacorporate, one-world, peace-on-earth" through luxuriating in a "cynicism" allowed by "cyber-decadence." Certainly, there was no pathos, no poignant and overgeneralized yearning, but rather a transmuted form of cynicism in *M2*'s clear promotion of high-tech consumerism:

> Call it a hyper-hip wet dream, but the information and communications technology industry requires a new *active* consumer or it's going to stall. . . . This is one reason why we are amplifying the mythos of the sophisticated, high-complexity, fast lane/real-time, intelligent, active and creative reality hacker. . . . A nation of TV couch potatoes (not to mention embittered self-righteous radicals) is not going to demand access to the next generation of the extensions of man.

Some of the fascination exerted by *M2* emerges from this shape-shifting, political and tonal "morphing," from the fancy footwork it takes to resolve the essential *ambivalence* of mondoid desire. Thus it is particularly telling that the first two editorials are in such contrary tonal relation to each other, and that they resolve the utopianism of the first with the cynicism of the second by making cynicism itself utopian.

Mondo cover number 9. Copyright © 1993 by Bart Nagel.

The New Gender Euphorics

Above: Jade wears an elegant ball gown designed by Kelvin Alejandro 415.922.8261

Heide and Stafford in suits from Thirtyone-Eighty

Fashion page from Mondo 2000. Copyright © 1993 by Bart Nagel.

This is, then, an optimistic cynicism. Reading *M2*, one might think that we live in the best of all possible worlds, or, perhaps, more precisely, that we live best only in possible worlds. *M2*'s ambivalence of desire, its nostalgia for the real possibilities and commitments of the past (the sixties), and its yearning for a real (rather than virtual) experience of the highly mediated present cohere in a peculiarly oxymoronic cosmology of the future. This cosmology explicitly resolves New Edge high-technophilia with New Age and "whole earth" naturalism, spiritualism, and hedonism. And it implicitly resolves the sixties' countercultural "guerrilla" political action and social consciousness with a particularly privileged, selfish, consumer-oriented, and technologically dependent libertarianism. Hiding under the guise of populism, the liberation politics touted in the pages of *M2* are the stuff of a romantic, swashbuckling, irresponsible individualism that fills the dreams of "mondoids" who, by day, sit at computer consoles working for (and becoming) corporate America. The Revenge of the Nerds is that they have found ways to figure themselves to the rest of us (particularly those of us intrigued by, but generally ignorant of, electronics) as sexy, hip, and heroic, as New Age Mutant Ninja Hackers (the name I gave them in my column for *Artforum*).

Focusing on electronic, quasi-disembodied forms of kinesis ("safe" travel without leaving your desk), interaction ("safe" sociality without having to reveal your identity or "true name"[3]), and eroticism ("safe" sex without risking an exchange of bodily fluids), the New Age Mutant Ninja Hacker's ambivalent desire to be powerful, heroic, committed, and yet safe within his (computer) shell leads to an oxymoronic mode of being one might describe as *interactive autism*. (This mode of being is briefly, but illuminatingly dramatized in the climactic "virtual reality" sex scene in 1992's *The Lawnmower Man*: while impossibly total sexual coupling occurs in virtual space, the two participants are seen physically separated in the "real" space of the lab, hugging and caressing their *own* data-suited-up bodies.) It is hardly surprising that *M2* privileges virtual reality and all that goes with it—virtual sex ("teledildonics"), virtual politics (which doesn't seem to affect the daily world except by its absence), and virtual community (a hierarchy of hackers, crackers, and phreakers).

Mondo 2000 focuses on the cybernetic union of carbon and silicon, an interactive feedback loop of biological and technological being achieved through the computer. Its raison d'être is the technoerotic celebration of a reality to be found on the far side of the computer screen and in the "neural nets" of a "liberated," disembodied, computerized yet sensate consciousness. This electronically constituted reality and consciousness is achieved through various prostheses that plug the human sensorium into interactive communion with the computer, so that the user transcends—and, all too often in this context, elides—not only his (or her) being in an imperfect human body, but also the imperfect world that we all "really" materially create and physically inhabit. At best, the encounters in virtual reality and cyberspace promoted by *M2* are video games that one can lose without real loss. At worst, they falsely promise a new Eden for cyborg Adams and Eves—enthusiastic participants in some computerized and simulated (in)version of the Back to the Earth movement.

The Cutting Edge: Getting Rid of the Meat. Although I know I have sounded pretty reactionary thus far, it needs stating that the "terminal" transformation of human subjectivity as it enters the electronic technosphere is not necessarily negative in its consequences and implications. Interesting things happen when identity can represent itself, to some extent, as liberated from, for example, normative categories of gender and race. (While she has subsequently tempered her initial enthusiasms, Donna Haraway pointed to these and other liberating possibilities in her seminal article, "A Manifesto for Cyborgs."[4]) As well, even at this early stage of development, the various formations of cyberspace and virtual reality not only provide novel recreational and aesthetic pleasures, but also have practical uses. Simulated worlds stimulate architects, medical researchers, and the air force. From ATMs and the largest electronic banking networks to bar codes and my beloved Powerbook, the datascape is (and has been for some time) as "real"—if not, as *M2* claims, *more* "real"— than the physical space occupied by my physical body. Indeed, elsewhere, I have argued extensively (from a phenomenological perspective) that the lived meaning of space, time, and subjectivity has been radically altered by electronic technologies in an experience that may be described, and cannot be denied.[5]

Nonetheless, the emergence of the celebratory (and generally eco-

nomically privileged) subculture represented by *M2*'s consistent vaca-
tioning in the datascape and in virtual worlds seems to me the mark
of a potentially dangerous and disturbingly miscalculated attempt to
escape the material conditions and specific politics (dare I, in this
context, say the "real" reality?) that have an impact on the present
social fragmentation of American culture, the body's essential mortality, and the planet's increasing fragility. Rather than finding the
gravity (and vulnerability) of human flesh and the finitude of the
earth providing the *material* grounds for ethical responsibility in a
highly technologized world, New Age Mutant Ninja Hackers would
look toward "downloading" their consciousness into the computer,
leaving their "obsolete" bodies (now contemptuously called "meat"
and "wetware") behind, and inhabiting the datascape either as completely disembodied information or as a cadre of "Be All You Can Be,"
invulnerable, invincible, immortal New Age/New Edge cyborgs with
the bodies of Arnold Schwarzenegger (and, for that matter, with his
politics, too).

Writing at a historical moment when the starving or dead bodies
of Somali children and the emaciated or dead bodies wrought by
Bosnia's civil warfare fill our television screens and the displaced
bodies of the homeless fill our streets, it is both comprehensible and
extremely disturbing that *M2*'s supposedly utopian celebration of the
liberating possibilities of the new electronic frontier promotes an ec-
static dream of disembodiment. This is alienation raised to the level
of *ekstasis*: "A being put out of its place." It is also an apolitical fantasy of escape. Historical accounts of virtual reality tell us that one
of the initial project's slogans was "Reality isn't enough anymore,"
but psychoanalytic accounts would more likely tell us that the slogan should be read in its inverse form—that is, "Reality is too much
right now."

Hence the ambivalence of mondoid desire. In a cultural moment
when temporal coordinates are oriented toward technological computation rather than the physical rhythms of the human body, and
spatial coordinates have little meaning for that body beyond its brief
physical occupation of a "here," in a cultural moment when there is
too much perceived risk to living and too much information for both
body and mind to contain and survive, need we wonder at the desire

to transcend the gravity of our situation and to escape where and who we are? It is apposite that one of the smarter articles in the early issues of *M2* philosophically entitles itself "Being in Nothingness," and tells us of the ultimate escape: "Nothing could be more disembodied or insensate than . . . cyberspace. It's like having had your everything amputated." This is dangerous stuff—the stuff that (snuff) dreams are made of. Indeed, *M2* is exceedingly—and apparently indiscriminately—proud that it is dangerous, for, as of its fourth issue, it quoted the preceding sentence as a "come on" to potential subscribers.

Haraway, author of the aforementioned "Manifesto for Cyborgs," has recently recognized the kind of impulses (dis)embodied by the *M2* subculture. In an interview in *Social Text*, she warns against cyborgism insofar as it plugs into dangerous forms of holism:

> Any transcendentalist move is deadly; it produces death, through the fear of it. These holistic, transcendentalist moves promise a way out of history, a way of participating in the God trick. A way of denying mortality.
>
> . . . In the face of the kind of whole earth threat issuing from so many quarters, it's clear that there is a historical crisis. . . . Some deep, inescapable sense of the fragility of the lives that we're leading—that we really do die, that we really do wound each other, that the earth really is finite, that there aren't any other planets out there that we know of that we can live on, that escape-velocity is a deadly fantasy.[6]

The holistic cyborg discourse of *M2* is thus deeply ambivalent about the New Age Mutant Ninja Hacker's technological (inter)face. Its dangerous excesses are constituted from what philosopher Don Ihde, in *Technology and the Lifeworld: From Garden to Earth*, recognizes as the *doubled desire* that exists in our relations with any technology that extends our bodily sensorium and, thereby, our perceptions—be it eyeglasses or microscopes, the camera or the computer. Describing this doubled desire, Ihde tells us that it

> is a wish for total transparency, total embodiment, for the technology to truly "become me." Were this possible, it would be equivalent to there being no technology, for total transparency

would *be* my body and senses; I desire the face-to-face that I would experience without the technology. But that is only one side of the desire. The other side is the desire to have the power, the transformation that the technology makes available. Only by using the technology is my bodily power enhanced and magnified by speed, through distance, or by any of the other ways in which technologies change my capacities. These capacities are always *different* from my naked capacities. The desire is, at best, contradictory. I want the transformation that the technology allows, but I want it in such a way that I am basically unaware of its presence. I want it in such a way that it becomes me. Such a desire both secretly *rejects* what technologies are and overlooks the transformational effects which are necessarily tied to human-technology relations. This illusory desire belongs equally to pro- and anti-technology interpretations of technology.

M2 ends up revealing negative as well as positive feelings about the amazing prostheses offered by electronic technology in general, and computers in particular. The New Age Mutant Ninja Hackers represent and embody this contradictory desire which is, at one and the same time, both utopian and dystopian, self-preservational and self-exterminating. New Age Mutant Ninja Hackers wish to become the machines that extend them and to cede their human flesh to the mortality it is heir to. But they simultaneously wish to "escape the newly extended body of technological engagement" and to reclaim experience through the flesh. Hence the New Edge reverts back to the New Age. Hence the extraordinary emphasis on kinesis and sex. *M2's* fourth issue features a piece called "The Carpal Tunnel of Love," in which Mike Saenz, developer of cybererotic software, tells us: "Virtual reality to the uninitiated, they just don't get it. But they warm immediately to the idea of Virtual Sex. . . . I think lust motivates technology. The first personal robots, let's face it, are not going to be bought to bring people drinks."

As Ihde points out, this double desire surrounding technology is constituted from "a fundamental ambivalence toward the very human creation of our own earthly tools." That is, "the user wants what the technology gives but does not want the limits, the transformations that a technologically extended body implies."[7] What is particularly dangerous about *M2* is that—despite its seeming self-consciousness— this ambivalence is unrecognized, if not completely disavowed. *M2's* dizzying pro-technology rhetoric hides its anti-technology dreams; its self-deception promotes deadly, terminal confusions between meat and hardware.

Negotiating the Edge: Merchandising Mondoid Libertarianism. Case, the maverick protagonist of William Gibson's cyberbible, *Neuromancer*, stands as the cult hero of those who voraciously read *M2* and imagine themselves cruising the datascape and sensuously experiencing the intense electronic high of information overload. That audience, according to an interview with editor R. U. Sirius,

> tends to be people in their twenties. A lot of computer kids, the kind of people who would go to performance works by, say, Survival Research Lab, and that sort of thing. We get a lot of old hippies too, who love the magazine and read it. People in their thirties, people in the computer industry. A large portion of our audience is successful business people in the computer industry, and in industry in general, because industry in the United States is high-tech.[8]

Envisioning themselves as individual and idiosyncratic (at the same time that they are apparently incorporated), as cowboy hackers (there aren't too many cowgirls), most *M2* readers must dream not only of electric sheep, but also of bucking corporate systems, riding the electronic range, and cutting through the barbed-wire master codes to keep information free, available to all (that is, all who have computer access and skills). Promoting future utopian "networks" in which everyone at every level of society is connected and plugged in to everyone else, the New Age Mutant Ninja Hackers, in the midst of this communitarian dream, have no real idea of how to achieve it. Instead, they privilege the individual—modeling themselves after some combination of *Neuromancer's* world-weary Case (and/or *Blade Runner's* Rick Deckard), entrepreneurial technomaverick Steve Jobs, and countercultural guerrillas who muck up "the system" and, at their worst, bear some relation to the very same eco-terrorists for whom *M2* expresses contempt.

M2 occasionally (and mostly for effect) declares itself anarchic and/or populist, but its position is really (or, in this case, virtually) libertarian. It stands against big government and big corporations (the villains of most of its purportedly political pieces), but ultimately seems in favor of a "night-watchman" state—one that functions minimally, but just enough to guarantee its citizens' "natural" rights to the "good life"—in *M2*'s case, hacking, drugs, sex, rock & roll (and probably guns). Although it dreams of a communitarian utopia, its major impulses are to secure maximum individualism and privatization, and it is blind to the historical structures that go beyond individual motivation and "do-it-yourself" entrepreneurship in determining "winners" and "losers." In this regard, *M2* talks about "access" in a vacuum and never relates it to economics or race or gender.

Consider the following description of cyberpunk "attitudes that seem to be related" (according to one of *M2*'s regular writers, Gareth Branwyn):

> *Information wants to be free.
> *Access to computers and anything which may teach you something about how the world works should be unlimited and total.
> *Always yield to the hands-on imperative.
> *Mistrust Authority.
> *Do It Yourself.
> *Fight the Power.
> *Feed the noise back into the system.
> *Surf the edge.[9]

This bumper-sticker libertarianism is neither progressive nor democratic. And, despite all the rhetoric of "networking," it is hardly communitarian. (A list of features of the "cyberpunk worldview" includes, at most, the notion of "small groups" as in: "Small groups of individual 'console cowboys' can wield tremendous power over governments, corporations, etc."[10]) Its ideolect is one that "winners" in the modern world adopt. Its dreams of personal freedom and its utter faith in self-help are grounded in privilege and the status quo: male privilege, white privilege, economic privilege, educational privilege, first-world privilege. Its dreams are grounded in the freedom to buy, and—especially—the freedom to sell. Its posture of rugged individualism (clothed by L. L. Bean) and personal transformation also has something to do with freedom from (yet within) the Protestant work ethic. Its entrepreneurial enthusiasms promote the easy attainment of spiritual grace and personal fortune through a transformative technology that takes the long hours of *bildung* out of the *bildungsroman*. As Rudy Rucker puts it:

> [N]one of us hackers or writers or rappers or samplers or mappers or singers or users of the tech are in it solely for the Great Work—no, us users be here for our own good. We work for the Great Work because the work is fun. The hours are easy and the pay is good. And the product we make is viable. It travels and it gets over.[11]

Merchandising the Edge: The Seductions of Selling Out. At the time I wrote my essay for *Artforum*, M2 had published only three issues and was already burnishing the glossy surface of its covers and contemplating a wider audience. In 1991, arousing the attention of both the media and a range of scholars interested (for various reasons) in contemporary SF, new technologies, and cultural studies, M2 was quick to see the academic writing on the wall. That first academically based advertisement for Ronell's *Telephone Book* was followed up in the glossy fourth issue with Professor Avital Ronell herself (opining on "Hallucinogenres"), posed glamorously in a head shot to die for (what was to become part of M2's signature style of male homage to smart women: part *Cosmopolitan*, part *Playboy*). Subsequent issues increasingly played to (and co-opted) the *Rolling Stone* crowd, featuring pieces on rock music and high-tech fashion, but they also continued their seduction of what a friend of mine has called the "leather theorists": Mark Dery began a column called "Guerrilla Semiotics" (which presupposed that mondoids knew what semiotics was), and in a later article called "Terrorvision" he explained Foucault's panopticon; Professor Larry McCaffery became an interviewer, while Professor Constance Penley became an interviewee. The fifth issue, in fact, conveyed the capitulation of *M2*'s libertarian worldview to its commercial smarts by featuring an unexpected "Acid Take on Camille Paglia," the kind of gun-toting academic and sexual persona one would have assumed the magazine would embrace—given their mutual rugged-individualist and sexist visions.[12] Indeed, the eighth issue is more blatantly into female bodies than ever, offering "Deee-lectronix: All New! All Nude! The Mondo Tech Centerfold!," a high-tech piece of erotica entitled "The Woman's Home Companion," a fashion layout (all dripping with a mix of irony and cum), and one of those respectful head jobs on singer Diamanda Galás. This glossiest issue yet, however, seemed to be losing most of its funky and high-tech advertisers.

I shouldn't have worried. Just in time for Christmas 1992, priced at $20, *Mondo 2000: A User's Guide to the New Edge* appeared as the coolest gift around. *Entertainment Weekly* gave it an "A" (compared to the "C" earned by *Jane & Michael Stern's Encyclopedia of Pop Culture: An A to Z of Who's Who and What's What, From Aerobics and Bubble Gum to* Valley of the Dolls *and Moon Unit Zappa*, which seemed to them like "a drag on a moldy roach").[13] The beautiful volume is a true Lover's Discourse of Cyberculture, an ecstatic New Edge Empire of Signs. Arranged alphabetically—from Aphrodisiacs to Zines (with "Cyberpunk, Virtual Reality, Wetware, Artificial Life, Techno-erotic Paganism, and More" in between)—are encyclopedia entries explaining it all in an extraordinarily appealing (and accessible) graphic version of hypertext: cross-referenced and -referencing, doubled and irregular columns, color-coded, beautifully illustrated (with, for *M2*, a certain reticent good taste), and served up on a glossy, slick, slippery paper that I admit I love to touch.

Throughout this sumptuous, sensuous tour of the New Edge (which has, in this volume, been considerably blunted, rounded, and contoured to fit the coffee table), in the midst of phrases or after a referenced book title, there appears that familiar green Masonic "God's Eye" that gives the dollar bill its particular mystique. This symbol, as R. U. Sirius says in his user's guide to the *User's Guide*, indicates "a product listed in the MONDO Shopping Mall" at the back of the book (with the extensive bibliography that now offhandedly lists Foucault and Derrida as well as Timothy Leary). The Shopping Mall, according to R. U. Sirius, is

> an access guide to *products*—yes, things you can *buy*. Educational toys, you could call them—to advance your understanding or just seduce you into joining this cultural New Thing. *Shopping Mall?!!!!* We could have called it something less crass: maybe "Tools for Access," like our respectable older cousins in the *Whole Earth Catalog*. But why be pretentious about it? We are present at the apotheosis of commercial culture. Commerce is the ocean that information swims in. And as we shall see in the Guide, the means of exchange in commercial culture is now *pure information.*[14]

Information has never been pure. And it is always materialized. I wonder as I hold this book, feel the sleekness of its pages, and the sensuousness of its artwork, why and how I am seduced again, so quickly, by something with which I have become so bored and at which I have become so angry. I only know that it's incredibly easy to be seduced by the easy, particularly when it parades as the complex. It would be restful to give in to my academic-doing-cultural-studies' sense of my own hip comprehension of "what's happening," to think myself "bad" rather than merely respected, to have fun wallowing about in my own prose. It would be wonderful to complacently protect myself from all-comers with an all-consuming irony, to transform my being without work, but with good lighting and makeup. I can't speak for *Artforum* or, for that matter, *SAQ*, but I am drawn to *Mondo 2000*, I realize, because it appeals to the worst in me, the laziest in me, the cheapest in me. In my sober and responsible moments, I bemoan our culture's loss of gravity and fear the very real social dangers of disembodied ditziness, but holding this Christmas present to myself, all I want is a head shot.

Notes

1   "What in the World: Vivian Sobchack on New Age Mutant Ninja Hackers," *Artforum International* (April 1991): 24–26. Portions of the present essay were originally published in this article.

2   Unless otherwise noted, references and quotations that follow are from the first three issues of *Mondo 2000*—1 (1989), its cover indicating Fall #7 (ostensibly as a continuation of *Reality Hackers*, which is figured in the illustration on the front cover), 2 (Summer 1990), and 3 (Winter 1991).

3   Reference here is to *True Names*, an SF novella published during the emergence of cyberpunk SF and concerned with a group of hackers whose computer pseudonyms hide their "true names" and physical identities, the knowledge of which constitutes the greatest threat and the greatest intimacy. See Vernor Vinge, *True Names and Other Dangers* (New York, 1984).

4   Donna Haraway, "A Manifesto for Cyborgs: Science, Technology and Socialist Feminism in the 1980s," *Socialist Review* 15 (1985): 65–107.

5   Vivian Sobchack, "Toward a Phenomenology of Cinematic and Electronic Presence: The Scene of the Screen," *Post Script* 10 (Fall 1990): 50–59. See also "Post-futurism," in my *Screening Space: The American Science Fiction Film* (New York, 1987), 223–305; and *The Address of the Eye: A Phenomenology of Film Experience* (Princeton, 1992), 300–302.

6   Constance Penley and Andrew Ross, "Cyborgs at Large: Interview with Donna Haraway," *Social Text* 25/26 (1991): 20.

7   Don Ihde, *Technology and the Lifeworld: From Garden to Earth* (Bloomington, 1990), 75–76.

8   R. U. Sirius, quoted in "Sex, Drugs, & Cyberspace," *Express: The East Bay's Free Weekly*, 28 September 1990, 12.

9   Gareth Branwyn, "Cyberpunk," in *Mondo 2000: A User's Guide to the New Edge*, ed. Rudy Rucker, R. U. Sirius, and Queen Mu (New York, 1992), 66.

10   Ibid.

11   Rudy Rucker, "On the Edge of the Pacific," in Rucker, Sirius, and Mu, eds., *User's Guide*, 13.

12   Issues 4 and 5 are not dated (most likely an effect of their irregular publication). Issues 6, 7, and 8 (the latest at the time this was written) are dated 1992.

13   Tim Appelo, "Far In and Out," *Entertainment Weekly*, 27 November 1992, 72.

14   R. U. Sirius, "A User's Guide to Using This Guide," in Rucker, Sirius, and Mu, eds., *User's Guide*, 16.

ERIK DAVIS

TECHGNOSIS, MAGIC, MEMORY, AND THE ANGELS OF INFORMATION

One of the most compelling snares is the use of
the term *metaphor* to describe a correspondence
between what the users see on the screen and how
they should think about what they are manipulating. . . . There are clear connotations to the
stage, theatrics, magic—all of which give much
stronger hints as to the direction to be followed.
For example, the screen as "paper to be marked
on" is a metaphor that suggests pencils, brushes,
and typewriting. . . . Should we transfer the paper
metaphor so perfectly that the screen is as hard as
paper to erase and change? Clearly not. If it is to
be like magical paper, then it is the *magical* part
that is all important.
—Alan Kay

While allegory employs "machinery," it is not an
engineer's type of machinery at all. It does not use
up real fuels, does not transform such fuels into
real energy. Instead, it is a fantasized energy, like
the fantasized power conferred on the shaman by
his belief in daemons.
—Angus Fletcher

Within the armour is the butterfly and within the
butterfly—is the signal from another star.
—Philip K. Dick

We begin with a digital dream. As computers, media, and telecommunication technology continue to collect, manipulate, store, represent, and transmit an ever-increasing flux of data, they are installing nothing less than a new dimension: the space of information. This proliferating multidimensional space is virtual, densely webbed, and infinitely complex, a vast and sublime realm accessed through the mediation of our imaginative and technical representations. How powerfully we engage this information space depends on how powerfully we both manipulate and inhabit these representations, these phantasms ghosting the interface.

For things do not work the same through the liquid crystal looking glass, with its codes, hypertexts, simulated spaces, labyrinthine network architectures, baroque "metaphors," colossal encyclopedias of memory. Inevitably, information theory mutates into an information praxis: How does one move through this space? What are its possible logics, cartographies, entities, connections? In constructing environments that mediate between brains and information space, computer interface designers are already grappling with the phantasmic apparatus of the imagination—these are questions for the dreaming mind as much as the analytic one.

Far beyond Palo Alto and MIT, in the margins and on the nets, phantasms hover over the technologically mediated information processing that increasingly constitutes our experience. Today, there is so much pressure on "information"—the word, the conceptual space, but also the stuff itself—that it crackles with energy, drawing to itself mythologies, metaphysics, hints of arcane magic.

Of course, science fiction has already explored such mythologies of information. But the three imaginative constructs I'll touch on— William Gibson's cyberspace, Vernor Vinge's Other Plane, and Philip K. Dick's mystical notion of VALIS (Vast Active Living Intelligence System)—are highly mobile concepts, far more penetrating and productive than mere "fantasy." Gibson's work actually created a social space, organizing the desires and intuitions of people operating in the widely disparate fields of journalism, law, media, psychedelic culture, and computer science. At the same time, information fantasies have entered social practice, many tinged with a distinctly apocalyptic fire. New Agers use crystals as personal computers that store and process spirit, while UFO churches and channelers transform incoming messages into cults of "living information." Citing Matthew 24:14 ("And this gospel of the kingdom shall be preached in all the world for a witness unto all nations; and then shall the end come"), many evangelical Christians believe that the communications technology that blasts the Word through the world's backwaters helps spark the endtimes, some even holding that the angels in Revelation refer to global satellites.

Neither original fictions like Gibson's nor popular myths arise in a vacuum. As I hope to show, by superimposing the notion of information on the vast arcana of esoteric, religious, and mythological traditions, curiously resonant stories, images, and operations emerge. In this regard I am inspired by Walter Benjamin's notion, outlined in "Theses on the Philosophy of History," that when one "grasps the constellation which his own era has formed with a definite early one," one "establishes a conception of the present as 'the time of the now' which is shot through with chips of Messianic time." My impulse is not only to contextualize the more spectral dimensions of cyberculture, but to call forth its millennial spark.

While the possible objects for an imaginative archaeology of information are vast—ranging from trickster tales to mystical conceptions of the Logos to divination—I'll concentrate on certain aspects of the hermetic imagination: the magical art of memory, demonic cryptography, and Gnostic cosmology. We derive the word "hermeticism" (perhaps even "hermeneutics") from Hermes, the trickster, craftsman, and divine messenger of pagan Greece. A central source of hermeticism is the *Corpus Hermeticum*, a collection of wisdom literature attributed to Hermes Trismegistus, a legendary author associated with both Hermes and the Egyptian divinity Thoth, the ibis-headed scribe of the gods. When the West rediscovered this material—which actually dated from late antiquity—Trismegistus was believed to be a spiritual contemporary of Moses. He was deemed so important that when Marsilio Ficino was translating classical texts at the onset of the Florentine Renaissance, Cosimo de' Medici ordered him to work on the *Hermeticum before* translating Plato.

The French scholar Festugière divided the *Hermeticum* into "popular Hermeticism"—astrology, alchemy, and the occult arts—and "erudite Hermeticism," a more elevated Gnostic philosophy that emphasized the ability of humanity to discover within itself the mystical knowledge of god and cosmos. Man was considered to be a star-demon in corporeal guise, able to recover his cosmic powers through gnosis, the moment of mystical illumination. The texts emphasized two loosely differentiated modes of gnosis. So-called optimist gnosis saw the world as a manifest map of divine revelation and held that, as John French puts it, "by inscribing a representation of the universe within his own *mens* [higher mind], man can ascend and unite with God."[1] This positive Gnosticism drove the proto-scientific impulses of later magicians, for whom the universe was alive with sentient stellar forces in constant communication with the earth, forces which could be discovered and manipulated by the magus.

The *Hermeticum*'s "pessimist" gnosis was derived from elaborate allegorical cosmologies that saw the world as a trap ruled by an ignorant, often malevolent demiurge. The true God was the distant Alien God, and to hear his liberating call, man had to awaken the "spark" or "seed" of light buried within. This moment of Gnostic revelation was not just an ineffable mystical oneness, but an influx of cosmic knowledge.

From the beginning, the hermetically inspired magician was immersed in data. In *Mind to Hermes*, the eleventh treatise of the *Hermeticum*, Mind promises that if "you embrace in thought all things at once, time, place, substances, quantities, qualities, you will comprehend God."[2] Part of the hermetic urge was encyclopedic, and magicians hoarded a stunning amount of information: ritual names, spells, and astrological correspondences; numerological techniques; ciphers, signs, and sigils; lists of herbs, metals, incense, and talismanic images.

But magicians needed to organize this vast arena, and some employed techniques derived from a classical art highly relevant to issues of computer representation: the artificial memory. As described by Cicero and other rhetoricians, and discussed at length in Frances Yates's remarkable *Art of Memory*, the art consisted of mentally creating a series of imaginative spaces, usually a vast building, rigorously constructed down to the right size and even the right lighting. Within these units were placed images of the things or words to be remembered, ranging from striking figures of bloody gods to simple emblems like anchors or swords. By "walking" through the phantasmic palace, one could locate the appropriate icon and then recover its store of words and information.

This virtual mnemonics evidently worked: the rhetorician Seneca could hear a list of two thousand names and spit them back in order. Later, in the Middle Ages, a truncated form of the art was transformed by the Scholastics into a didactic technique for allegorically representing the church's innumerable vices and virtues. Rather than use the palaces of the classical world, the Schoolmen often lodged their data in the multilayered onion of the cosmos itself, that dense vertical bureaucracy of hell, purgatory, and heaven. Yates argues that Dante's *Divine Comedy* was in many ways a product of the art of memory, as it followed the classical rule of "striking images on orders of places."[3]

The brilliant medieval Neoplatonist Raymond Lull took a different tack in his mnemonic art, which he claimed would enable the user to know everything that was going on in the universe and retain the information. Lull's art consisted of an abstract and incredibly complex system of wheels within wheels. The rims of these wheels were inscribed with letters which stood for the nine qualities of God that Lull had seen in a vision, qualities which reflected and organized the sum of all knowledge. But "Doctor Illuminatus," as Lull was called, added a fascinating twist: by shifting the wheels, one could create endless combinations of concepts. Lull's art was thus an ancestor of symbolic logic and influenced Leibniz's development of calculus. Recognizing Lull's work as one of the computer's "secret origins," the German philosopher Werner Künzel translated his *Ars magna* into the programming language COBOL. In *Magical Alphabets*, Nigel Pennick points out that Lull's combinatorial wheels anticipate Charles Babbage's nineteenth-century "difference engine"—which used a system of gears to perform polynomial equations—and "hence can be considered the occult origin of modern computers."[4]

Yates makes a similar suggestion when she describes the highly systematized and profoundly magical memory charts in the *De umbris idearum* of the Renaissance genius Giordano Bruno (who ended his days on a Vatican pyre, a "martyr to science" who was actually a flagrantly heretical mystic). Bruno's systems were of "appalling complexity," combining Lull's interlocking wheels with a dense iconography of star-demons derived from astrological applications of the art of memory ("demons," here as throughout this essay, does not imply evil, but like "daemons," describes spiritual entities that can range from gnomes to planetary rulers to archangels). Bruno's system was meant to be internalized in the imagination, for like most hermeticists, Bruno believed that "the astral forces which govern the outer world also operate within, and can be reproduced or captured there to operate a magico-mechanical memory." Yates sees a "curiously close" spiritual link between Bruno's memory system and the "mind machines" discussed in the 1960s.[5]

At the very least, this link attests to the continuity between the impulses of magic and the scientific drive toward technological and symbolic mastery, a drive which in many ways is realized in the universal machine. "The Renaissance conception of an animistic universe, operated by magic, prepared the way for the conception of a mechanical universe, operated by mathematics."[6] Yet today, as our own mind-machines push the boundaries of the atomized, mechanical paradigm toward self-organization, holistic complexity, and artificial life, Bruno's vision of a densely interconnected universe alive with constant communication begins to flicker on the screen, like some ghostly landscape arising from a hazy childhood recollection.

≡≡≡≡

In his *Confessions*, Augustine gives a remarkable sense of what it must feel like to use the artificial memory, describing "the plains, and caves, and caverns of . . . memory, innumerable and innumerably full of innumerable kinds of things." Augustine calls this an "inner place, which is as yet no place," and catalogs the images, knowledges, and experiences that exist there. "Over all these do I run, I fly; I dive on this side and that, as far as I can, and there is no end."[7]

If Augustine sounds like one of William Gibson's cowboys, he should, for cyberspace is a space of memory, a "graphic representation of data abstracted from the banks of every computer in the human system. . . . Lines of light ranged in the non-space of the mind, clusters and constellations of data."[8] Through their Nintendo-like decks, Gibson's cowboys run and fly. "Put the 'trodes on and they were out there, all the data in the world stacked up like one big neon city, so that you could cruise around and have a kind of grip on it, visually anyway, because if you didn't, it was too complicated, trying to find your way to a particular piece of data you needed."[9]

While the concept of using digital space to represent abstract data can be traced back to Ivan Sutherland in the 1960s, a particularly rich form of that concept was conjured up in a 1990 *New York Times* article on a Columbia research project partly funded by Citicorp: a virtual reality system that would allow traders to use a special glove to manipulate 3-D representations of options portfolios that would change as variables, such as interest rates, shifted. And the virtual-reality flagship company VPL was working with an actuary company that wanted to represent discrete collections of information as trees within a vast forest tied to its data base.

With this (unrealized) image of an insurance agent wandering through a forest of premiums, we're back in the allegorical heart of the medieval art of memory, when Lull created the *Arbor scientiae*. These visual charts attempted to schematize the total encyclopedia of all knowledge into a forest of trees, organized under the abstract qualities of God (*bonitas, virtus, gloria,* and so forth). Adolf Katzellenbogen writes that trees work as metaphors because "the highly articulated structure of the growths of nature could lodge complicated systems of abstraction and their upward development could be interpreted step by step—or rather, branch by branch."[10]

Such allegorical knowledge-maps take an interesting turn when they become allegorical narratives. For it's only a few steps from Lull's overdetermined grove to the bowers, forests, and caves in Spenser's *Faerie Queene*, a poem Coleridge described as taking place in a domain "ignorant of all artificial boundary, all material obstacles. . . . [I]t is truly in land of Faery, that is, of mental space."[11] For all their lush and evocative description, these spaces are not so much sensual as they are dense visualizations of abstract conceptions of sin, temptation, and redemption. As Angus Fletcher explains in his remarkable *Allegory*, "[F]or the suggestiveness and intensity of ambiguous metaphorical language allegory substitutes a sort of figurative geometry. It enables the poet, as Francis Bacon observed, to 'measure countries in the mind.' "[12]

Yet for all the strict hierarchies implied in the geometric cartographies of Dante, the *Faerie Queene*, or *Pilgrim's Progress*, the spaces of allegory remain fundamentally phantasmic, dreamlike and metamorphic, as if the very rigidity of their codes produces a surreal countermovement. Fletcher points out that even though allegorical elements are highly ordered, their causal connections and behavior are far more magical than rational. This magical ordering describes the mindset of the Renaissance magus and his allegorical science, as well as the rigorous pseudoscience that undergirds the frequently allegorical nature of science fiction. As Joanna Russ says in an article for *Science Fiction Studies*, "[S]cience is to science fiction . . . what medieval Christianity was to deliberately didactic medieval fiction." SF not only allegorizes science, but, "like medieval painting, addresses itself to the mind, not to the eye." Russ recognizes that this allegorical character in part produces SF's capacity for eliciting emotions of wonder and awe.[13]

Neuromancer is one of SF's most sublime allegories, though, like VPL's actuarial forest, it represents not science but the technologically driven information economy of global capitalism. Yet though *Neuromancer*'s "real" world is a place of vicious corporations, violent mercenaries, and social dystopia, the allegorical realm *within* the text nonetheless becomes a locus of demonic agency, as the sentient godhead that emerges at the end of *Neuromancer* fragments into *Count Zero*'s voodoo deities. This is the magic gap of allegory, for though cyberspace collects data and cash, its shapes conjure up alien logics, distant realms. With its infinite boundaries, its vast hierarchies of "corporate galaxies" and the "cold spiral arms" of military systems, its grids and buildings, cyberspace is more than a virtual database—like Dante's *Comedy*, it is a cosmos.

═══════

Earlier literary commentators used the term "allegorical machinery" to describe both the overdetermination of allegorical narrative and the fated mechanical nature of its agents. Computer interfaces can also be seen as allegorical machinery—both fuse (and confuse) images with abstractions, tend toward baroque complexity, contain magical or hyperdimensional operations, and frequently represent their abstractions spatially. Like allegory, interfaces blend mimetic symbols (in the Mac's case, trash cans and folders) with magical symbols (a phoenix in a didactic alchemical engraving is no mere image, but like an icon in HyperCard, "opens" onto a particular operation or unit of information). And some in the avant-garde of computer interface design are developing "agents," programmed anthropomorphic functions that help the user manage information space. As computer interfaces become more robust, the Mac's desktop "metaphor" may open like some sigil-encrusted gateway onto a huge realm of allegory.

It is therefore no surprise that, when we look at one of the computer's earliest virtual spaces, we discover the allegorical mode in all its magical splendor. Adventure was a text-based fantasy game created by programmers on the mainframes of Stanford's AI lab in the 1970s. By typing simple commands, players could probe Adventure's underworld cartography, gather treasure and spells, solve puzzles, kill trolls. Adventure was similar to Dungeons and Dragons, an impressively virtual game that consists of little more than dice rolls, simple math, printed manuals, and the imaginations of the players interacting with a virtual map described by the "dungeon master." In Adventure, the computer was the dungeon master, greeting the player with this description:

> YOU ARE STANDING AT THE END OF A ROAD BEFORE A SMALL BRICK BUILDING. AROUND YOU IS A FOREST. A SMALL STREAM FLOWS OUT OF THE BUILDING AND DOWN A GULLY.

This image is schematic but strangely potent, and it may remind us of another traveler, at the end of another road, about to begin another grand adventure:

> When I had journeyed half our life's way,
> I found myself within a shadowed forest,
> for I had lost the path that does not stray.

So does Dante begin his descent into the underworld of the Inferno.

Dante's underworld and a computer game resonate because both inhabit the peculiar environment of coded space. As Fletcher notes, allegory is "a fundamental process of encoding our speech."[14] Allegory's coded levels of meaning are not distinct from its surface; rather, the two levels interpenetrate each other. Neither reading is fully realized; both are held in an ambiguous tension that Fletcher believes creates the frequently enigmatic, surreal, and magical quality of the mode.

Dante's images compel us to tear through the surface imagery and unpack distinct meanings: historical personages, medieval theology, Italian politics. But the poetry, the phantasm, always comes back. Appropriately, when the Dartmouth Dante Project created a searchable on-line Dante database that linked six centuries of commentary with Dante's text, they embedded the tension between text and interpretation in cyberspace. Though the project was later discontinued, Dante became for a while a multidimensional cluster of poetry, information, and commentary, a coded space that, like the *Comedy* itself, was searched.[15]

Adventure's magical spaces also cloaked an underlying code, not just the puzzle that had to be cracked to pass to the next room, but the computer itself. For computers are nothing if not hierarchies of code, higher-level programming languages descending into the decidedly unnatural machine language of ones and zeros. Steven Levy writes in *Hackers*: "In a sense Adventure was a metaphor for computer programming itself—the deep recesses you explored in the Adventure world were akin to the basic, most obscure levels of the machine that you'd be travelling in when you hacked in assembly code."[16] This magical metaphor, or allegory, seemed to fit the computer like a glove, and continues to influence cyberspace. Adventure laid the way for countless fantasy games, so that today even an elementary-school computer spelling game like Wizards is organized around a magical model of powers, spells, and levels. Adventure also inspired the "wizards" and virtual cartographies of the MUDs, or "multi-user domains," that populate the Internet. And it helped conjure up Vernor Vinge's Other Plane, the only SF cyberspace cartography that rivals Gibson's.

In the novella *True Names*, Vinge describes the Other Plane as a virtual representation of "data space" accessed by game interfaces called Portals. The reigning metaphor is a magical world of "sprites, reincarnation, spells and castles," as well as Spenserian woods where errant knights easily lose their way. The hacker denizens of the Coven perform various pranks for fun and profit, and take on colorful handles like Mr. Slippery and Wiley J. Bastard; like Dungeons and Dragons players, they construct the imagery of their characters, most choosing to represent themselves as magicians and witches.

As Mr. Slippery's description of the path to the Coven makes clear, the Other Plane is a space of technoallegory, where imagery is directly linked to abstract functions. "The correct path had the aspect of a narrow row of stones cutting through a gray-greenish swamp. . . . The subconscious knew what the stones represented, handled the chaining of routines from one information net to another, but it was the conscious mind of the skilled traveller that must make the decisions that could lead to the gates of the Coven."[17] At these gates, Mr. Slippery encounters the allegorical agent Alan, a subroutine represented as a chthonic elemental creature who tests Mr. Slippery's authenticity by trading spells and counterspells.

Unlike the hard lines of Gibson's cyberspace, which are as objectively apparent as video game imagery, the Other Plane requires that the traveler cooperate in the imaginative generation of the world.

> You might think that to convey the full sense imagery of the swamp, some immense bandwidth would be necessary. . . . In fact . . . a typical Portal link was around fifty thousand baud, far narrower than even a flat video channel. Mr. Slippery could feel the damp seeping through his leather boots, could feel the sweat starting on his skin even in the cold air, but this was the response of Mr. Slippery's imagination and subconscious to the cues that were actually being presented through the Portal's electrodes.

This process of eliciting phantasms with a minimum of signals dovetails with VR designer and theorist Brenda Laurel's insistence on the positive role of ambiguity in computer interfaces. Arguing against a high-bandwidth overload, Laurel—who began her career as a fantasy game designer—recognizes that one of the imagination's greatest powers is its ability to generate psychedelic perceptions with a minimum of sensory cues. Using our ability to see faces in rocks and clouds as one example, Laurel argues that there is a threshold of sensory ambiguity that boots up fantasy, a threshold that virtual interfaces should emulate.[18]

Mr. Slippery notes that "magic jargon was perhaps the closest fit" to this process; for Vinge, magic's manipulative power operates in the ambiguous gap between sensation and internal imagery. In *Eros and Magic in the Renaissance*, Ioan Couliano paraphrases Giordano Bruno: "Magic action occurs through indirect *contact* . . . through sounds and images which exert their power over the senses of sight and hearing. . . . Passing through the openings of the sense, they impress on the imagination certain mental states. . . ."[19] The magician would not only impress fantasies on other people, but on himself through his virtual memory art.

Some Coven members in *True Names* argue that their magic jargon is simply a more natural and convenient way for manipulating dataspace than the "atomistic twentieth-century notions of data structures, programs, files, and communications protocols." This "naturalness" stems from the structure of magic, its artificial mnemonics, phantasmic manipulations, and allegorical conceptions. As Fletcher points out, modern science depends on a disjunction between the synthetic fantasies of the imagination and the rigor of analytic systemization, whereas allegory fuses these two modes.

The allegorical pressure on coding also dovetails with one of Vinge's central concerns: cryptography. On the Other Plane, power is not knowledge—power is code. When Mr. Slippery follows the Red Witch Erythrina as she opens up a castle's secret passages through cryptic gestures and spells, he enters a space of encryption. And when Mr. Slippery first accesses the Other Plane, he makes sure his encryption routines are clouding his trail. "Like most folks, honest citizens or warlocks, he had no trust for the government standard encryption routines, but preferred the schemes that had leaked out of academia—over NSA's petulant objections—during the last fifteen years." Vinge's cryptographic hunch (he was writing in 1980) is borne out in current cyberculture. While hackers have long explored restricted-access dungeons, and phone-phreaks have hoarded phone spells, cypherpunks have begun creating anonymous remailing systems that will ensure that all traffic is untraceable and all participants remain anonymous. As Vinge suggests, cyberspace's ultimate secret code is one's True Name, one's real human identity.

Though Vinge may not have realized it, magic spells are not mere metaphors for encryption schemes. Hermeticism is rife with secret codes and unnatural languages, most stemming from the complex numerological methods that Kabbalists used to decipher the esoteric messages they believed were buried in Jewish Scripture. Two of these methods for mystical exegesis should be mentioned: Gematria and Temurah. Temurah consisted of simple letter transposition according to a number of schemes, while Gematria took advantage of the strict numerological equivalents for each Hebrew letter. By replacing words with their numerical equivalents, one could discover esoteric correspondences (for example, the words for Serpent and Messiah both have the numerical equivalent of 358).[20]

No greater proof of the deep relationship between cryptography and magic exists than the *Stenographia* of Trithemius, the dreaded abbot-necromancer of Würzburg whose famous and immense monastery library was packed with heretical works on magic. Appropriately, the *Stenographia* is a bizarre, multivalent text. As was recognized by later scholars, the demonic incantations that fill the first two books of the work are nothing more than arduous encryption schemes, the name of the demon heading the text indicating which decipherment key to employ. As far as magic is concerned, the names of the demons and their invocations are meaningless.

But in the latter portion of the *Stenographia*, Trithemius describes a complex and recognizably coherent scheme of demonic magic in which the images of cosmic forces are etched in wax in order to capture and manipulate their energies. Thus the cryptography and the demonic magic cover for each other, producing a highly ambiguous and enigmatic coding space. And Trithemius directed his demonic codes toward a curious goal: long-distance telepathic communication. When properly directed, he claimed, his seals and spells invoked entities such as Saturn's angel Oriphiel, who would create an astral network that delivered messages anywhere within twenty-four hours, a guarantee worthy of Federal Express. Nor was Trithemius's astrological magic limited to communication alone—as D. P. Walker notes, "[I]t was also the means of acquiring universal knowledge, 'of everything that is happening in the world.' " [21] Trithemius thus aimed his coded ethereal communications toward the grandest dream of the *Hermeticum*: to know everything instantaneously and thereby, presumably, to know God.

Returning to Vinge, we find that a similar hermetic expansion toward universal knowledge occurs in the climax of *True Names*, when the combined forces of Erythrina and Mr. Slippery battle the mysterious Mailman, an enigmatic and powerful entity who attempts a takeover of the world's dataspace (in the end, the Mailman proves to be a creature made of code, an out-of-control NSA self-protection program). During the battle, Mr. Slippery and Erythrina take over more and more data-processing facilities until they begin to drown. "To hear ten million simultaneous phone conversations, to see the continent's entire video output, should have been a white noise. Instead it was a tidal wave of detail rammed through the aperture of their minds." Mr. Slippery figures out how to distribute his consciousness through the system until "the human that had been Mr. Slippery was an insect wandering in the cathedral his mind had become. . . . No sparrow could fall without his knowledge, via air traffic control; no check could be cashed without his noticing over the bank communication net." Interestingly, as Mr. Slippery's consciousness expands toward totality, Vinge's imagery shifts from pagan magic to Christian figures of cathedrals and fallen sparrows.

After further battles, the Mailman's processors are destroyed, and the victorious duo gaze on Earth, serenely viewed on all frequencies. The babbling voices return as Mr. Slippery and Erythrina put human communications systems back on line. "Every ship in the seas, every aircraft now making for safe landing, every one of the loans, the payments, the meals of an entire race registered clearly on some part of his consciousness. . . . By the analogical rules of the covens, there was only one valid word for themselves in their present state: they were gods."

When Shakespeare wrote *The Tempest*, he may have modeled Prospero on Dr. John Dee, the greatest English magus of the Elizabethan era. Scientist, secret agent, geographer, antiquarian, and court astrologer, Dee was the quintessential Renaissance man. Possessed of the largest library in England, he typified the hermetic pattern of information addiction, and his interests ranged from Euclid to navigation to Lull to mechanical toys, particularly machines that could simulate bird calls.

In *De Occulta Philosophia*, one of the most influential source texts for Renaissance magicians like Dee, Agrippa defines three different types of magic, "Naturall, Mathematicall and Theologicall." Natural magic held that stellar forces influenced nature, and that by manipulating the natural world, one could attract these influences. Mathematical magic—"mathesis"—grew from the Pythagorean mystical philosophy that number was God's hidden symbolic language of creation. By the time of the Renaissance, much mathematical magic was utilitarian—what we would recognize as "real" math. As John French notes, while a brilliant man like Dee recognized the distinct difference between these two modes of number, he absorbed both into his magical philosophy, so that cabbalistic numerology and the gears that powered robot birds were both expressions of divinity's secret code.

However, it is Dee's more bizarre "Theologicall" attempts at angelic communication that interest me here. Agrippa emphasizes that theological or demonic magic—of which the *Stenographia* is a prime example—is the most difficult and dangerous kind of magic. Drawing heavily on the Kabbalah, the magus attempted to contact the powers residing in the supercelestial angelic hierarchies that existed beyond the elemental powers of the earth and the celestial zone of the zodiac. Invoking archangels, powers, and principalities led magicians toward divine wisdom, but it also exposed them to the deceptions of evil spirits. Adam McLean points out in his introduction to *A Treatise on Angel Magic* that most magicians were extremely concerned about distinguishing truthful angels from dissembling devils.[22]

A True & Faithful Relation of what passed for many Years Between

Dr. John Dee . . . and Some Spirits presents Dee as a pious man motivated by a Gnostic desire for revelation. Yet Dee was also the first
to apply the cryptographic dimension of high—or "Theologicall"—
magic to espionage.[23] As a secret agent of Elizabeth's court (his code
name was 007), according to Richard Deacon, Dee maintained a network of informants on the continent and collected a great deal of data
concerning Spanish threats to England and discoveries in the New
World. In 1692 Robert Hooke decoded a number of angelic names
and conversations from *A True & Faithful Relation* and proclaimed
the work an encrypted record of Dee's secret missions. One angelic
conversation that Dee sent to England from the Continent may well
have described Spanish plans to burn the Forest of Dean.[24]

But like Trithemius, Dee's taste for cryptography was fused with
metaphysical quest. As Dee put it, he had "long been desirious to
have help in philosophicall studies through the company and information of the Angels of God."[25] Dee accessed his information through
a ludicrously complex form of spiritualist channeling. Briefly, he enlisted a rogue named Edward Kelley as his "scryer." Kelley would
stare into a crystal sphere, called the "shew-stone," and describe
visions and messages that Dee would record. The angels were not
exactly interested in clarity—they communicated in "Enochian," a
unique language with its own alphabet and grammar, encompass-
ing a complex directory of angels, Aethyrs, kings, seniors, and Calls.
Enochian was laboriously dictated to Dee through complex grids
called the *Liber logaeth*. Finally, the nineteen "Calls" that formed the
heart of the system were communicated backward. In the end, Dee
and Kelley channeled at least twenty-six books, most of which, according to Deacon, are "not only totally unintelligible, but do not
seem to be related to any of the usual cabbalistic or numerological
systems." Dee devoted himself to their decipherment, having been
promised that if successful, he would "have as many powers subject
to him as there [were] parts of the book."

What to make of all this? As with all of the magic and Gnostic
experiences I've mentioned, I turn over the question of what Dee
and Kelley were "actually" doing to the notorious twentieth-century
magus-trickster Aleister Crowley, who wrote of magical entities and
powers: "It is immaterial whether they exist or not. By doing certain
things, certain results follow." What's important here is the quali-

tative nature of the supercelestial realms, as well as the agents and coded operations at its interface. Because "Theologicall" magic conceptualizes the divine mind as a decidedly unnatural, hyperdimensional structure, its magical operations and representations try to fit that structure. Dee and Kelley's Enochian system, as well as Bruno's and Trithemius's, is characterized in part simply by its vast hermetic complexity. These magical machines, at once rigorous and phantasmic, were created by projecting systematic techniques of numerology and cryptography into a kind of free space of mystical abstraction, which produced a treacherous density of names, numbers, hierarchies, correspondences, and functions. This complexity not only mirrored the immensity of divine wisdom, but amplified and strained the magician's mind toward a divine change of state. In Dee's case, the angelic communications embodied this information density in their indecipherability—as the angels told Dee, ". . . [T]herein is comprehended so many languages they are all spoken at once."

On the one hand, the temptation to compare the representation of supercelestial realms with cyberspace is intellectually suspect because rational mathematics, network architectures, and programming codes are so technically distinct from the mystical mathematics, celestial architectures, and demonic codes of angel magic. But perhaps, from a qualitative perspective, complexity space is complexity space—any information system, when dense and rigorous enough, takes on a kind of self-organizational coherence that resonates with other systems of complexity. As computer visionary Ted Nelson writes concerning representations of hypertext: "Once we leave behind 'two-dimensionality' (virtual paper) and even 'three-dimensionality' (virtual stacks), we step off the edge into another world, into the representation of the *true structure and interconnectedness of information*. To represent this true structure, we need to indicate multidimensional connection and multiple connections between entities."[26] This sense that there is a "true structure" of information is one of the most pervasive metaphysical myths of cyberspace.

Angel magic gives us a hermetic image not only of information space, but of its agents. Angels are immaterial beings composed of intelligent light; they have human form, yet are voiceless. Because they have no soul and are motivated by neither will nor passion, angels, like allegorical agents, are "fated" to reproduce mechanically their mode of being. In *Allegory*, Fletcher points out the proto-scientific function of the demon: "Coming from the term that means 'to divide,' *daemon* implies an endless series of divisions of all important aspects of the world into separate elements for study and control."[27] Many magical texts consist of endless lists of these star-demons, their appearances, numbers, and powers, their hierarchies of Orbs and Aethyrs and offices. These agents mediate the complexity of supercelestial information. They are the original images of artificial intelligence—not the sentient AIs of SF, but the text-based expert systems, independent software objects, and audiovisual interface agents we are so keen to develop—passionless entities made of intelligent light.

As Manuel De Landa argues in *War in the Age of Intelligent Machines*, though there are many names for software objects that operate autonomously (actors, agents, demons), the term "demons" is perhaps the best because "they are not controlled by a master program or a central computer but are rather 'invoked' into action by changes in the environment."[28] Like stellar demons, digital demons are at once independent and programmed ("fated"), operating autonomously yet responding automatically to certain cues with certain acts. As the ecologies of such event-driven demons increase in complexity, computers are able to react to the environment in an increasingly "lifelike" manner. De Landa claims that demons enable computers to respond far more interactively to human users *and* to function far more powerfully outside human control (the killer robot being a particularly terrifying example of the latter). Like their spiritual counterparts, software demons can both serve and subjugate.

Like John Dee, computer interface designers are more interested in conjuring demons that serve. Visionary designer Alan Kay suggests that in order for us to take advantage of the increasing complexity of computer processes, there must be a "qualitative jump" from the manipulation of tools to the management of agents, which Kay defines as "autonomous processes that can be successfully communicated with." Such agents would "act as guide, as coach, and as amanuensis," and could either be tabular or anthropomorphic. As an example, Kay describes a system that would monitor news and private messages in order to collate a private newspaper. Kay also emphasizes that as agents are given more irrevocable power over information (the ability to regularly delete files, for example), the stakes are raised considerably.

> At the most basic level the thing we most want to know about an agent is not how powerful it can be, but how trustable it is. In other words, the agent must be able to explain itself well so that we have confidence that it will be working on our behalf as a goal sharer rather than as a demented genie recently escaped from the *Arabian Nights*.[29]

All this puts Dee's conversations in a strange new light. Dee, seeking their "company and information," would invoke angels with an elaborate system of coded Calls. He spent much of his time interrogating these beings in order to make sure they were trustworthy, and not devils in disguise. In "The Directory," a section of a late seventeenth-century occult manuscript recently published in *A Treatise on Angel Magic*, the author outlines a form of Dee's interrogation process, noting that if the spirits disappear, or remain silent, there's a problem. (In *True Names*, Mr. Slippery first suspects something nefarious about the Mailman when there is a long pause in the entity's answers to Mr. Slippery's questions.) In accessing angelic agents through the interface of coded Calls and "shew-stone glass," magicians like Dee may have stumbled on the first Turing test—only rather than testing the ontological status of these entities, they tested their true names.

≡

The magus's highest aspiration was gnosis: divine knowledge, universal memory. But the Gnostic impulse that motivated Bruno's and Dee's exploratory proto-science can be found in far more purist or "pessimistic" forms, which seek a divine wisdom that absolutely transcends a dark and evil material world. The Gnostic emphasis on memory remains, but it shifts from the virtual encyclopedia to the trigger-signal that catalyzes anamnesis, the soul's recollection of its celestial origins.

Ancient Gnosticism's more dualistic cosmologies held that the world is not a glittering web of divine correspondences, but a trap ruled by false, ignorant gods—including the Jehovah of Genesis. The

the words of our letter"—is delivered before the letter itself is opened, suggesting that Gnostic triggers have a dimension of *meta*-information —information about information. Like Alice's cake, or a talking mushroom, Gnostic information says "eat me."

But the letter boots up information already contained within the soul of our hero—Valentinus's recollection of true origins and true destiny. This interior spark thus functions like a radio transponder, which can receive and transmit signals, but lies dormant until it receives a specific signal that activates it. But while the call comes from out of the blue, the hero must also choose to "break the seal" of the letter—to break the code inscribed on the surface of things. And he must be prepared to find Gnostic information in the most marginal places—lying in the dust of the road, for instance.

Many Gnostic texts did not just tell tales of the informing gnosis, but sought to "quiver" with its "movements," to directly impart "the Voice which exists within a perfect intellect."[34] Some of these writings possess a peculiar power that lies less in their cosmological import than in their rhetoric of immediacy—an attempt to represent the unmediated presence of the Gnostic mind. No greater example of this intensity exists than "Thunder, the Perfect Mind," a fourth-century tractate that eludes scholarly classification but has strong Gnostic elements. The poem is delivered in first-person, and consists mostly of paradoxical statements of identity ("I am the whore and the holy one / I am the virgin and the wife," and so forth). At one point, the informing voice describes her own mode of information:

> I am the voice whose sound is manifold
> > and the word whose appearance is multiple.
> I am the utterance of my name.
>
> .   .   .   .
>
> Hear me, you hearers,
> > and learn of my words, you who know me.
> I am the hearing that is attainable to everything;
> > I am the speech that cannot be grasped.[35]

Here, the animate Logos seems to describe not its contents or forms, but its underlying nature, a luminous flux of information density, of manifold sounds and liquid speech. Yet for all the immediacy of the "I am," an alien quality lingers, as if the speaker is both close to home, and far, far away.

═════

In its obsession with simulacra and encoded messages, as well as its almost libertarian hatred of traditional authority and a corresponding emphasis on spiritual autonomy, Gnosticism anticipates cyberculture. Ihab Hassan has shown how the notion of direct Gnostic revelation is resurrected now that "communication itself is becoming increasingly immediate."[36] But while Hassan and a few SF writers have pursued this link, no one has plunged into information Gnosticism with such abandon as the brilliant SF writer Philip K. Dick. Though Gnosticism is only one dimension of Dick's dense and tangled oeuvre—only now beginning to receive the attention it deserves— the mythic mode lies at the heart of many of his themes and devices: "living" books, false worlds, divine invasions.

In the essay "Man, Android and Machine," Dick suggests that Gnostic information is both a space and a being. Taking up the popular Christian thinker Teilhard de Chardin's image of the noösphere— a bubble of human thought that envelops the earth like a virtual atmosphere—Dick suggests that something strange occurred when technology entered the picture:

> . . . [T]he noösphere . . . no longer served as a mere passive repository of human information (the "Seas of Knowledge" which ancient Sumer believed in) but, due to the incredible surge of charge from our electronic signals and information-rich material therein, we have given it power to cross a vast threshold; we have, so to speak, resurrected what Philo and other ancients called the Logos. Information has, then, become alive.[37]

The whole encyclopedic space of thought, juiced up by technology, becomes the ultimate example of artificial life.

In *The Divine Invasion*, Dick creates an even richer theological image of living information space: a three-dimensional, color-coded biblical hologram.

> The total structure of Scripture formed, then, a three-dimensional cosmos that could be viewed from any angle and its con-

> tents read. According to the tilt of the axis of observation, dif-
> ferent messages could be extracted. . . . If you learned how, you
> could gradually tilt the temporal axis, the axis of true depth,
> until successive layers were superimposed and a vertical message
> —a new message—could be read out. In this way you entered
> into a dialogue with Scripture; it became alive. It became a sen-
> tient organism that was never twice the same.[38]

In this image of hypertext heaven, Dick shows how a space of information density achieves an animate quality through the structure of
an open-ended dialogue.

But "living information" was no mere metaphor within Dick's brilliant though decidedly unstable mind, for in 1974, sitting at home
in Orange County, he apparently experienced such a force. According to Dick's later testimony, seeing an *ichthys*, or fish-shaped Christian icon, on a delivery woman's necklace "triggered" the influx of a
rational and benign mind: VALIS, or Vast Active Living Intelligence
System. Among other things, VALIS—which Dick sometimes com-
pares to a computer or an AI system—linked him telepathically to
an early Christian living under Roman oppression and informed him
(through a Beatles song on the radio) that his son Christopher had a
potentially lethal health problem.

In our culture, we call individuals like Dick schizophrenic, but
in the confines of his literary works, his apparent schizophrenia
achieves an unparalleled oracular glow. After 1974, most of Dick's
work, both his novels and over two million words of tortured philosophical maunderings in his largely unpublished "Exegesis," was a
response to the VALIS experience, though Gnostic themes and structures are clearly latent in his earlier work. In *VALIS*, the greatest
and strangest of these late works, he fleshes out his information mysticism in the "Tractates Cryptica Scriptura," a twelve-page excerpt
from his "Exegesis."

In the "Tractates," Dick maintains that our universe is a space of
information, and the phenomenal world a hologram, "a hypostasis
of the information" that we, as nodes in the true Mind, process. But
humans have lost the ability to read this divine language, and both
ourselves and our world are occluded. For Dick, the ancient demi-

urge is recast as the irrational "Empire": Rome, the Nixon administration, the State as such. Dick did not emphasize the material or Satanic aspect of demiurgic powers, but rather their ability to create false worlds. In the introduction to *I Hope I Shall Arrive Soon*, a collection of late short stories, he writes that "we live in a society in which spurious realities are manufactured by the media, by governments, by big corporations, by religious groups, political groups— and the electronic hardware exists by which to deliver these pseudoworlds right into the heads of the reader, the viewer, the listener."[39] As demonstrated by the illusory and demonic nature of his constantly imploding fictional worlds, Dick transforms Gnostic pessimism into a skeptical weapon wielded from within the fathomless simulations of Baudrillardian hyperreality.

Just as the nameless hero of the "Hymn of the Pearl" found the Logos lying by the side of the road, VALIS penetrates the simulated world through the margins. The True God must mimic "sticks and trees and beer cans in gutters—he presumes to be trash discarded, debris no longer needed." Dick says at the end of *VALIS* that "the symbols of the divine show up in our world initially at the trash stratum." So, too, do the images and peripheral details of Dick's fictions—circulating through the trash stratum of SF pulp—glow with a powerful allegorical density, and many narratives are propelled by the decoding of these clues. One of *VALIS*'s most fascinating chapters describes a scene in which the protagonist, Horselover Fat, and some friends see a trashy SF movie called *Valis* and then unpack its subliminal messages, their bizarre conclusions leading them to make contact with the filmmakers and the savior-figure, Sophia. For Dick, decoding is more than reading; it is being infected by code. VALIS is nothing less than a virus that "replicates itself—not through information or in information—but as information." Once triggered, it parasitically "crossbands" with human hosts, creating "homeoplasmates."

Dick is not the only one to imagine information as a kind of virus (itself a quasi-living body of code). In addition to Burroughs's famous phrase ("language is a virus"), there's scientist Richard Dawkins's understanding of *memes* as thoughts which, like genes, propagate and compete in the competitive environment of culture. In *The Selfish Gene*, Dawkins quotes N. K. Humphrey:

> . . . [M]emes should be regarded as living structures, not just
> metaphorically but technically. When you plant a fertile meme
> in my mind you literally parasitize my brain, turning it into a ve-
> hicle for the meme's propagation in just the way that a virus may
> parasitize the genetic mechanism of a host cell. . . . [T]he meme
> for, say, "belief in life after death" is actually realized physically,
> millions of times over, as a structure in the nervous systems of
> individual men the world over.[40]

Memes have already become a somewhat trendy notion in cyberculture, but what is intriguing is Humphrey's insistence that they be
conceived "not just metaphorically but technically." In Dick's fiction, metaphors are transformed into technical operations. Even more
interesting is the meme Humphrey uses as an example. For of all the
artifacts of human culture, it is the great memes themselves that perhaps come closest to eternal life. And one of the greatest of those
is the one that claims that, just as memes survive in the minds of
human hosts, so can human consciousness survive in the abstract
space of the meme.

≡≡≡≡

Information's final infection is apocalypse. As Hans Jonas points out,
the Gnostic individual internalizes eschatology, radically modifying
subjectivity itself into an alien immediacy that creates a simulacrum
of the final days. So wherever you encounter the Gnostic mode,
you're likely to find an apocalyptic trace. This millennialist infection
has long been evident among evangelical Fundamentalists, but now it
is spreading in more mutant forms throughout one of the most reviled
and unexamined fringes of cyberculture: the New Age project.

Even if we characterize the New Age movement in its broadest
sense—as an eclectic network of spiritualism, theosophy, therapy
techniques, goddess myths, brain gadgetry, alternative medicine, hermetic wisdom, and hippie mysticism—incorporating it into cyberculture may strike some as extreme. Yet New Age elements are rife
throughout the post–1960s Bay Area culture that laid the groundwork
for much of what we call cyberculture. A psychedelic, do-it-yourself
spirituality directly feeds the more utopian elements of this northern

California subculture of VR designers, computer artists, and computer programmers, whose forums include *The Whole Earth Review*, *Mondo 2000*, and the WELL (a Sausalito-based electronic bulletin board that serves as a colloquium for denizens of cyberculture). For many of these folks, computers are the latest and among the greatest tools available for the achievement of the Aquarian goal: the expansion of consciousness by whatever means necessary.

But the influence of the New Age movement on cyberculture extends beyond that of the psychedelic fringe. As Andrew Ross suggests when he calls the movement an "alternative scientific culture," New Agers are driven in part by a desire to propound an account of reality that both includes and transcends scientific method and technology. Many New Agers restlessly consume weird pop science in their quest for a new metaphysics, while more entrepreneurial Aquarians develop countless transformational technologies, in the literal and the metaphorical sense—brain machines, as well as self-improvement regimens like neuro-linguistic programming or Tony Robbins's "Personal Power" program. The pervasive (and often unrecognized) influence of New Age thought lies in the fact that these aesthetic, social, and philosophical transformations of science (and self) occur in a layperson's, middle-brow context. Ross argues that to ignore this "kinder, gentler science" while reveling in the hip alienation of cyberpunk or "avant-garde"—or even normative—scientific accounts is to perform a subtle kind of intellectual elitism. Meanwhile, the New Age movement grows.

In attempting to reprogram human subjectivity, many New Age practices unconsciously translate contemporary concerns about the formation and maintenance of identity into a scientific and technological milieu. For the more futuristic New Agers, the self is an information-processing entity that changes nature, depending on the information flows it receives and the various media to which it connects. This emphasis on communication flows stems in part from the New Age role as the religion of the Information Age. It also explains the crucial role played by one particular occult technique: channeling.

Little about the New Age is new, and channeling is no different. From the oracles at Delphi to the table-rapping of the nineteenth century, spiritualism has long been the most immediate yet controlled mode of nonrational communication, at once technically structured and visionary. There is often a trace of SF in these practices: the angelic channeler John Dee believed that specially constructed mirrors could draw magical power from the sun and transmit messages and objects to distant stars and other worlds.[41] Contemporary channelers not only spiritualize information, but also the means of communication. Ross says that one of the curious aspects of New Age channeling is that, besides the messages themselves, New Agers celebrate channeling's "ability to resolve the technical problems of communication."[42]

Ross argues that this attitude reflects both mainstream Information Age ideology and the dominant scientific language that the New Age is in part attempting to displace. But beneath these forces, this emphasis on the technical dimension of channeling shifts the arena of enacted spiritual transformation from the interior of the soul to the interface, to the act of communication. All channeling could be said to proceed from this kind of info-gnosis. But it is when New Agers turn their "etheric antennae" toward the most distant sources—extraterrestrials and angelic beings—that the apocalyptic and science-fictional dimensions of info-Gnosticism emerge.

Written on a clunky manual typewriter in the 1970s by a rural New England carpenter named Ken Carey, the best-selling *Starseed Transmissions* is possibly the best and most seductive of the channeled New Age ET texts. Carey claims that the book's source was a series of transmissions from beings who embrace the language both of angelic hierarchies and of extraterrestrial frequency modulations; the text is delivered as the monologue of an alien angel. According to *Transmissions*, these entities are subtly penetrating our culture, attempting to wake us up to the imminent collapse of history, thought, and matter as we phase into the next millennium. The Information Age not only lays the digital web-work for what Carey's angels (and chaos theorists) call a "singularity," but it foreshadows the form of the next phase of existence: immaterial and luminous, at once infinitely complex and absorbed into a monad. In order to pass through our "metahistorical" moment, the aliens insist, we must cease identifying ourselves with the outmoded "programmed product(s) of human culture." Restrained by something like *Star Trek*'s Prime Directive from intervening in terrestrial history, the angels are nonetheless able to provide information concerning not only our situation, but also how we can intuitively achieve "direct contact with the source of all information."

At the very least, *Transmissions* is a solid addition to the tradition of SF Christianity that includes works by Olaf Stapledon, C. S. Lewis, and Philip K. Dick. Carey's book also dovetails with the apocalyptic visions of "the transcendental object at the end of history" found in psychedelic explorer Terence McKenna's witty, provocative, and hermetically inspired writings. Moreover, the angels' gospel of love adds a positive emotional dimension to the potentially stark unfolding of Gnostic information, as well as compensating for the dark paranoia about aliens that saturates both pulp SF and the UFO fringe. *Transmissions* suggests that the supreme Otherness of the extraterrestrial can be embraced at the interface—an act of acceptance that recalls an ancient Mandaean Gnostic fragment that tells how "Adam felt love for the Alien Man whose speech was alien and estranged from the world."[43]

But *Transmissions* is also a strangely compelling meditation on the modes of information. Carey writes in his introduction: "Regardless of one's opinion on the plausibility of extraterrestrial or angelic communion, it might be pointed out that the simple act of structuring information in this manner opens up communicative possibilities that are virtually non-existent in a conventional mode." This applies equally to Dee's conversations and to the assertion that because human languages are insufficient for the Word, having been "designed to facilitate commerce," the angels provide a new language: "Living Information." This information will not only provide instructions during the apocalypse, but will awaken memories of our own stellar origins, buried beneath the "spell of matter" induced when we chose to incarnate as human individuals. Carey's aliens are quite frank about how they are subliminally affecting human minds, sneakily spreading their infectious meta-information throughout terrestrial culture.

In this sense, Carey's transmissions are delivered more as a propagandistic virus or a set of trigger-signals than as a collection of

beliefs. Like some Gnostic texts, Carey's seeks a rhetoric of immediacy, of direct contact. This is most obvious in the pervasive use of
the second-person, a technique that actively seeks both to invade and
to reconfigure the reader's "you":

> It is critical that you remember your origin and purpose. Your
> descent into Matter has reached its low point. If all that you
> identify with is not to be annihilated in entropic collapse, you
> must begin waking up.[44]

Transmissions attempts to create a flip-flop at the slippery edges of
identity ("You are not the form you animate, but the force of animation itself"). By alternately addressing the "you" that is an ordinary
human ego and the awakening "you" that Bruno would have called a
star-demon, *Transmissions* would reconfigure the subject as an entity
that is ultimately identical to the alien. This is no different in substance from an ancient fragment of the apocryphal "Gospel of Eve":
"I am thou and thou art I, and where thou art I am, and in all things
am I dispersed. And from wherever thou willst thou gatherest me;
but in gathering me thou gatherest thyself."[45]

In *The Postmodern Condition* Jean-François Lyotard claims that
"the self . . . is always located at 'nodal points' of specific communications circuits. . . . No one, not even the least privileged among
us, is ever entirely powerless over the messages that traverse and
position him at the post of sender, addressee, or referent."[46] The
New Age rhetoric of *The Starseed Transmissions* takes this notion a
step further, suggesting that the circuits into which we tune actually *produce* the self and its experiences. But with its hand on the
remote control of reality, the New Age subject tends to dissolve into
the multidimensional information space that lurks behind all of our
descriptions: cyberspace, Other Plane, memory palace, angelic hierarchy, SF schizophrenia. Carey's Alien God puts it this way: "This
new information is not additional data that you will act upon. It
is, rather, the very reality of your new nature. You are not to act
upon my information in the future, you are to be my information
yourselves."

Notes

1   John French, *John Dee* (London, 1972), 71.

2   Ibid., 76.

3   Frances Yates, *The Art of Memory* (Chicago, 1966), 95.

4   Nigel Pennick, *Magical Alphabets* (York Beach, 1992), 214.

5   Yates, *Art of Memory*, 224.

6   Ibid.; see also her *Giordano Bruno and the Hermetic Tradition* (Chicago, 1964).

7   Quoted in Yates, *Art of Memory*, 47.

8   William Gibson, *Neuromancer* (New York, 1984), 51.

9   William Gibson, *Mona Lisa Overdrive* (New York, 1988), 13.

10   Adolf Katzellenbogen, *Allegories of the Virtues and Vices in Medieval Art* (London, 1939), 67.

11   Samuel Taylor Coleridge, *Miscellaneous Criticism*, ed. T. M. Raysor (London, 1936), 36.

12   Angus Fletcher, *Allegory* (Ithaca, 1964), 180.

13   Joanna Russ, "Towards an Aesthetic of Science Fiction," *Science Fiction Studies* 6 (July 1975): 113–16.

14   Fletcher, *Allegory*, 3.

15   See my "Cyberlibraries," *Lingua Franca* (February–March 1992): 46–51.

16   Steven Levy, *Hackers* (New York, 1984), 141.

17   Vernor Vinge, *True Names*, in collection of the same title (New York, 1987), 60.

18   See Brenda Laurel, *Computers as Theater* (Menlo Park, 1991).

19   Ioan Couliano, *Eros and Magic in the Renaissance*, trans. Margaret Cook (Chicago, 1987), 91.

20   See, for example, Israel Regardie, *A Garden of Pomegranates* (St. Paul, 1985), 106–34.

21   D. P. Walker, *Spiritual and Demonic Magic from Ficino to Campanella* (London, 1958), 89.

22   *A Treatise on Angel Magic*, ed. Adam McLean (Grand Rapids, 1989).

23   Richard Deacon, *John Dee* (London, 1968), 3.

24   See Deacon, *John Dee*, 1–25, for a convincing argument on this point.

25   Quoted in Deacon, *John Dee*, 142.

26   Theodor Holm Nelson, "The Right Way to Think about Software Design," in *The Art of Human-Computer Interface*, ed. Brenda Laurel (Menlo Park, 1990), 241.

27   Fletcher, *Allegory*, 59.

28   Manuel De Landa, *War in the Age of Intelligent Machines* (Cambridge, 1991), 120.

29   Alan Kay, "User Interface: A Personal View," in Laurel, ed., *Human-Computer Interface*, 206.

30   See Hans Jonas, *The Gnostic Religion* (Boston, 1963), 45.

31   Quoted in Jonas, *Gnostic Religion*, 77.

32   See *The Other Bible*, ed. Willis Barnstone (New York, 1984), 275.

33   Ibid., 308–13.

34 Ibid., 592.

35 Ibid., 594–99.

36 Ihab Hassan, *Paracriticisms* (Urbana, 1975), 135.

37 Philip K. Dick, "Man, Android and Machine," in *Science Fiction at Large*, ed. Peter Nicholls (New York, 1976), 216.

38 Philip K. Dick, *The Divine Invasion* (New York, 1981), 70–71.

39 Philip K. Dick, "Introduction: How to Build a Universe That Doesn't Fall Apart Two Days Later," in *I Hope I Shall Arrive Soon* (New York, 1985), 4.

40 Richard Dawkins, *The Selfish Gene* (Oxford, 1976), 192.

41 Deacon, *John Dee*, 37.

42 Andrew Ross, *Strange Weather* (New York, 1991), 37.

43 Quoted in Jonas, *Gnostic Religion*, 89.

44 Ken Carey, *The Starseed Transmissions* (New York, 1982), 35.

45 Quoted in Jonas, *Gnostic Religion*, 60.

46 Jean-François Lyotard, *The Postmodern Condition: A Report on Knowledge*, trans. Geoff Bennington and Brian Massumi (Minneapolis, 1984), 15.

PETER SCHWENGER

AGRIPPA, OR, THE APOCALYPTIC BOOK

All techniques meant to unleash forces are techniques of disappearance.
—Paul Virilio

Black box recovered from some unspecified disaster, the massive case opens to reveal the textures of decay and age. Yellowed newspaper, rusty honeycombing, fog-colored cerement enveloping a pale book. On the book's cover, a burned-in title: *Agrippa (A Book of the Dead)*. Within it, page after page printed with cryptic letters.

TGTGG
CCATA
AATAT
TACGA
GTTTG

These are the combinatory possibilities of genetic codes, as re-coded by scientists. The pages are singed at their edges; more fragments of old newspaper are interspersed. And at intervals, engravings by New York artist Dennis Ashbaugh reproduce the commercial subjects of a previous generation, subjects that will later acquire a fuller meaning: a telephone ad ("Tell Daddy we miss him"), a diagram for the assembly of a pistol, an advertised magnesium gun "for nighttime photography" (Figure 1). Black patches like burns smudge these images. With exposure to light the images gradually fade; the black patches reveal themselves to be the rhythmic chains of the DNA molecule as captured in microphotography (Figure 2). Embedded in the last pages of the book is a computer disk containing a text by cyberpunk novelist William Gibson. When activated, it runs once; then a built-in computer virus destroys the text, leaving a blank disk (Figure 3).

No matter, for now, what the evanescent content of that disk may be. Its specific content is less important than the fact of its disappearance. In a jibe at the art world's commercialism, publisher Kevin Begos, Jr., suggested to Ashbaugh that "what we should do is put out an art book on computer that vanishes." Ashbaugh took him seriously, took him further; Gibson was enlisted shortly after. For all its complex resonances as an object, then, *Agrippa* is based on this one idea: a book disappears.

The idea has precedents. Maurice Blanchot's essay on "The Absence of the Book" argues from writerly experience that a work always becomes something other than what it is intended to be—what it is intended to be being, of course, a book. But the book (icon of law, presence, textual-cultural wholeness) is always betrayed by what Blanchot calls "the disaster." This disaster has to do with the necessary falling short of a work's concept at the same time that an unexpected otherness beyond the work is evoked. A book never realizes its desired full presence; its realization occurs only and paradoxically through absence—"the prior deterioration of the book, the game of dissidence it plays with reference to the space in which it is inscribed; the preliminary dying of the book."[1] In the end the original concept, and even the very idea of "concept" must be exploded, Blanchot argues, citing Mallarmé's curious statement that "there is no explosion but a book."

Mallarmé also said that "the world exists in order to be put into a book." And he made this book—Le Livre—the ongoing preoccu-

Figure 1. Etching by New York-based artist Dennis Ashbaugh, printed in the book housing the disk on which *Agrippa*'s text is stored. Photo courtesy of Kevin Begos Publishing, Inc. Reprinted with permission.

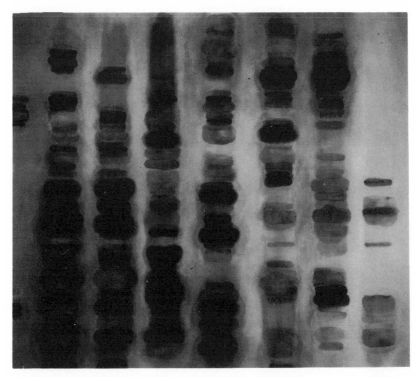

Figure 2. *Gene-Meddling Microbe* by Dennis Ashbaugh. Photo copyright ©
by Megan Boody; provided by Kevin Begos Publishing, Inc. Reprinted with
permission.

pation and project of his last twenty years, a project which came
to nothing. Le Livre never appeared; its absence may have been the
very point of it. The book's nonappearance is linked to the disappearance of the world, a crucial component of Mallarmé's art—so Sartre
argues.

> Meaning is a second silence deep within silence; it is the nega-
> tion of the world's status as a thing. This ever unspoken meaning,
> which would disappear if one ever attempted to speak it . . . is
> quite simply the *absence* of certain objects. What is involved here

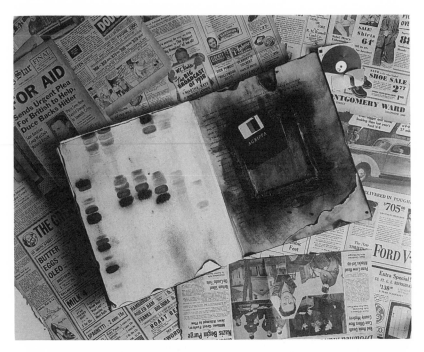

Figure 3. *Agrippa*, a collaborative artists' book by William Gibson and Dennis Ashbaugh. Photo copyright © by Megan Boody; provided by Kevin Begos Publishing, Inc. Reprinted with permission.

is not the mere absence of a particular being but a "resonant disappearance."[2]

Sartre is here quoting Mallarmé's "disparition vibratoire," which was for him the condition of any possible meaning or truth. Speaking of his own writing, Mallarmé said that "whatever truth emerged in the process did so with the loss of an impression which, after flaring up for a brief instant, burned itself out."[3]

Kevin Begos has acknowledged the influence of both Mallarmé's book and Blanchot's "Absence of the Book." One more book was needed to catalyze *Agrippa*, however—an old photograph album discovered by Gibson on a trip back to his home town of Wytheville, Virginia. His computerized text reproduces its commercial title page:

ALBUMS
C. A. AGRIPPA
Order extra leaves by letter and name

The print is dim, scrawled over with something indecipherable. The opening words of Gibson's text describe the opening of the album:

> I hesitated
> before untying the bow
> that bound the book together
> A Kodak album of time-harmed
> black construction paper

These words describing a hesitation themselves hesitate before they begin scrolling past. Then, one by one, the old photographs are rendered in words, each with its caption—though these captions are sometimes indecipherable, their obscurity described along with the rest of the book's "time-harmed" textures. This electronic book, book of the future, evokes through its words the ghost of antiquated pages.

That this ghostly book is a photo album means that it is already a book of the dead. In the photographs a whole world of people and objects is depicted in intense specificity: shadows cast over the brim of straw hats, grass that needs cutting, electric wires strung over street intersections. Yet all these things fall into a Mallarméan absence. Viewing a photograph, Roland Barthes says, "I shudder . . . *over a catastrophe which has already occurred*. Whether or not the subject is already dead, every photograph is this catastrophe."[4] The black box of the camera is a temporal mechanism; Gibson speaks of the fall of the shutter as dividing time.

The description of the album's discovery is followed by the recollection of an earlier discovery by Gibson: As a boy he opened a drawer to find another mechanism of disappearance, his father's pistol. He took it out of the drawer and it unexpectedly discharged; when he dropped it, it went off again. Beyond the biographical fact, there may be a link here to another pair of explosions half a world away: Gibson's father worked on the Manhattan Project. Another possible disappearance of the world is adumbrated, not literary but literal; the singed, disastrous look of the black box's contents takes on a new significance. This "relic from the future," as Begos has called it, replicates a typical pattern of nuclear-war fiction. Relic of a past event which is yet to take place in the future, the nuclear narrative is transmitted backward to us in the present, which is that future's past. The paradoxes shuttle and blur into "time no more," as announced by the angel of the apocalypse; and that "no more" is echoed in the last resonances of a disappearing world.

The men who moved the world closer to disappearance have, most of them, themselves disappeared; Gibson's father died when his son was six. To the degree that *Agrippa* is a memoir of Gibson's father, its irreversible passing is like his life, or any life. We can reread a human life only in memory. We can, of course, *write* of a human life, write "in memory of." When we do, we inhabit a paradoxical space, according to Jacques Derrida:

> [D]oes the expression "in memory of" mean that the name is "in" our memory—supposedly a living capacity to recall images or signs from the past, etc.? Or that the name is in itself, out there somewhere, like a sign or symbol, a monument, epitaph, stele or tomb, a memorandum, aide-mémoire, a memento, an exterior auxiliary set up "in memory of"? Both, no doubt; and here lies the ambiguity of memory, the contamination which troubles us, troubles memory and the meaning of "memory."[5]

Following a distinction in Hegel, Derrida suggests that there are two kinds of memory: mechanical memorization (*Gedächtnis*), associated with writing, and interiorized recollection (*Erinnerung*), associated with mourning. For Derrida, these are at odds with each other: "[T]he inscription of memory [is] an effacement of interiorizing recollection, of the 'living remembrancing.'"[6] Or, as Paul de Man puts it, art "*materially* inscribes, and thus forever forgets, its ideal content."[7] But the process can be reversed: writing that disappears can make another kind of memory appear. This is an *un*forgetting, in Heidegger's terms—the return from Lethe—*aletheia* or truth, a version akin to Mallarmé's truth. To lose the text commemorating a loss is not, then, to redouble loss; it is to move away from the loss that is always inherent in memory's textual mechanism. It is once again to take into one's keeping the memory that is interiorized recollection.

What I have just said may give the impression that Gibson's text is exclusively past-bound, father-oriented, in one way or another an act of mourning. This is not so. At a certain point in the album, and in his own book, the photographed small-town streets which are his father's memories fuse with Gibson's own memories. He then detaches himself from those past streets, remembers the process of forgetting them. By way of the draft board office on the town's main street, Gibson recalls his one-way trip to the Canadian border; when he crosses that border, time is divided as if by a shutter. He describes the unfamiliar feel, the texture, of his first days in Toronto. Finally, a leap into an even stranger future, so remote from these that it might be a scene from one of Gibson's own novels. In a Far Eastern city, a typhoon speeds "horizontal rain" at the speaker's face. Yet this destructive future elicits neither mourning nor fear. In the last words to scroll by, the speaker is "laughing in the mechanism."

What mechanism? The word "mechanism" is repeated at intervals in *Agrippa*, and the idea is implicit throughout it.

—The camera is a mechanism for dividing time.

—The gun, when it discharges, enforces in the silence that follows an "awareness of the mechanism."

—Behind the gun, the bomb—and a mechanism extending beyond the bomb casing to the Manhattan Project and the forces that produced it.

—On a still night in Wytheville, the boy can hear the clicking as traffic lights change a block away, and this too is described as an awareness of the mechanism. How far away does the mechanism extend?

—The photograph album is referred to as a mechanism; any book is a mechanism.

—Language is a mechanism; for Jacques Lacan, it is the mechanism we are born into, the set of the structuring principles of our lives.

—An affinity between chains of signifiers and chromosomal chains. If we are born into the mechanism of language, we are born *out of* a genetic mechanism—out of which we cannot move, for it composes us.

—The mechanisms of our genes and our nervous systems, insofar as they are mechanisms, are linked to those of the computer in a cybernetic field.

When the disk has run its course, everything in the text—book, camera, gun, explosion, father, town, time, memory—is encrypted into a mechanized code much like that on Ashbaugh's pages, before it contorts and vanishes. Always, and in all its versions, the mechanism is involved with absence and its ultimate end is disappearance.

That disappearance is apocalyptic: I am using the word not only in its sense of overwhelming destruction, but also in its original Greek sense of revelation. The last book of the Bible has forever linked destruction with revelation—as Blanchot does, as Mallarmé does. Moreover, it does so repeatedly through a *book*. The Book of the Apocalypse describes the opening of a book; that opening, seal by seal, unleashes a series of terrible endings. The Last Judgment is initiated when the Book of the Dead is opened. And finally the sky disappears "as a scroll when it is rolled together." Microcosmic apocalypse, *Agrippa* too is destroyed by being opened, its images fading, its text scrolling past us into irreversible emptiness. But if there can be no rereading, the reading we have finished may not be finished with us. After the final destruction of heaven and earth in the Bible a new heaven and earth come to pass; and something like this comes to pass in reading, even if what is read can never be read again. Blanchot has said that writing is "the opaque, empty opening into that which is when there is no more world, when there is no world yet."[8] He hovers here between "no more" and "not yet," between loss and potential: the emptiness is apocalyptic, in both its senses. Through the necessary destruction of the text (all texts), something comes to pass. Though the question of what comes to pass is ultimately beyond us, the question of *how* it comes to pass is not.

A book, says Blanchot, is "a ruse by which writing goes towards *the absence of the book*."[9] The ruse in *Agrippa*, as in other books, has to do with framing. The final disappearance of *Agrippa* takes place within multiple frames, some literal, some literary: the black box, the corroded coffin in which the shrouded book is laid; the book's cover and title; the time-bound pages of newspaper, commercial images, genetic codes; the embedded disk of magnetic code; the code of language; rhythm and recurrence—all that I have articulated of what this work articulates, and more. All of these are mechanisms which, rightly combined, explode into revelation, the immanence of something *beyond*. But in the revelation of what lies between or beyond these framing elements, they are annihilated. For what is apprehended is exactly what is other than these separate elements, a sum that exceeds these parts. We move toward the famous conclusion of Wittgenstein's *Tractatus*—a tautology that is saved from the "intense inane" by being itself framed, the product of a certain process in time. At the end of the process that is *Agrippa* we are left not merely with emptiness, but with our awareness of that process both in and beyond the mechanism. Knowing that there *has been* a process in time, the blank page (as in Isak Dinesen's tale) may be the most eloquent text. "The most beautiful and perfect book in the world," says Ulises Carrión, "is a book with only blank pages, in the same way that the most complete language is that which lies beyond all that the words of man can say."[10] In the very act of disappearing, then, *Agrippa* makes something appear.

Notes

This work was supported by the Social Sciences and Humanities Research Council of Canada. Special thanks to Veronica Hollinger and Sasha Sergejewski.

1   Maurice Blanchot, "The Absence of the Book," in *The Gaze of Orpheus and Other Literary Essays*, ed. P. Adams Sitney, trans. Lydia Davis (Barrytown, NY, 1981), 151.

2   Jean-Paul Sartre, *Mallarmé, or the Poet of Nothingness*, trans. Ernest Sturm (University Park, PA, 1988), 140.

3   Letter from Mallarmé to Eugène Lefébvre, 17 May 1867, in *Stéphane Mallarmé: Correspondance, 1862–1871*, ed. Henri Mondor (Paris, 1959), 245–46.

4   Roland Barthes, *Camera Lucida: Reflections on Photography*, trans. Richard Howard (New York, 1981), 96.

5   Jacques Derrida, *Mémoires: For Paul de Man*, trans. Cecile Lindsay, Jonathan Culler, and Eduardo Cadava (New York, 1986), 50.

6   Ibid., 56.

7   Paul de Man, "Sign and Symbol in Hegel's *Aesthetics*," *Critical Inquiry* 8 (1982): 773; cited in Derrida, *Mémoires*, 67.

8   Maurice Blanchot, *The Space of Literature*, trans. Ann Smock (Lincoln, NE, 1982), 33.

9   Blanchot, "Absence of the Book," 147.

10   Ulises Carrión, quoted in *Artists' Books: A Critical Anthology and Sourcebook*, ed. Joan Lyons and Gibbs M. Smith (Rochester, 1985), 38.

SCOTT BUKATMAN

GIBSON'S TYPEWRITER

Our writing materials contribute their part to our thinking.
—Nietzsche

Typewriter: It types *us*, encoding its own linear bias across the free space of the imagination.
—J. G. Ballard

hat's Not Writing, That's Typing! This is what we know about it: It's green (actually green and black), with celluloid keys of canary yellow. It's heavy; it's flammable; it's a "tough and elegant" Swiss machine from the shop of E. PAILLARD & CIE S. A. YVERDON. It was once owned by a journalist, but it remained in the family. It was expensive. It's a Hermes 2000. William Gibson wrote *Neuromancer* on it.

It is a tale often told in cybercultural enclaves and English departments: William Gibson wrote *Neuromancer* on a manual typewriter. *Really? Yes!* There is something charming about the anecdote, and it is not difficult to locate the source of that charm. A simple bit of irony is at work in the apparently singular fact that this novel all about computers, the novel that invented cyberspace (sort of), the hippest, highest novel of the 1980s, should have been written on such an antiquated device. That this primal work of electronic culture was produced, not on a word processor or even an electric typewriter, but rather on an archaic piece of nineteenth-century technology, seems worthy of continual note.

But there might be more at stake in the compulsive repetition of this little cyberfable. Ironies are rarely simple, while we know that laughter or amusement can mask anxieties that lurk only slightly beneath the surface. In this instance, the anxieties center upon contemporary relations to history, technology, and language. In the telling of this story, two separate communities come into existence. The first, comprised of hackers and cyberdroolers, shares a dedication to the sheer coolness of new technologies. *Come on*, they say, *a TYPE-WRITER?!* The story enables those involved to position themselves as part of the new breed (*What's a typewriter?*). It's a funny story of personal idiosyncrasy, like finding out that Gibson rode a unicycle and wore pantaloons while he wrote. And then there is the more conservative community—English professors, let's say—that forms around the relief generated in linking this high-tech figure to the traditional world of letters (*typewritten* letters) and literature.

What our two anecdotal communities share is their regard of the typewriter as an obsolescent technology. For the more conservative group, *Neuromancer* is reinserted into canonical understandings of literature, as the terrors of the electronic age are displaced to a safe distance. The cyberheads become hacker undergrounders through the story: its telling constructs them as cyberspace cowboys with abilities superior to even those of *cyberspace's architect*. For this group, *Neuromancer* is situated as an instantiating text, as history is reduced to an ironic gloss. The very urgent history of mechanical technology becomes an absurd footnote within a cybercultural history that believes only in the newness of all phenomena, as though the world itself had been entirely reborn in the electronic era.

To an extent, I am sympathetic to (and complicit in) the construction of this ahistorical teleology. The ultimate effect of the electronic refiguring of the world remains indeterminate; the boundaries of new technological powers are still uncertain, while all ontological categories are seemingly put up for grabs. There is no question that *something* new is at work while we all slip into a state of terminal identity. But, despite this future-shocking onslaught, the discourse surrounding (and containing) electronic technology is somewhat surprisingly prefigured by the earlier technodiscourse of the machine age. Machines have become the metaphors that enable comprehension of postindustrial technological proliferation—even the high-tech, rust-proof sheen of *Mondo 2000* is just a seductive exercise in denial. Hence an examination of earlier technocultures is the movement of the moment (see Gibson and Sterling's novel *The Difference Engine* for Victorian-era cyberpunk, or "steampunk"). The disappearance of history was, after all, proclaimed over ten years ago by Jameson, Baudrillard, and their progeny. While a new "cultural dominant" has yet to emerge, many salient characteristics of postmodernity have waned, or shifted terrain. Within this tumult, history can make— has been making—its necessary return. Perhaps its disappearance was little more than a trope of the postmodern text.

Some attention to the typewriter may therefore be warranted in order to type history back into *Neuromancer*. What emerges from a consideration of Gibson's typewriter, or at least what can be teased out of that consideration, are several overlapping tropes that tie cyberculture to its historical forebears. Reinstating the history of the typewriter indicates that *Neuromancer*'s disembodied informational cyberspaces are anticipated by the "obsolescent" rhetorics and technologies of what Mark Twain, the author of the first typewritten manuscript, once called "machine culture."

≡≡≡≡

The Industrialization of Language in the Nineteenth Century. The history of the nineteenth century is, of course, marked by the pervasive spread of industrial technologies, which affected more than the conditions of production or even consumption. As the historical research of Wolfgang Schivelbusch demonstrates, industrialization resulted in a phenomenological reconfiguring of urban existence (through the introduction of new building materials, the impact of the railroad, and the electric lighting of both interior and exterior spaces), as well as a pervasive reconception of spatiotemporal experience (through the convenient/marvelous/traumatic experience of railway travel and the related technologies of the telegraph and the cinema).[1] To these we might add that the telegraph, telephone, automated typesetting machine, and typewriter constituted a far-reaching industrialization of *language* in the nineteenth century. As Nietzsche remarked, in a typewritten letter from 1882, "Our writing materials contribute their part to our thinking."[2]

While Schivelbusch rejects technological determinism, he maintains that technological development so marks the nineteenth century that it must become the central issue for historians of that era. This same reasoning certainly also applies to the subsequent, and equally rapid and pervasive, developments of the Electronic Age.

The Typewriter and Its History: Improvements Wanted. The repression of the typewriter's historical significance in the *Neuromancer* anecdote has its analogue in the annals of technological history. No serious academic investigation of the typewriter has been published, to my knowledge, and almost all curious writers seem to rely upon the same two texts: *The Typewriter and the Men Who Made It* (hmm . . .) and, even better, *The Wonderful Writing Machine* (wow!), both highly positivist texts from the 1950s. The saga of the typewriter's development lacks a heroic central figure, such as Edison, Whitney, or Bell (or Alan Turing, Steve Wozniak, or Bill Gates). In fact, the saga seems more of a case study of American manufacturing methods in the later nineteenth century: not exactly biopic material.[3]

There had been a number of attempts to construct writing machines in the eighteenth century. The first machines were developed for use by the blind and were designed to make a tactile impression on the page. The machine was to make it possible to process information despite a loss of vision and/or visibility. A similar desire operates through the metaphor of Gibsonian cyberspace: a space in which the invisible processes of information circulation are recast in visual and tactile terms (the metaphor resides in the status of cyberspace as a *narrated*, rather than an *actual*, space). Typewriters accomplish their goals by spatializing information—the letters of the alphabet are dispersed in a standardized arrangement, each immediately available to the user. Information is rendered accessible, despite the lack of visual interaction. "Spatially designated and discrete signs—that, rather than increase in speed, was the real innovation of the typewriter."[4]

This arranged keyboard was the 1873 innovation of a Milwaukee newspaper editor, Christopher Latham Sholes (or the "father of the typewriter," as he is inevitably called). Earlier prototypes were usually characterized by a dial and a lever. Dial a letter, press the lever, and an impression is made on the paper (hidden from view). Release the lever, and the paper advances one space. The method was slow and far removed from the flow of writing by hand. The machines were inefficient extensions of existing modes of human communication (to be McLuhanesque about it). Sholes had responded to a challenge published in *Scientific American* that exhorted its gadget-oriented readership to produce a writing machine that would improve on existing models (it was a 1987 *Scientific American* article that introduced virtual reality, or cyberspace, to a more general readership).[5] Inspired by the key of a telegraph sender, he constructed an array in which each piece of type was operated by a separate lever, all spread out before the user's gaze and hands.

Sholes was a colorful advocate of strange technological happenings. "Think of it!" he exclaimed, in predicting the arrival of telegraph lines to Milwaukee. News from the East Coast would reach the city ten minutes after it was sent. "Language fails to convey anything like the sensations which the certainty of such an event must create." (This is not just a case of the technological sublime in action—Sholes was also interested in other forms of communication, as his active participation in the spiritualist fads of the middle-century attests.[6]) We witness in Sholes's rhetoric a vested interest in an information revolution: his euphoria is a function of the *speed* and *power* of information technologies which would immediately empower the citizenry—a position espoused today by technoprophet Alvin Toffler. Late in his life Sholes foresaw the obsolescence of his own medium, as news would be delivered to each home via little wireless teleprinters (this became a favorite fantasy of the early twentieth century within the pages of *Popular Mechanics* and endless SF stories).

Advances in industrialism produced the enabling technologies that were fundamental to the execution of a reliable and durable type-writing mechanism. (One history asserts that the "typewriter was the most complex mechanism mass produced by American industry, pub-lic or private, in the nineteenth century."[7]) But a successful industrial invention implies equally successful economic exploitation. News-paper publisher James Densmore worked with Sholes and his partners on simplifying the typewriting mechanism so that the device could be successfully and economically manufactured. Densmore then mar-keted the invention to the Remington Firearms Company, which, in the years following the Civil War, was retooling its munitions facto-ries to produce sewing machines and other complex machinery for American industry.[8]

———

A Typewriter Warmed in Hell: Typewriters Go to War. The juxtaposi-tion between the technology of firearms and the machinery of the typewriter is provocative. In *Neuromancer*, a disassembled typewriter in Deane's office—Gibson's own machine making a cameo appear-ance—hides a weapon: " 'It's on all the time,' Deane said mildly, taking a gun from behind the exposed works of his old mechanical typewriter and aiming it carefully at Case. It was a belly gun, a mag-num revolver with the barrel sawn down to a nub." And, from Bruce Bliven's *The Wonderful Writing Machine*:

> In millions of homes the typewriter is really as important as the washing machine; it's just that the members of the family seldom think of mentioning that fact. A young man or woman would hardly consider going off to college without a portable. (Sometimes the same machine that Father used, with the tat-tered remnants of the school colors still sticking to the battered case.) And—perhaps the ultimate test—when man goes into war he keeps his typewriter close by his side. The captain of a battle-ship insists that there be fifty-five typewriters on board before he feels fully equipped to meet the enemy. On the ground, as the army moves forward, there are more writing machines within four thousand yards of the front lines than medium and light artillery pieces combined.[9]

≡≡≡

Learning to Type. Initial returns on the typewriter were surprisingly small. Businesses were originally loath to make the capital investment (machines and training), and were further concerned that typewritten correspondence would lack a "personal touch" and might prove offensive to clients. Journalists were surprisingly slow to adopt the new machine. Nietzsche procured an early machine to compensate for his failing eyesight, but he was unable to adapt to its rigors.

What rescued the machine from oblivion were the economic shifts that America underwent following the Civil War. In the move from an agrarian to an overwhelmingly industrial economy, businesses expanded enormously. The male office worker, traditionally a clerk who copied documents by hand, was simply unable to cope with the new volume of business-related paperwork. Of course, there was a vast, literate, potential work force available for employment at lower wages—middle-class women.[10] There was thus a major shift in the composition of the work force with the introduction of this new information-processing technology (cyborg fans will want to note that the women who worked on typewriters were *themselves* known as typewriters).

In his history, Richard Current stresses the increased output of information that resulted from the introduction of the typewriter: "[T]he writing machine swelled tremendously the output of recorded words." He further notes that once-concise attorneys and businessmen, now dictating to a typist, revealed a tendency to wax loquacious. More documents, more words, more typewriters (the machine and the worker). As Current argues, the "multiplication of records not only measured but made possible a growing complexity of life. In particular, it facilitated the rise of both Big Business and Big Bureaucracy."[11] Industrial culture and informational culture arose together in a flood of typewritten symbols. Future shock and the overload of the Information Age here made their initial appearance. In the late twentieth century, computers developed into text-processing machines precisely in order to *control* the informational cyberblitz produced by all the typewriters in the world.

—————

Information Overload in the Atomic Age. The Wonderful Writing Machine describes the rise of a profession that accompanied the indisputable success of the typewriter in the twentieth century. As "the growing accumulation of old typewriting began to overwhelm businessmen and business offices," a new figure emerged—the files disposal expert. "He is a man, essentially, who knows how to throw typewriting away." This "essential man" is a figure of the Atomic Age. Bliven writes (with striking glibness for 1954): "The files disposal business boomed in about 1947 when the atom bomb threatened to clean out everybody's files with one whoosh, and businessmen thought that, if they didn't have such an awfully bulky lot of stuff to keep, they might save a few of the more important things in caves or underground vaults." [12] Here, in miniature, is the cold war experience of abundance and expansion subverted by a continual sense of physical vulnerability and paranoia. Protecting the files would at least close the potential information gap in a post-apocalyptic international business setting.

—————

The Différance Engine. In his recent *Discourse Networks 1800/1900,* Friedrich Kittler has applied the language strategies of poststructuralism to the technologies of discourse. For Kittler, the introduction of the typewriter to the field of textual production has had profound and lasting effects, which are described in terms that bring us to the edge of cyberspace. What first characterizes typing as an act of writing is an effect of *disembodiment*: the first typewriters did not permit the user to see the printed characters until several lines later. Not until Underwood's refinement did "visible writing" become a possibility. Angelo Beyerlin, Germany's foremost typewriter manufacturer, wrote:

> In writing by hand, the eye must constantly watch the written line and only that. It must attend to the creation of each written line, must measure, direct, and, in short, guide the hand through each movement. For this, the written line, particularly the line being written, must be visible. By contrast, after one presses

down briefly on a key, the typewriter creates in the proper position on the paper a complete letter, which not only is untouched
by the writer's hand but is also located in a place entirely apart
from where the hands work.[13]

Even a visible-writing typewriter hides the empty space that lies
before the writing (the field of potentiality). Thus, "Underwood's
innovation unlinks hand, eye, and letter" in a historically unique
moment of disjuncture. The hands appear *here*, while the writing appears *there*. Typing produces an information space divorced from the
body: a proto-cyberspace.

This disembodiment results from the emphatic standardization
already described as a consequence of the keyboard array. If the act
of handwriting had been a "continuous transition from nature to culture"—that is, from prelinguistic thought to sign—then the act of
typing was "selection from a countable, spatialized supply." Following the precepts set forth by Derrida in *Speech and Phenomena*, Kittler
makes a valuable distinction between a handwriting that *appears as* a
direct emanation from the body, from nature, and a typewriting that
is clearly mediated by cultural systems.

The described effect of a disembodied textual mechanics separates
Kittler from the more utopian version of typing history provided
by Marshall McLuhan. Like Richard Current before him and Kittler
after, McLuhan emphasizes the structural impact of the typewriter
and related technologies (though his main source seems to have been
The Wonderful Writing Machine: "A modern battleship needs dozens
of typewriters for ordinary operations"). As one might expect, however, McLuhan's emphasis on technology as "the extensions of man"
leads him to stress, not the displacements of disembodiment, but
rather the *integration of functions* that occurs through typing: "At the
typewriter, the poet commands the resources of the printing press.
The machine is like a public-address system. . . . As expediter, the
typewriter brought writing and speech and publication into close
association. Although a merely mechanical form, it acted in some
respects as an implosion, rather than an explosion."[14] All these disparate functions are brought together and introjected within an increasingly empowered body. Cyberspace becomes the ultimate terrain for

this implosive integration of functions, as humans and data are made equivalent. McLuhan's utopian technoneurology serves a function similar to Gibson's cyberspace, as a metaphor that "naturalizes" technology to compensate for the human's alienation from the speed, power, and pervasiveness of contemporary technological configurations. (Gibson's formations seem by far the more richly complex of the two.)

Typecasting

The keyboard standardized the appearance and spacing of letters, and some worried that the typewriter spelled an end to the ability to write. The typewriter would thus yield a loss of bodily control, or perhaps even a loss of the body itself. The result, however, was a handwriting that aspired to the perfection of the typewritten standard. The typewriter thus makes potential cyborgs of us all, in our attempt to match its machine-tooled perfection. Ironically, the computer age has also introduced personalized fonts, developed from the handwriting of the user. The computer now simulates the human's fallible and uniquely shaky scrawl, albeit in a newly standardized and storable form. Is it live, or Personal Font?™

(For the nostalgic, however, the computer can recall and reproduce the hyperbolic regularity of Machine Age typewriting. What exactly *is* the Courier font, in all its clunky glory, doing on my Mac?)

Speed-Typing. In 1839, Michel Chevalier wrote about the American in motion:

> . . . [H]e is always in the mood to move on, always ready to start in the first steamer that comes along from the place where he has just now landed. He is devoured with a passion for movement; he must go and come, he must stretch his limbs and keep his

muscles in play. When his feet are not in motion, his fingers must be in action; he must be whittling a piece of wood, cutting the back of his chair, or notching the edge of the table, or his jaws must be at work grinding tobacco. "We are born in haste," says an American writer. "Our body is a locomotive going at the rate of twenty-five miles an hour; our soul, a high-pressure engine." [15]

Ever the technophile, Twain was one of the first to purchase a type-writing machine (the story of his purchase appears, with suspiciously minimal variation, in every typewriter history). He praised it with reckless enthusiasm. But Twain's attitudes toward technology were truly ambivalent; as his *Connecticut Yankee* demonstrates, mechanization can produce unparalleled devastation. Nevertheless, one biographer argues that

> [t]he Yankee and the Machine were twinned in his mind. Both were tests of a perfectible world in which, contrary to all his insights and experience, friction and mechanical difficulties were equivalents of ignorance and superstition. Both expressed a secular religion which had as an unexamined article of faith a belief not in eternal life but in *perpetual motion*. [16]

Perpetual, agitated kinesis marks the American spirit. The body is a machine, perfectible and progress-oriented, while—at the same time—the machine becomes a body. [17]

The symbiosis of typewriter (machine) and typewriter (user) probably reached an apex with the *speed-typing* exhibitions that swept the country for about thirty-five years, beginning in the late 1800s. "Typewriter speed queens and kings were celebrities of a minor luminosity." [18] Before the battles, typewriter manufacturers had been content to boast that typing was twice as fast as the hand, but now these typewriter/cyborgs, these carbon-paper cowboys, left the natural hand far below on the evolutionary ladder. One charming and slightly scary photo shows the 1926 Amateur (!) Champion, Stella Willins, posing in a motorcycle sidecar with her typewriter (of course) perched precariously before her. It's as though her typing must be measured in mph instead of wpm. Kinesis alone produces the technologized subject.

Unlike *Neuromancer's* renegade cowboys, these jocks were largely corporate-owned—perhaps they belonged to the Underwood Speed Training Group, or a similar organization. They did, however, have their own "decks": "Each typist had his own racing typewriter. . . . He carried it to matches, or on exhibition tours, in a big plush-lined case . . . and he worried about it the way a concert violinist worries about a Stradivarius. . . . The machines were stock models but souped up, like a hot-rod racing automobile. . . ."[19] Bliven describes the intense concentration the "speed queens" (and kings) displayed during a match, their fingers endlessly moving in conditioned-reflex perfection. "The slightest trace of self-consciousness was a fatal drawback." In *Neuromancer*, Case, too, yearns for the "bodiless exultation of cyberspace," the dissolution of self within the information vectors of the machine. For Gibson, though, this is both a dissolution of self and a self regained.

≡≡≡

Keep Jane's Fingers Dancing. Of course, there is another step in this cyborg dance. Despite the sporting aspects of these thoroughbred competitions, speed-typing also represents the apotheosis of the Taylorist vision in which every gesture is designed to maximize productivity. *The Wonderful Writing Machine* reports that "motion studies" of the new electric typewriter revealed a 6 percent energy savings: "Which is pure bonus as long as the boss doesn't expect his patient stenographer to accomplish 20 per cent more, now that he's broken down and bought her an electric."[20] Throughout Bliven's book, secretaries are presented as a naive, patient, but secretly controlling group of girls ("or ladies, to be more polite"), coddled by bosses who can't afford to lose them. Yet the increase in the speed of office information processing called for a commensurate increase from the human user. The not-so-shocking truth is that the shift to electric typewriters was *not* grudgingly performed by gruff but lovable bosses giving their secretaries a "pure bonus," but by managers determined to maximize profits. The trend has obviously continued: Jeremy Rifkin reports that where a secretary once averaged about thirty thousand keystrokes every hour, a worker at a VDT terminal is expected to average eighty thousand.[21] Some "bonus."

Surveillance of worker output is also much easier in cyberspace, since every terminal can measure and report the number of keystrokes to a central managing position. *Processed World* magazine once featured a parodic ad for "Press®," a product designed to monitor employee pace:

> If Jane's [keystroke] count drops below your chosen margin for more than three minutes, a subliminal warning flickers at the top of the screen. And if Jane still hasn't pulled herself together after two more minutes, a healthy 1-second jolt of 50 volts pulses out of her specially modulated keyboard and grounds harmlessly through her chair. It's guaranteed to get her moving again![22]

=====

The Mysterious Interior of Machine #HH 5166247. The Wonderful Writing Machine features a chapter that concentrates on the labor of "final adjusting" as it is performed by Horace Stapenell ("a modest man"), an employee ("one of the best") of the Royal Typewriter Company in Hartford, Connecticut. The author provides Horace's name, address, and biography before moving into a detailed explanation of his job. Just as Horace is a fairly ordinary guy, so the machines he works on are "standard-width carriage machine[s] with a standard keyboard." Those Johnny-come-latelies, the portables and the electrics, get their adjustments, mysteriously enough, "in other departments in other parts of the factory." Horace works in Department 10-C, and "10-C men hang around together." The chapter then becomes a tour through the inside of the typewriter, as we watch Horace make minute adjustments to bring the entire complex mechanism into alignment. The lines must be straight, the spacing even, the mechanism smooth and unresistant.

Horace is a real typewriter cowboy ("typewriters have been the focus of his whole working life"), fully jacked into his machine ("[a]ll his senses except taste are involved"). Once again, a symbiosis operates as man and machine are each narrated simply in terms of the other. The figure of the human exists to present the space of the machine, and the machine is thereby humanized. Unlike that of the human typewriters and secretaries, Horace's work is measured by how *slowly* he proceeds: he "spends as much as three hours adjusting a single typewriter." And despite the monotony of his labor, Horace has developed his own system, subtly different from that of the other workers around him ("[t]hey are the distinctions between working at a craft and *working as a machine*").

The chapter details all the operations that Horace is likely to make, elaborately fetishizing each mechanism of the complex whole. The chapter frankly reads like ad copy: the more clarity the descriptions offer, the more the machine is mystified and mythicized. An assembly-line worker is inscribed within the rather different history of skilled handcraftsmanship, while the "standard" typewriter is itself invested with the precise workmanship of a town clock in Switzerland. It is as though the loss of the *hand* in the switch from handwriting to typewriting calls for its reappearance at some other part of the "discourse network," and so the writing machine is maintained by a particularly careful, knowing, but human hand.[23]

≡≡≡≡

Dylan Goes Acoustic (or, Clapton Unplugged). Thus the wonderful writing machine is invested with all the romance of a pretechnological mechanical marvel, like an elaborate automaton. In his volume on postmodernism, Jameson offers an interesting reading of the modernist text:

> Modern art . . . drew its power and its possibilities from being a backwater and an archaic holdover within a modernizing economy: it glorified, celebrated, and dramatized older forms of individual production which the new mode of production was elsewhere on the point of displacing and blotting out. Aesthetic production then offered the Utopian vision of a more human production generally; and in the world of the monopoly stage of capitalism it exercised a fascination by way of the image it offered of a Utopian transformation of human life.[24]

Despite the postmodern trappings of *Neuromancer*, Istvan Csicsery-Ronay, Jr., has located a significant modernist impulse at work in the subtextual celebration of art and creation that underlies much of Gibson's writing.[25] Its mode of production on a manual (hand-powered) typewriter links the work to Jameson's theory of modernism and uneven technological development. The typewritten manuscript belongs to a different historical moment from the postmodern cyberspaces of *Neuromancer*; in this sense, Twain was far more progressive than Gibson. When, around 1883, Twain produced the first typewritten manuscript, *Life on the Mississippi*, he was distancing himself from older modes of textual production, while with *Neuromancer*'s manuscript, Gibson proclaims his fidelity to those modes. (It's tempting to regard *Neuromancer* as the *last* typewritten manuscript, even if it isn't true.)

≡≡≡≡≡

The Mechanics of Fiction. Spatialization of information, disembodiment, exaggerated kinesis, information overload (cyberblitz), and the passage into the realm of the machine—these are the familiar tropes of Gibson's *Neuromancer*. But these figures are prefigured by a range of earlier discourses surrounding emergent information technologies, including those from the late nineteenth century (Twain, Sholes) as well as the middle of the twentieth (McLuhan, Bliven) and later (Jameson, Kittler).

Twain had invested a fortune in a typesetting machine developed by a James Paige (with fulsome praise, Twain compared it to all the most marvelous recent inventions, including the "difference engine" developed by Charles Babbage): the machine "became 'an inspired bugger,' 'a cunning devil,' and, after passing through a 'sick child' stage, a 'magnificent creature' ranking second only to man." Justin Kaplan argues that through this anthropomorphism, Twain expressed both his hopes and "his basic layman's ignorance, his credulity in the face of what seemed to him a divine mystery only because he knew hardly anything about mechanics."[26] Twain thus relied on nature for the conceptual metaphors that would render the mechanical susceptible to thought; he reached with eagerness for the inconceivable, but could do so only in terms of the already conceived.

Gibson might be understood to do the same, but instead of nature, he draws upon the paradigm of industrial technology. Thus cyberspace is as mathematically precise as a blueprint ("the cool geometric intricacy of Zurich commercial banking"), and despite "the horizonless fields," its data systems comprise "an endless neon cityscape" and even "the old RCA Building" makes an appearance—"The Kuang program dived past the gleaming spires of a dozen identical towers of data, each one a blue neon replica of the Manhattan skyscraper." Case, the cyberspace cowboy, loses his body but becomes a vehicle:

> Case had the strange impression of being in the pilot's seat in a small plane. A flat dark surface in front of him suddenly glowed with a perfect reproduction of the keyboard of his deck.
> "Two, an' kick ass—"
> Headlong motion through walls of emerald green, milky jade, the sensation of speed beyond anything he'd known before in cyberspace. . . . The Tessier-Ashpool ice shattered, peeling away from the Chinese program's thrust, a worrying impression of solid fluidity, as though the shards of a broken mirror bent and elongated as they fell—
> "Christ," Case said, awestruck as Kuang twisted and banked.[27]

The relentless kinesis is one aspect of *Neuromancer*'s postmodern amphetamine rush, but it also evokes the locomotives, automobiles, and airplanes of the Machine Age, when, as industrial designer Norman Bel Geddes proclaimed, *"Speed is the cry of our era, and greater speed one of the goals of tomorrow."* If cyberspace is a "consensual hallucination" that enables computer users to make sense of both their actions and the circulation of information, then that hallucination works by continually referencing the kinetic urban landscapes of machine-age modernity.

Gibson shared Twain's "basic layman's ignorance" of the new machine's real operations. He relates in an interview: "When I started writing this stuff, I'd never touched a computer. And I think it gave me a certain strange edge in terms of imagination, in that I wasn't really hindered by what was possible." After he got a computer, he began to understand their real-world mechanics: "I somehow thought that they were these silent, crystalline engines. I never really thought about how they worked. [Elsewhere, Gibson writes that he "assumed the data was just sort of, well, *held* in a *glittering mesh* of silicon."] And then I realized it was this piece of clumsy Victorian technology. . . . And at that point I sort of lost something, you know?"[28]

Rust Never Sleeps. While Gibson wrote *Neuromancer* on a manual typewriter, the Voyager Company has enabled me to read it on my Powerbook. A single floppy contains the entire trilogy: *Neuromancer*, *Count Zero*, and *Mona Lisa Overdrive*. Using the search function, I pretend to determine the prevalence of machine culture references in Gibson's writing. Did you know that there are twelve references to *rust* in the first book, nineteen in the second, and a whopping *twenty-six* in the last? "Accelerated decrepitude," as someone in *Blade Runner* once said.

The Adding Machine. An acknowledged influence on Gibson's writing is William Burroughs. Together, Burroughs and Brion Gysin developed the cut-up and fold-in methods of rearranging typewritten text, releasing the words from their mechanically determined linearity. "You cannot *will* spontaneity," wrote Burroughs, whose family was responsible, incidentally, for the Burroughs adding machine. "But you can introduce the unpredictable spontaneous factor with a pair of scissors."[29] The typewriter is liberated from the mechanics of instrumental reason through these dadaist interventions. In "Technology of Writing," Burroughs advised new writers, "One more thing: Sinclair Lewis said: 'If you want to be a writer, learn to type.' This advice is scarcely necessary now. So then sit down at your typewriter and write."[30] David Cronenberg's 1992 film of Burroughs's *Naked Lunch* featured a typewriter that talked out of its ass.

The virus is one of Burroughs's most pervasive metaphors: the cut-up is a virus that destroys syntax and the rational domination of meaning. Burroughs once advocated the use of the Silence Virus to escape from the controllers of language, who are also then the controllers of the self (David Porush has observed that the "noise" generated by the cut-up is a form of silence).[31] In 1992, Gibson released *Agrippa*: a software text with a built-in computer virus that would erase the text as it was read, and a book of illustrations that would fade more slowly, over time.[32] The permanence of data is undermined, subverted by Gibson's own viral play. Gibson now becomes an exterminator, a files disposal expert.

━━━━━
━━━━━
━━━━━

Afterword: Gibson's Afterword. Nothing kills a critical analysis like an author who beats you to it. The Voyager Company's electronic edition of the cyberspace novels features a new afterword, written by Gibson in the summer of 1992. He discusses his Hermes 2000 in loving terms, his subsequent forced experiment with a nightmarish Royal, and his present acquaintance with an Apple computer. He recognizes the perceived irony of his writing *Neuromancer* on a manual machine, but rejects it: "Some readers, evidently, find this odd. I don't." The books "may pretend, at times, and often rather badly, to be about computers, but really they're about technology in some broader sense." At the heart of *Neuromancer* lies the continuity of machines and history. "I suspect they're actually about Industrial Culture; about what we do with machines, what machines do with us, and how wholly unconscious . . . this process has been, is, and will be."[33]

Notes

Let me thank Ed Halter, David Samuels, and Alex Juhasz for their suggestions and ideas. I must also acknowledge a particular debt to Mark Seltzer's *Bodies and Machines*, which was an invaluable source of material.

1   Wolfgang Schivelbusch, *The Railway Journey: The Industrialization of Time and Space in the 19th Century* (Berkeley, 1986), and *Disenchanted Night: The Industrialization of Light in the Nineteenth Century* (Berkeley, 1988).

2   Cited in Friedrich A. Kittler, *Discourse Networks 1800/1900* (Stanford, 1990), 196. In this essay I will not be concentrating upon issues surrounding the materiality of language, or the Logos.

3   This is precisely how it is treated in a somewhat meager industrial history. See Donald R. Hoke, *Ingenious Yankees: The Rise of the American System of Manufactures in the Private Sector* (New York, 1990).

4   Kittler, *Discourse Networks*, 193.

5   "We want a machine which could print as easily as we can now write" ("More Improvements Wanted," *Scientific American*, 8 October 1851, 7); cited in Hoke, *Ingenious Yankees*, 134.

6   Bruce Bliven, Jr., *The Wonderful Writing Machine* (New York, 1954), 4.

7   Hoke, *Ingenious Yankees*, 133.

8   The implications of so-called "armory practice" in manufacturing have been debated in economic history. The military had little reason to economize, and thus its development of labor-intensive mass production may not have been the most

democratic *or* efficient model to apply to civilian production. The evidence seems to suggest that the Remington Company used both armory practice and new methods of organization to produce its typewriters as efficiently as possible (see Hoke, *Ingenious Yankees,* for a more detailed analysis).

9   Bliven, *Wonderful Writing Machine,* 22–23.

10 Margery Davies further argues that women could become typists because the machine was new enough to avoid any sex-specific connotations. See *Woman's Place Is at the Typewriter: Office Work and Office Workers 1870–1930* (Philadelphia, 1982).

11 Richard N. Current, *The Typewriter and the Men Who Made It* (Urbana, 1954), 120–21. Current notes that the typewriter, of course, was not the only such enabling technology (122).

12 Bliven, *Wonderful Writing Machine,* 153.

13 Cited in Kittler, *Discourse Networks,* 195.

14 Marshall McLuhan, *Understanding Media* (New York, 1964), 259–62.

15 Cited in Schivelbusch, *Railway Journey,* 112.

16 Justin Kaplan, *Mr. Clemens and Mark Twain* (New York, 1966), 281.

17 Mark Seltzer, *Bodies and Machines* (New York, 1992), 3–4.

18 Bliven, *Wonderful Writing Machine,* 116.

19 Ibid., 174.

20 Ibid.

21 Jeremy Rifkin, *Time Wars: The Primary Conflict in Human History* (New York, 1987), 117.

22 "Keep Jane's Fingers Dancing," in *Bad Attitude: The Processed World Anthology,* ed. Chris Carlsson with Mark Leger (London, 1990), 181.

23 All quotations in this section are from Bliven, *Wonderful Writing Machine,* 176–200.

24 Fredric Jameson, *Postmodernism, or, The Cultural Logic of Late Capitalism* (Durham, NC, 1991), 307.

25 Istvan Csicsery-Ronay, Jr., "The Sentimental Futurist: Cybernetics and Art in William Gibson's *Neuromancer,*" *Critique* 33 (Spring 1992): 221–40.

26 Kaplan, *Mr. Clemens and Mark Twain,* 283.

27 William Gibson, *Neuromancer.* Electronic ed. (New York, 1992), 228, 510–11.

28 Peter von Brandenburg and Marianne Trench, *Cyberpunk* (a documentary distributed by the Voyager Company [1990]); and William Gibson, "Author's Afterword," *Neuromancer,* 541.

29 William Burroughs, "The Cut-Up Method of Brion Gysin," *Re/Search* 4/5 (1982): 35.

30 William Burroughs, "Technology of Writing," in *The Adding Machine: Collected Essays* (London, 1985), 37.

31 David Porush, *The Soft Machine: Cybernetic Fiction* (New York, 1985), 101.

32 For more on *Agrippa,* see Peter Schwenger's "*Agrippa,* or, The Apocalyptic Book," in this special issue.

33 Gibson, "Author's Afterword," 541–42.

MARC LAIDLAW

VIRTUAL SURREALITY: OUR NEW ROMANCE

WITH PLOT DEVICES

Virtual reality?

This is all I know:

There's something like a dark empty stage in the middle of your brain. As I start to speak, a little light flickers over it, illuminating a man in the shadows. The lights come up a bit more, and now you can see he's wearing glasses of a trendy old-fashioned sort with wire lower rims and heavy black plastic uppers. He has brown hair, dark eyes, a close-trimmed beard. That's about as much as you can make out at first. Then you realize that his mouth is moving in time with the words you hear: yes, it's his voice. My voice. Thanks for letting me into your sensorium.

This is virtual reality, of an old and reliable sort. I'm programming a display of images using the English language, which comes far more naturally to me than using CAD (computer-aided design) software to make pictures glow upon a screen or inside a cybertronic helmet. This is virtual reality, but the chances of your mistaking it for actual reality are about as slim as the chance that you'll forget you're wearing that heavy plastic helmet whose last wearer apparently had pesto for lunch and smoked a big cigar to top it off.

You will always be able to close the book—or shut off the screen—you're reading. Eyes grow tired, if nothing else. But VR technology is young. What happens when the clumsy helmet becomes a snug full-body datasuit, capable of transmitting illusory sensations so convincing that the false reality is indistinguishable from the real? What happens when TV turns invasive, when your Sony Watchman crawls into your eyes and the antennae wrap themselves around your nerves? Can fiction possibly prepare us for such breakthroughs?

I have no particular interest in, or understanding of, technology as such—least of all the complex, constantly evolving new forms of technology that are making virtual reality a household word. When I investigate technology (which is rarely), I want to read or talk to the people who really know what it's all about—the creative geniuses and workaholics who invent and work with the stuff. Why ask a science fiction writer about science when you can ask a real scientist?[1] All you should really ask a writer about is *writing* and its technologies: narrative styles and strategies. Happily, it is here, in a discussion of literary technique, that the virtual realities of technology and fiction can intersect.

For me, virtual reality is mainly a wonderful *plot device*, one that allows surreal effects without recourse to dreams or hallucinations. VR is a fine way of exploring, within the context of technology-oriented science fiction, the nature of reality.

In my first novel, *Dad's Nuke* (1985), I explored some applications of an immersive VR technology, one in which suburbanites donned clumsy hoods and typing gloves to enter a simulated world which, once entered, was extremely realistic, and gave access to a network of connections with other users. It offered a semblance of reality, a "virtual" reality, but was an entirely distinct and separate thing from the "actual" reality of the characters. In moments of mental duress, however, they could sometimes confuse the two; and the technology itself contributed to this confusion by generating convincing images of their actual environments.

In the following scene, Connie Johnson goes in search of her husband, entering his virtual workspace for clues to his whereabouts.

This is not his actual workspace, but a blind he's erected to fool anyone (like Connie) who might come snooping for him. His actual work environment is embellished with pornographic images, sexy secretaries, and other WASP male fantasy icons. But Connie, lacking the proper passwords, can't get into that environment.

"On," she said, and the system began to purr. Light spilled over the desk, speckled her hands. She found the IMR-gloves resting on the arms of the chair and put them on; and then, somewhat clumsily in the gloves, she struggled to get the hood over her head. For a second she suffocated in darkness, but the eyepieces moved into place with slight suction and she found light flashing into her eyes, pulsing, and she relaxed. Her hands tingled. Electricity raced through her spine.

Where was she?

Black curtains parted ahead of her and she moved into a dusty, yellow-lit hallway. With a start she became aware of her body—a heavy-set male physique, dressed in a gray suit. Everything seemed dim and out of focus, including herself. Her steps were heavy, plodding, and hardly carried her down the hall.

She approached a door, one of many, moving with incredible slowness. *Mr. Johnson* was painted on the frosted glass pane. Monday, she kept thinking.

Monday. Sigh.

Poor Bill, she thought in spite of herself. Every day he comes to this.

She was almost afraid to open the door, but she did. There might be a clue to his whereabouts.

The place lit up as she entered. She gazed into a room that surpassed the hallway in drabness. Steel desks, cork partitions, rows of filing cabinets. The hands of an enormous antique clock were frozen at five after eight. Stacks of paper covered the nearest desk, and on the topmost sheet of the tallest stack she saw in huge red letters:

NEED YOUR COMMENTS ASAP.

Her hands, in the gray sleeves, trembled. She felt exhausted, weak, thirsty, as though the dust of the office had settled into her pores. She backed out of the room, turning off the light as she went, and continued down the hall in search of a fountain. A constant clicking sound emanated from the walls on all sides, no louder than the rattling of her teeth, and her headache finally seized her.

With a moan she turned to the nearest door, where the sound of clattering—it must be a typewriter—was very loud.

CENTRAL FILES

Someone here should be able to help her.

She went in, but found herself in an aisle of filing cabinets. There was no one typing, no room in fact for a desk, and the sound she heard came from beyond a door at the far end of the room. When she saw the name on it—*Men*—she started to leave, but the clamor coming from behind the door kept her a moment longer. It sounded like someone scrabbling at the knob, a trapped person hoping to get out. What if it were Bill?

She crossed the room quickly, her steps sounding loud and clear to her ears.

"You can come out," she said in her manly voice. "I unlocked it for you."

The door opened swiftly in the hand of a shadow. Beyond the opener were layers of blackness, darkening successively into the distance. It hardly looked like a restroom.

Four figures stood in the dark. None of them was her husband.

"Hello?" she said.

As they came forward they put out their hands, but she hardly cared when she got a look at their eyes.

Bits of raw meat.

In the hallway, everything was quiet and dim and slow again, the yellow light full of dust. She ran toward the curtains at the far end of the hall, wishing that her body were lighter, her legs more agile. Motes of dust hammered against her face. At last she staggered into the dark, and came to herself in the gloves and the hood, at Bill's desk.

The most comforting thing that can be said about this scene is that Connie was at least able to extricate herself from the hood and gloves and return to the normalcy of her life. (Unless, that is, the VR set fed her the illusion that she had exited the system, and given her only a convincing simulation of escape—in which case she is in for a rude awakening, eventually.) It is an immersive technology, which one can take on or put off.

But the technology in *Dad's Nuke* is deliberately clumsy, a parody of the slick brain-jack technology that William Gibson popularized in *Neuromancer* (1984). (Likewise, the office environment, a faithful description of the office where I surreptitiously wrote that scene, is in dreary opposition to Gibson's breathtaking cyberspace.) When I wrote this book in 1984, it seemed to me that clumsy was the way to go. Little did I know that datagloves and VR technology were about to spring into the public eye, where they still remind me uneasily of the Johnsons' bulky hoods and typing gloves.

My literary approach to cybertech altered as the real stuff became available. I grew especially tired of the glib VR fantasy games that became more and more common in science fiction of the late 1980s, taking the place of the hoary old dream sequence. Characters began to spend entire novels immersed in VR fantasy game programs where nothing was real. It seemed necessary to inject more reality into the material, which meant injecting the material more deeply into reality.

In my latest novel, *Kalifornia* (1993), the technology is no longer immersive but actively invasive. Polynerves, a network of organic "wires" running in parallel to the human nervous system, are ubiquitous in the book. To be without them would be like living without a TV or a telephone . . . or a cellular telephone. No longer can you shut off the TV or close the covers of your magazine: the media are *inside* you.

> Prone on his warm squishy jellobed futon, Sandy Figueroa filled his lungs with tasty resinous redweed primo, inhaled and kept inhaling, gulped a little bit more, lungs cramping now, like a pearl diver filling his chest before a particularly deep and difficult plunge. Then, lying back, releasing the hookah's filter tip, he closed his eyes and let his body-channels switch at random.
>
> Getting zee'd to ride the wires was his favorite indoor pastime, and he rarely did one without the other. The livewire frequencies modulated in accord with his thoughts, which, after the deep drag, had turned totally chaotic. Half a thousand channels

flipped through him in half a second, none quite in synk with his mood. He waited for something to grab him.

Most of the broadcasts were garbage, a polluted ether of advertising and you-are-there gameshows. Bad media lurked in his polynerves like an Alzheimer's prion, waiting to crystallize. He lost a little control and a bit more discrimination when he was zoned. That was part of the fun, but it made for a hairy ride. The redweed put an edge on his mood, making it easier for the freakshows to grab him. Now, for instance, he was snared by—

Bugs!

Jessie Christo! They crawled from his pores, tickled his feet, cast off his nails like manhole covers and scurried for the shelter of his face and genitals. He didn't know whether to cover his nose or his crotch. In a panic, he tried to change channels, but his fright mired him in the signal, making it virtually impossible for him to tune into anything else. There was no waking from this nightmare until it had run its course.

This was no horror show; they didn't grip so ruthlessly. This was a commercial.

Suddenly, a cooling aerosol spray covered him from head to foot. A purple-brown cloud of lilacs and chocolate dissolved the chittering little monsters an instant before they reached his face or pubes. Iridescent wings, scaly carapaces, manifold eyes and quivering antennae—all vanished, leaving him limp and grateful for the spray, whatever it was.

"*Doctor McNguyen's Soothing Anti-Psychotic,*" whispered a sexy voice in, curiously, only one ear. "*Now in aerosol cans.*"

There are more than merely the two "actual" and "virtual" realities active in this scene, for a third kind of reality is generated at the point where they intersect—the equivalent of surrealism's "dreaming with open eyes." However, with about fifty more years of exposure to these technologies than the befuddled suburbanites of *Dad's Nuke*, the denizens of *Kalifornia* are more practiced at distinguishing the various shades of reality.

Since, as some philosophies assert, our reality may itself be an illusion created by the senses and compounded by ignorance, then VR is a particularly fitting metaphor for an exploration of reality. The possibility of confusing virtual and actual modes satisfyingly mirrors the manner in which our minds are duped into believing that they have an objective existence. If reality is a cosmic illusion, then its details need be no more fine-tuned than the best of our sensors to fool us into believing it. Our senses may be very coarse filters, but the mind itself—building up models from a combination of all available information—seems more sensitive, and ultimately it is the mind that must distinguish between reality and fabrication. When the mind has only sensory data to work with, its conclusions are no better than the signals it receives; but when it can merge completely with the forces that generate reality—whether virtual or actual—then it becomes part of the creative process, an active interpreter of nature.

In the following scene from *Kalifornia*, a media prophet abandons her body completely in order to experience an undiluted stream of information, not yet formed into any particular shape. Here I engage in what I consider a chief practical fictional application of virtual reality: namely, CAF, or Computer-Assisted Foreshadowing.[2]

=====

The Seer raged, raged at her studio audience. She had to *grab* their attention. They lived in her flesh, but the sight of it bored them. They preferred the veil to the face beneath it. They craved the illusions she cooked up for them, preferring insubstantial fantasies to solid food. And they loved it best when she insulted them for their bad taste.

"It's criminal, the mental degeneration I see here!" she cried. "Am I the only one who still has a mind of her own? Let's talk concepts, let's talk eons of time. You're devolving. You'll be blind and white as cave fish soon, your bodies will shrivel up, your eyes will cloud over, you'll be nothing but a bunch of body-temp insulation for your wires."

The audience laughed in tentative agreement.

"Oh, Shiva!" she cried in mock exasperation. "Do you even hear what I'm saying?"

Pulses of acknowledgement lit up the tall response boards along

Web I by Ferret. Copyright © 1993 by Ferret. Printed with permission.

the walls, like lightning flashing in stained-glass windows. She noted the boards with satisfaction.

"I see that some of you are still breathing. But how much of this is *really* getting through?"

Fewer flickers this time. She glanced at the ratings monitor to make sure that the audience was still with her; they were too self-conscious to give their all just yet. She signaled her thruput man with a pinching gesture: *peel me a few off the top.*

Her vision darkened. Her wires began to warm and purr. She slid sideways into the astral realm, sailing the pure ether of information, skimming the Akashic records.

Shadows filled the studio, blotting out the audience, the techcrews, the walls of equipment. Her normal sight was displaced by a fly's-eye view, a composite of signals skimmed from the vast population of her audience. "Receive-Only" was a misnomer; most people never thought of the fact that they were all potential senders. Wires were wires, if you knew which switches to throw. They had been designed that way, with the distant goal of continuous two-way operation, just as the telephone companies had provided early push-button phones with symbol keys that no one used for years. It was all a matter of opening their eyes and using them as her own.

She looked out at dingy living rooms with stuccoplast walls; she leaned against splintered doorframes, stroked mangy dogs, squatted in an alley as her guts heaved.

"I'm disappointed in you," she said, closing her fingers to constrict thruput to a more manageable stream. "I mean, you people, you people . . . my God, you have no respect. Someone out there right now, yes you, shitting in a backstreet. Yeah, I see you— damn right I do! You ever stop to think that's disrespectful? You don't find me shitting on the program, do you? You don't tune in to find that kind of stuff going on. We all know it happens, we're adults here, but do I shove your faces in it? How would you like me to treat you with that disrespect? You're so tied up in me that each and every one of you would crap your pants or your reclining chair or your kitchenette, wherever the hell you are. If you want me to take care of your bowel movements for you, all right, I'll do it. But get this, people. *I'm not going to wipe your collective ass!*"

She completely closed the gap between her fingers and the signal window shut. Herself again, free of the leeches, she faced her equipment, her crew and the restless studio audience.

"It's time to do a little skimming," she said.

The ratings monitors hummed as the audience grew. All over the state, people who'd tuned in with half a mind now got completely snagged. She was scooping receivers from a hundred competitors for this, her most popular segment.

Nobody outdid the Seer at her job. No one else had her particular talent for illusion-weaving.

She gave the newcomers time to settle in.

"We're going through the fire today, folks. Anybody doesn't like it, tune out now. I'm warning you so that you can pretend to be responsible free-willed adults capable of making your own decisions. The fire is painful. It's the fire of truth. You're not going to like this. Well, a few of you might, but I think by and large you're going to find it very unpleasant."

The ratings increased steadily. As usual.

"In fact, I think you're going to hate it. It's going to *hurt* you!" The lack of response infuriated her. "I mean, people, why do you put up with this every day? This has got to be the worst experience of your day. Why do so many of you sign on for the ride? For a few bits of throwaway enlightenment? What's it worth? You want out of here, people, you want to forget about me for good. Tune in on someone else, someone calm, someone who takes things for granted and never looks too deep. Tune in on *yourselves.*"

There. She had them now—she'd hit a nerve. Even the studio audience looked angry, gnashing to get into her. She didn't want so much as a dribble of thruput at the moment. She stoked the hostility to an almost unmanageable level. That's showmanship. That's suspense!

"You don't like to hear that, do you? You don't like to be told to think for yourself. It goes right against the grain. It rubs against all the training and habits that you think are nature itself. Well let me tell you something, people. You don't know the first thing about nature. If you did, you wouldn't live the way you do. You're the first of your kind—the prime degenerates, the first true two-dimensionals, the most devolved ever. You remember TV? Kind of a curiosity now, but your grandparents may talk about it. Those were the days, right? TV worked the brain cells and the muscles, too. With TV, you had a choice. You could shut it off. You could reach right out and change a channel just like that, of your own free will; you could look at a dozen different things. But *you* had to *decide* to *do* it. You couldn't be wishywashy. And those images . . . nothing but flat pictures on a box: you had to use your imagination, your experience, your knowledge of the world to pretend they were real, that those flat little things were living, breathing, life-sized people. All that was healthy! That was the peak of our evolution! That was exactly the sort of thing our sun and planet and minds and bodies evolved a hundred-billion years to achieve: TV watching. We were built for it, people. It didn't involve invasive technology; it didn't mean growing polynerves. Nope. It was natural, stimulating, healthy."

She paused. The audience was peaking. Time to fly.

"But things have changed since then, folks. Things have definitely changed."

She held up both hands, flicked her fingers wide open, and the techs went to work.

In an instant, they routed her out of the main signal and sealed her into a safe, muffled pocket of consciousness so that she wouldn't lose any personality or suffer psychic erosion in the flow of raw traffic. All the time, thruput was rising. With the Seer out of the way, it snapped up to full. She couldn't conduct the signal herself; her mind would have disintegrated in the blast like a dirt clod dipped in a torrent.

Darkness filled the room, filled her mind, rushed out through the airways and filled her audience. It was intense, total as system death, but it lasted only an instant. Then the equipment came up to full and started the mind-numbing shriek of sensory feedback: the fire through which she daily dragged her fans.

All the receivers who tapped into the Seer were suddenly turned into senders, their signals thoroughly mixed and sent out again. Her audience, for a painful moment, was able to look through all its eyes at once. The fire was too much for most of them, so many solipsists sitting at home nursing on wires, thinking themselves the center of the world and liking it that way. Now a blinding light dawned in their heads. Democracy. They experienced the reality of a vast population, knew at firsthand that their cherished ego was nothing but an illusion made of silken self-deception. They saw that even solitude was an artifice, requiring the construction of incredibly elaborate barriers. They were little more than motes in a duststorm of humanity. Not only were they not the center of the universe, but the universe had no center.

Oh, if they could only have harnessed this power to govern themselves. That was the *promise* of the wires. But no ordinary politician had found a way to do this without going mad. It remained the domain of "magic"—or art, which is how she secretly thought of it. She was a weaver of the wired world's dreams.

Eyes within eyes within eyes; nerves inside of nerves. Each signal cannibalized itself and amplified along the axis of pain. Fine distinctions broke down to gross generalizations. The Seer kept silent but her flesh began to howl. The feedback's siren call reached her even in the sanctum of her signal cocoon. She couldn't resist the pure power of an audience, and this was that power distilled to its ultimate. 200 proof. The purity of broadcast consciousness climbed an infinitely steep curve, tugging her along.

She hit the floor without feeling it, bringing the audience down with her. She went into convulsions, swallowing the white heat. She exploded, sailed out in every direction at once, fragmented into exactly as many particles as there were people in her audience. She felt she was all of them.

Hands grabbed her; a hard rubber pad was jammed between her teeth; her arms were strapped down to the sides of the throne. The crew, bless them, gave her release. She could truly ride the wires now, let her body fall away, leave the audience numb and trembling while she found new things for them to chew when they came back to their old selves, cleansed and purified by the fire, ready for the visions that she wove.

Free.

Floating in radiant darkness.

Seeing. . . .

She saw wires. Wires running everywhere. Wires in the shape of human beings, wires like nerve schematics suspended in space, wires of all colors sending and receiving, receiving and sending, three-dimensional antennae of lovely fractal complexity held in place by the faint sheen of a flesh-and-blood matrix that seemed almost ugly compared to the pristine wires.

Around the wires, energizing the darkness, spreading out through space, she saw a glow of divine electromagnetism. Polarities reversed, setting compass needles swinging, betraying True North. All the plasmic roads led to Power and the Flow.

Where the current tended she saw the current trends.

Voices. In the distance.

The staccato chatter of binary conversation, an on-again:off-again ideology, fell uninterpreted through what remained of her conscious mind. It slipped down between the widening cracks in her subconscious and encountered her own wires, which drank the clamor thirstily. Turgor in her polynerves, a subtle, satisfying expansion. Data rose from the wires like steam. She leaned over the vent, the fuming fissure in the floor of her subconscious, as if she were a Delphic oracle receiving psychoactive vapors. Dreams filled her soul. Visions and voices came at last.

—no longer look into the eyes or through the eyes, but by the legerdemain of will swim through the eyes, head and arms and legs, to explore the curve of vision. I see around myself as the mother who bore me once saw round the corners of time. I have broken the wall—

—and I desire you as you owe me any love, that you suffer me to enjoy him. If you accuse me of unnaturalness in that I yield not to your request, I am also to condemn you of unkindness, in that—

—in the soffits of the six windows is a beautiful chorus of angels, busts in medallions, altogether twenty-four, making music, censing—

—this string zero one seven this—

—man, the woman, the children at the aerial table resting on a miracle that seeks its definition—

Raw traffic. The Flow from which she drank. Meaningless, even to the Seer. Her skill was that of spinning colorful strands from this woolly haze; her talent was for weaving these separate strands into a living fabric.

It was pure gossip, stray rumors and innuendo that, combined, seemed integral parts of a secret that was hers alone to reveal.

She shuttled in darkness, hands on the enormous invisible loom. Intuition inspired her. She hardly saw what was in her hands; she gathered the strands and wove them. This was something no one else could do. There was pure pleasure in seeing what emerged from the chaos:

A narrow band of stars obscured by tumbling blackness.

Dogmen slipping down metal stairs.

A girl's smile blazing like a weapon.

Almost ready.

A complete thought, an idea cribbed from the wireborne cosmos, floated before her, still unfurled, like a crumpled tapestry. She grasped it by metaphorical corners and shook it out to see the whole picture.

And dropped the cloth, screaming.

She fled back to consciousness, groped her way blindly into flesh again, pulled her body on like a clammy wetsuit. Heart pounding, tongue thick in her throat, she spit out the rubber pacifier and opened her eyes.

Terrified.

The audience waited for her words. Waited for the oracle to speak, to illuminate them, to bring some bright speculation to their dreary lives. To give purpose to their passage through the fire.

She didn't know what to say.

There was no way to tell them what she'd seen. Not that it was unclear. She could describe it, yes—she simply didn't dare.

If what she knew were true, and if, being truth, she revealed it, she would die. And while much of what she wove was pure deception, enough to make her doubt what she'd just seen, some

Web II by Ferret. Copyright © 1993 by Ferret. Printed
with permission.

part of it always came true, and that was enough to keep her silent.

For the first time in her life, the Seer feared the wires. Feared what they had told her. Feared they might speak again. Feared what they could do.

Her audience waited.

She had to tell them something. Anything. She must distract them.

She rose and faced them. Raised her arms.

An expectant hush. Walls shining with lights.

Tell them anything.

She threw back her head, closed her eyes, groped. . . .

Screamed, sybillic:

"Elvis lives!"

≡≡≡≡

Computer-Assisted Foreshadowing is one particular narrative trick that VR has made possible. Some of the images that the Seer glimpses during her ride through the fire will bear fruit later in the book, and I hope that these quick tastes will simultaneously excite a reader's anticipation of the story to come and offer a clearer understanding of certain events when they finally occur. Similarly, in the office simulation scene excerpted from *Dad's Nuke*, the people with raw-looking eyes are at work in another part of the story, making their way toward Connie's realm. For a moment the two worlds (and two plot streams) intersect, quite literally.

This sort of surreal foreshadowing has typically been accomplished through dream sequences or hallucinations. Personally, I can think of few dream sequences in fiction that are even remotely convincing. Most are too linear, too obvious. The best are ambiguous, contrived to show a character's state of mind, and these work on a purely psychological level. The worst are meant to be taken literally, providing some kind of clue to the story. In sloppy horror stories (not to mention films), characters are always falling asleep and glimpsing the trouble that is about to come, in laboriously contrived dream sequences. What could be more unreal than this? How often do *you* have literal, accurately precognitive dreams? For purposes of foreshadowing, VR technology offers a definite advance over the dream sequence.

This is not to suggest that virtual reality in fiction bears—or should bear—any resemblance to extant or projected technology, or owes very much to recent advances in science. (I certainly hope the wires of *Kalifornia* don't seem dated in ten years.) Like many of the technological staples of science fiction (spaceships and computers in particular), VR's evolution as a fictional device owes at least as much to purely literary antecedents as to the development of the real virtual technologies on which fictional models are based. SF writers have been using things like VR for years, under one name or another: parallel universes may serve much the same function; drugs are popular gimmicks for altering perceptions; and a whole array of VR-like devices can be found in the literature.

Philip K. Dick has used all of these "gimmicks" to explore his multilayered vision of reality, so full of fraudulent demiurges and cosmic hoaxes. However, Dick also had the skill to completely jettison the clunky baggage of technological SF explanations when he wished. The deluded human mind was often the only device he needed to journey through layers of illusion, and Dick's ability to "travel light"—without recourse to any kind of gimmick (apart from mental illness and/or mere insight)—is enviable. The best of Dick uses every possible effect—electronic, drug-induced, schizophrenic, meditative, divine—to disrupt any definite answer to the question "What is real?" Consider the Perky Pat toys of *The Three Stigmata of Palmer Eldritch* (1964), Barbie-like model homes into which outer-space suburbanites project themselves with the aid of drugs; or the time-distorting chamber that recreates the world for an autistic boy in *Martian Time-Slip* (1964); or the parallel worlds of *Eye in the Sky* (1957), where a number of separate twisted realities are created by the fusion of several neurotic personalities with a "bevatron" power generator; or the astonishing "Hermetic transform" in *The Divine Invasion* (1981), where the god-child Emmanuel deftly "reprograms" reality so thoroughly that no one ever remembers things being otherwise.[3] These latter two tricks, and many other combinations derived from and related to them, are played out to wild effect in *Ubik* (1969), not to mention the entire illusory town in *Time Out of Joint* (1957). In Dick, the list goes on and on, but he is only the weirdest representative of a grand tradition.

It is worth noting that both immersive and invasive reality-simulation technologies exist in the more recent *Neuromancer* by William Gibson. Gibson's cyberspace "Matrix" is immersive, a vast computerized "dataspace" accessible by computer jocks; this exists alongside the invasive "simstim" technology, which relies on physical implants.[4] Simstim allows people (that is, entertainment consumers) to live the glamorous lives of their idols, seeing through their eyes. Of course, simstim and its cousins (including the "wires" in *Kalifornia*) have their roots in Huxley's "feelies," which are certainly the best-known VR technology in fiction. One could even argue that the feelies played the same part in the development of virtual reality that years of pulp sci-fi spaceships played in molding the minds of those inventors and aerospace engineers who would later grow up to send ships and satellites into space. How many youngsters, reading *Brave New World* (1932) by force or curiosity, encountered the feelies and thought to themselves, I wonder if that's possible? I wonder if I could make that happen?

> The house lights went down; fiery letters stood out solid and as though self-supported in the darkness. THREE WEEKS IN A HELICOPTER. AN ALL-SUPER-SINGING, SYNTHETIC-TALKING, COLOURED, STEREOSCOPIC FEELY. WITH SYNCHRONIZED SCENT-ORGAN ACCOMPANIMENT.
>
> "Take hold of those metal knobs on the arms of your chair," whispered Lenina. "Otherwise you won't get any of the feely effects."
>
> The Savage did as he was told.
>
> Those fiery letters, meanwhile, had disappeared; there were ten seconds of complete darkness; then suddenly, dazzling and incomparably more solid-looking than they would have seemed in actual flesh and blood, far more real than reality, there stood the stereoscopic images, locked in one another's arms, of a gigantic negro and a golden-haired young brachycephalic Beta-Plus female.
>
> The Savage started. That sensation on his lips! He lifted a hand

to his mouth; the titillation ceased; let his hand fall back on the knob; it began again. The scent organ, meanwhile, breathed pure musk. Expiringly, a sound-track super-dove cooed "Oo-ooh"; and vibrating only thirty-two times a second, a deeper than African bass made answer: "Aa-aah." "Ooh-ah! Ooh-ah!" the stereoscopic lips came together again, and once more the facial erogenous zones of the six thousand spectators in the Alhambra tingled with almost intolerable galvanic pleasure. "Ooh. . . ."

Huxley's use of the feelies in *Brave New World* is nearly devoid of importance as a plot device; it serves merely as yet another example of the novel's cold technologies, a deepening of Huxley's metaphors of alienation through the Freudian/Fordian mechanization of experience, with no application outside the scene in which it is featured. The speculative forays of "mainstream" writers into science fiction often result in intellectually clever but rather bloodless exercises; being less psychically deformed by the demands of the genre market to produce a breakneck plot, they may content themselves with introducing a single device, or pursuing one stiff line of social extrapolation, and standing back to admire the oddly static results of their experiment. New inventions in much SF of this sort are often simply spotlit and rotated slowly on the showroom floor. The genre writer knows that most genre readers feel they have "seen it all," and their fabrications must not only look striking, but actually *strike* as well. Had down-and-dirty Dick been the author of *Brave New World*, he probably would not have introduced the feelies without letting them run amok . . . even slightly. But then, Huxley gets high points for pioneering, and *Brave New World* is rarely boring.

By the time William Gibson came to employ simstim, the feely tradition had developed far past the point where it was sufficient to introduce the invention and point at it, marveling. Gibson intuitively used simstim as a narrative device, taking for granted its place in the society he imagined.

One of the most striking passages in *Neuromancer* is Molly Million's venture into the orbiting station Straylight while the protagonist, Case, linked to her via computer, experiences the journey through her flesh.

. . . He saw enough of her arms and hands to know that she wore the polycarbon suit again. Under the plastic, he felt the familiar tension of thin tight leather. There was something slung under her arm in a harness or holster. She stood up, unzipped the suit and touched the checkered plastic of a pistol-grip. . . .

The low, vaulted hallway was lined with dozens of museum cases, archaic-looking glass-fronted boxes made of brown wood. . . .

Molly paid little attention to the cabinets and their contents, which irritated him. He had to satisfy himself with her disinterested glances, which gave him fragments of pottery, antique weapons, a thing so densely studded with rusted nails that it was unrecognizable, frayed sections of tapestry.

This is a live-action feely, and it serves as an extremely economical storytelling tactic: through a third-person limited viewpoint (that of Case, our narrative conduit, whose thoughts and sensations bombard us), we are carried into the body of a second character (namely, Molly, whose thoughts remain opaque to Case and to us alike, unless she speaks aloud). Molly is filtered through Case, and the reader thus exists in two characters simultaneously. This conflation of viewpoints is a remarkable and alluring narrative device (more convincing than telepathy, another old-fashioned SF rationale that has been used to accomplish similar ends) because it instantly suggests new ways of doing things in a story—and new things to do.[5] I couldn't resist a few variations on this ploy in *Kalifornia*:

The fetal wires had been live since the seventh month of gestation, broadcasting to the infant's mother on a private umbilical wire that was shielded from any other receivers. Poppy could enter her daughter through this wire, which served as a two-way channel until the cord was cut. Through infant eyes, heavy-lidded, she peeked at orange darkness, her fluid-filled ears picking up the pounding of her mother's and her own heartbeat. This part of Poppy was not entirely Poppy. The girl child had a life of her own. Her soul was a bright fish that couldn't be caught in the seine of wires. Sometimes Poppy wondered if her daughter ever crept up the umbilicus and into her mother's wires, to look out through Poppy's eyes, to listen with her ears.

Writers have their own uses for technology. A new gadget in a science fiction story *may* spring from an article in *Scientific American*, but it is just as likely to issue from the need to achieve an effect that would otherwise be impossible, in a story that cannot be told in any other way. Some of the details in my own stories are obviously extreme ramifications of trends and technologies I see today; but far more satisfying and meaningful to me are the inventions that arise out of the needs of the story, without reference to research. The beauty and attraction of science fiction is the ease with which it allows metaphor to take on flesh—or perhaps a metal housing. As a philosopher, Philip K. Dick may have felt the need to continually challenge consensus reality; but as a writer, he had more pressing needs: to make a living by doing his questioning in the context of a science fiction novel. So he wired together some scrap parts that had been lying around in the pulp magazines, drew on some of psychology's wilder rationales, piped in enough drugs to render the senses exquisitely vulnerable, and *voilà!*—reality fell to pieces. Similarly, William Gibson needed a cinematic, visual way of exploring a place his protagonist could not enter without violating the logic of a third-person limited viewpoint, so he put that character inside his lover's flesh. I'm fairly certain that neither writer referred to contemporary scientific literature when his books put him in a tight spot. Each needed immediate solutions to any craftsman's basic problem: How can I make this work? And those answers almost always come, serendipitously, from some combination of past example and the moment's inspiration. When a story works, of course, the gantries roll back, the supporting structures crumble, and everything seems all of a piece.

Notes

1   Alternatively, you can wait for writer/scientist Rudy Rucker's forthcoming novel, *The Hacker and the Ants*, which concerns a VR hacker whose mid-life crisis becomes inseparable from a technological catastrophe. The devices in this book are presented with nuts-and-bolts verisimilitude, utterly convincing and (because this is Rucker) equally absurd.

2   Now, before you think that I esteem my work too highly and seek to shore up my accomplishments by flanking them with Huxley, Dick, and Gibson (whose excerpts are dwarfed by my own), I beg you to learn the genesis of this essay. Mark Dery first solicited an article relevant to the theme of this issue; I declined for lack of time. Mr. Dery then requested a substantial piece of prose; I had nothing suitable. He then asked to print a chapter of *Kalifornia*, to which I agreed. But that seemed like a cheesy way of discharging a promise, and when the time came to choose a selection, nothing seemed to stand well on its own, without lengthy surrounding material. This article *is* that surrounding material.

3   . . . He saw outside him the pattern, the print, of his own brain; he was within a world made up of his brain, with living information carried here and there like little rivers of shining red that were alive. He could reach out, therefore, and touch his own thoughts in their original nature, before they became thoughts. The room was filled with their fire, and immense spaces stretched out, the volume of his own brain external to him.

   Meanwhile he introjected the outer world so that he contained it within him. He now had the universe inside him and his own brain outside everywhere. His brain extended into the vast spaces, far larger than the universe had been. Therefore he knew the extent of all things that were himself, and, because he had incorporated the world, he knew it *and controlled it.*

4   One of the most memorable predecessors of Gibson's "cyberspace" may be found in Harlan Ellison's seminal nightmare of the Information Age, "I Have No Mouth, and I Must Scream" (1967), in which a party of explorers is marooned in the interior of an infinitely malevolent computer. This story alone demonstrates clearly the enormity of the debt the so-called cyberpunk movement owes to Ellison in matters of attitude, style, and substance.

5   Later in this sequence, but less coherently excerptable, is another example of "dreaming with open eyes." While Molly stares into the face of a murdered girl, Case sees the stranger's face melt and change into that of someone he knows. Here, the computer responsible for the link between Case and Molly has deliberately altered the broadcast. This is a favorite surreal VR effect, and while on one level it may reflect the ongoing debate about the authenticity of photographs and digital imagery, it also adds an element of hallucinatory strangeness to any scene—an indispensable ingredient in much science fiction. There is a similar—and even more disorienting—scene in Dick's *A Scanner Darkly* (1977), where a drugged Bob Arctor sees his lover's face shift in a "nightmare," then later sees the same effect recorded by a scanning device, apparently showing objective reality altered by his insanity—or by the device itself.

PAT CADIGAN

CHAPTER 14, *SYNNERS*

This is an excerpt from a novel called *Synners*, which is, to summarize as simply as possible, about the entertainment industry in the future. You've probably already heard many times about how virtual reality—Sensurround™ on steroids—is going to revolutionize the way we entertain ourselves. We're going to be a part of the entertainment, they tell us—well, practically—instead of onlookers and audience members. It will be interactive as well, so we'll not only be in it, but we'll be determining what course it takes.

It might turn out to be as good as everyone says; it might be the biggest thrill since the invention of the roller coaster, or the parachute—hell, it might make the art we know even better, and give rise to art forms we can't even conceive of right at this moment.

But whatever it turns out to be, I guarantee you our real lives are going to complicate matters. No matter where we go, or how we go there—to Alpha Centauri via rocketship in suspended animation or to new levels of artistic expression via the *Synners* hotsuits and headmounted monitors—it's the human animal taking the trip. We may enhance or embellish our intellects to make them work faster and smarter, we might change our bodies to the point where they're unrecognizable, and we might even separate the two entirely for who knows what reason, but I promise you: even if the human of one hundred years from now is a sentient entity contained within a piece of silicon, s/he's going to have a personal life.

She was supposed to settle into a routine now.

She was supposed to accept everything the Beater had told her, leave Mark alone, do the videos, hope for the best. Hope for the best. What the fuck kind of talk was that? She couldn't ask him; he was suddenly unavailable, closeted with Rivera, busy, busy, busy, and she couldn't ask Mark, because Mark had been spirited away again.

Her own goddamn fault, most likely, for opening her big mouth to the Beater. He'd gone to Rivera, and Rivera had probably waved his magic corp-wand and removed the only person who could have given her an answer.

She looked for him anyway, on the off-chance that he was simply dodging her to avoid being smacked around. Looking for Mark had become a fucking way of life in the past few years. She didn't really know how to do anything else, except make the videos, and somehow, making the videos was too hard when she didn't know where he was.

Fuck it all, she thought, walking the boulevards, scoping the clubs, making at least one nightly run to the Mimosa, scouting the hit-and-runs. Fuck it all, let Mark come to her if he ever decided there was something she should know. Twenty-umpt years could make you tired; she had a right to be tired. And then she looked some more.

"Ain't seen him," said Loophead's little percussionist, rapping her sticks on the table. It was some empty night between one empty day and another in a nameless little Hollywood joint trying to hold its own with a combination of videowall and live music. The postage-stamp-sized dance floor was packed with boulevardettes, and attitude-mongers pretending they were Somebody, and vidiots who had finally had to go somewhere, and a couple of hungry kids with handcams hoping to capture something they could manipulate into some semblance of a video, probably on hardware built from paper clips and masking tape and held together with spit. Then they'd watch it on one of the public-access channels while the rest of the world watched just about anything else.

The little percussionist's name was Flavia Something. She dressed like a cavewoman on food stamps, and she took her sticks everywhere. They beat out a sequence of shifting rhythms on the tabletop as if of their own will, unperturbed by the conflicting beat coming from the band up front. All of Loophead's music grew out of percussion.

"When you comin' over, do the new one?" Flavia asked her. "You come do the video with us on our turf. Finish wherever you want, but you *do* with us, okay?"

"I thought Mark had your next," Gina said, taking a healthy swig from the bottle of LotusLand in front of her. Flavia tapped the bottle as she put it down, hesitated, and then tapped it again, liking it. As if she could hear it over the thrash.

"Told you, ain't seen him. Can't do video with the invisible man." Flavia's shrug was exaggerated, but the sticks never stopped. On another night, some time ago, Flavia had taken Mark to bed with her, sticks and all. Gina remembered it; Flavia remembered it; Mark didn't.

Up front, a kid in rags and plastic wrap made an old-fashioned stage-dive into the dance-floor crowd, helped along by a kick from the group's hoarse vocalist. The kid sank by uneven degrees into the bobbling mass of jerking bodies and resurfaced several feet away, hopping up and down like a maddened kangaroo. There was a distinct heelprint on his forehead.

"A synner in the making," Gina murmured.

Flavia tapped a stick directly in front of her. "You gonna syn, syn bravely. I forget who said that. Vince Somebody, I think, died in a terrorist raid in Malaysia."

Gina shook her head. "Somebody else. Died like a dog, probably."

The group came to a screaming halt and cleared the stage in a minor brawl as the video screen went on. One of Mark's. Gina finished the rest of the LotusLand, putting on a solid tox while she watched the big curved screen. The texture of the stony shore came through vividly even in this format.

"*Rocks*," Flavia said, and made a face. "I get it already, wish he'd stop doing it, do something else."

"Pass a law."

The perspective traveling along the shore came to a slow stop and focused on a smooth red gold stone, stutter-zooming in close enough to show the graininess of the surface, changing, melting into unreadable symbols that merged with the patterns she was getting from the hallucinogen in the LotusLand. The symbols resolved themselves into regular shapes, an aerial view of a foreign land that began to roll, earth and sky switching places like the flapping of a huge wing.

≡≡≡≡

Canadaytime dragged her out of a hit-and-run in the ruins of South Bev Hills just before the cops would have. Valjean claimed not to know where Mark was, but had she ever known him to miss one of his parties?

Plenty of fucking times, she told him.

Well, then, one of the better ones, how about that?

Plenty of fucking times. But she let them take her because it was a different empty night, and Valjean had been known to turn up with Mark stashed in one of his many bedrooms.

She wasn't sure it qualified as one of Valjean's better parties, but he had a cam crew saving all of it anyway. Do a finish on it later—not her, some drone; she did his videos, but she wouldn't do his fucking parties—make it better than it could have been, the insty-party channels were hungry for all they could get. Plenty of people out there, strung out on the dataline, they'd never get to a party like this, they'd never have lives like this. Here's the real secret, folks, she thought, as a kid with a cam to her face stalked her like a machine of prey: none of us will ever get to a party like this, none of us will ever have lives like this; this isn't what happened; nothing happened except the dataline.

Valjean had a screen for every porn channel, jammed together in the wall so that food porn overlapped med porn overlapped war porn overlapped sex porn overlapped news porn overlapped disaster porn overlapped tech-fantasy porn overlapped porn she had no idea how to identify. Maybe nobody did, maybe it had just bypassed the stage where it would have been anything other than porn. Meta-porn, porn porn?

I don't know what it is, but it makes me horny, and that's all that matters.

"Fucking *right* there's nothing fucking wrong with porn," said Quilmar. Quilmar was one of the stone marathoners. He'd taken so many years off his age, he'd have been nine when he'd cut his first single (okay, maybe eight and a half), and he'd had it polished and tightened so much, his lovers said the dimple in his chin was actually his navel. Maybe, Gina thought, the Beater hadn't been so fucked after all to do what he'd done. "Porn is the fucking secret of life, sister-mine. If you can't fuck it and it doesn't dance, eat it or throw it away. That's the fucking order of the universe, and I'm at the fucking *top* of the food-fuck-and-dance chain."

Then he tried to corner her in Valjean's long, narrow kitchen but he got a little bit confused, and she left him dry-humping the refrigerator door. Wait till he tried to throw *that* away.

"Talent squeezes out brains." Jolene, looking older, but good-older, wiser, full of dignity. "Shit, *you* told me that the first time I helped you drag Mark home. How's he surviving the corporate life?"

When she couldn't answer, Jolene took her up to the top floor, to Valjean's secret oxygen supply, and gave her a few hits off the mask. This was how she kept track, she thought, by who was helping her find Mark and how toxed she was herself. The O$_2$ helped; there was a little more in it than God's pure oxy. She and Jolene sat out under the eaves and looked down the canyon, held hands, didn't say much. Didn't have to.

"I get some work," Jolene was telling her after a while. Jolene's head was resting on her shoulder. Gina was a flaming hetero, but Jolene liked to keep her options open, as Jolene herself said. Being with someone who wasn't afraid of knowing you needed to be touched was okay whether your options were nailed down or wide open and flapping in the fucking breeze. "I get work from some of the indies, outlaws most of them with one leg over the fence, thinking about going legit. Don't get much legit air, but that's where the scene is getting to be. The Dive'll have people crawling through the clubs on their hands and knees to steal from us soon. Except you, Gina, because you're there already, aren't you?"

"Yah. They tell me to come, but I'm already there."

"Walk," Jolene said, suddenly urgent. "Walk away, what are they gonna do, throw you in debtors' prison?"

Gina nodded. "Does the phrase 'contempt of court' do anything for you?" She drew up her knees, rested her chin on them. "You know you could theoretically spend the rest of your life in the can on a c-of-c charge? Die of old age in the can for nothing more than saying, 'Fuck, no.'"

"You're lost, girl."

She laughed. "Oh, no. What it is, is, I been found. That's the fucking problem, I'm found, and they're gonna keep me. And Mark's the one so found he's lost for good."

≡≡≡≡

!! U B THE * !!
Many Main-Run Features Starring U!
Available Now:
Raid on Buenos Aires * Thrash-Out * Love Kills
The Buddy Holly Story (3rd—and BEST!!—remake)
1000s of others available, come in and BROWZE!!!!
Complete Rock Video Catalog, Too!
(Take-Out Xtra)

She read it through and then went back to the first line, puzzled. U B the asterisk? Was she too toxed or not toxed enough?

You be the ass to risk.

Gina nodded. For all she knew, she was looking at the secret of life. You be the ass to risk. Love Kills. 3rd—and BEST!!—remake.

Complete Rock Video Catalog, Too! Where old rock videos went to die, hers, Mark's, everyone, here in the wannabee parlors, in the wannabee pipe on the dataline for those who could foot that kind of FOB.

Quilmar hadn't had it quite right. If you can't fuck it, and it doesn't dance, eat it, *be* it, or throw it away.

A woman with tiny old-fashioned movie reels twined in her hair and arcs of silvery spectrum mylar instead of eyebrows was trying to get a rabbity-looking guy in a rented bodyshield to step through the beaded curtain in the open doorway. "Anyone can say they'll make you a star, but we're the only ones who can really do it, whaddaya say? What you wannabee?" The mylar wiggled up and down, the beads swaying in the doorway clacked lightly, and the traffic on the boulevard nattered and chattered and popped.

"Come on, homeboy, it's so easy. What you wannabee? You wannabee Buddy Holly? You wannabee a raider on Buenos Aires, you wannabee a killer and get away with it?" She pushed up the sleeves of her slatternly kimono and took both his hands. "Come on, homeboy, tell me. I'm your Hollywood landlady with a full pot of coffee or whatever else you drink and all the time in the world to listen to you. Just tell me what you wannabee."

The guy looked around like he was afraid someone was going to catch him at this. "You got full-body hotsuits?" he asked. "Full coverage?"

"Homeboy, where are you *from*? We got the full coverage, the *full* coverage, they don't make 'em better than the ones we got. Ain't no part of you gonna be neglected, just tell me what you wannabee."

He looked around again, and his gaze snagged on Gina where she was standing by the sign. The woman frowned a little, no mean trick with mylar eyebrows. "That stuff with you?" she asked him.

"No," he said, but uncertainly, as if he weren't really sure. Gina wanted to laugh. Yah, I'll tell you what *him* wannabee. Him wannabee somebody who doesn't live in Culver City or Inglewood or some other damned place like that in a three-roomer with a two-screen dataline subscription, not knowing what to do with himself when he's used up all the series and the movies and the videos and the insty-parties and wondering why he can't go out and find a life like what he sees on a high-res screen, or at least why he can't afford a hotsuit with full coverage.

The guy's expression was a mixture of defiance and embarrassment as the woman pulled him through the curtain. The beads rippled, and then the woman poked her head through them again.

"You wannabee getting off my sidewalk, okay, homegirl?"

Gina gave her the sign of the horns and moved off, laughing to herself.

"What's so funny, homegirl?" A real homegirl, a green-haired boulevardette wrapped in a red trash bag with the words *Hazardous Waste* stenciled in large repeat all over it and the same thing tattooed on her forehead.

"I'm lucky I can dance," Gina said.

———

They were all dancing in Forest Lawn, whether they actually could or not. The music was cranked up so loud that the cops had to be comatose not to hear it. Hit-and-run, but Mark wasn't there, either. Some little snipe named Dexter with a laptop had her backed up against Liberace's tomb, claiming he was a fucking orchestra, and off to one side a familiar figure with a cam was trying to look like he wasn't taking her picture.

He looked good tonight, too, and she could hear the sexy laugh in her mind, and what the hell, she could pretend there wasn't anything he wanted to know about, at least for the duration. But even if there hadn't been, all he'd be for her was another furnished room: whatever she needed, none of it hers.

"What's new?" he asked, coming over.

"You mean, what's news."

"However you want it," he said, sounding honest.

She glanced at the snipe, who was standing by on a wish and a prayer. "Whack the road," she told him, and he moved off trying to look too chill to be hurt.

"This how you get to night court?" she asked. "Go someplace you know the cops'll give you a ride from?"

He smiled, looked down the rise to where most of the jumping was taking place. The pickle stand was still in business, but the group had packed up their keyboards and motored; the music was coming out of a box now, but the kids weren't working out any less for it. She saw Clarence or Claw sweating in the middle of a frantic group of kids trying to peak before the cops got around to crashing the party.

"I got something might interest you," he said, after a bit.

"If I tell you what I know," she said. "Don't bother. I still don't know dick."

He looked at her speculatively for a long moment and then shrugged. "Would you tell me if you did?"

"What do I look like to you, *General News? Pop-Cult Index?*"

"*Dear Mrs. Troubles.*"

She grinned. "Fuck you."

"I wouldn't rule it out."

You win the game, Mark had said once, *as soon as you get them to say it. Then you do whatever you want.* Which would have explained a lot, except she'd never said it to Mark, not once.

He waited, and she waited, and then he shrugged again. "Take a look." He set the cam on preview mode and gave it to her. She looked through the eyepiece and saw him sitting in the sand, leaning back on his hands and staring dreamily upward. "I took that tonight. From the state he was in, I'd say he's probably still there."

She gave the cam back to him. "Thank you."

He looked startled for a second and then covered it. "I thought you'd want to know. I did a little research on you. And him. It's kinda hard to do any research on one of you without getting the other. Tell me something, how did a soul sister come by a name like Ay-ee-see?"

"Eye-*ay*-see," she said. "It was easier than you'd think." She hopped down off Liberace's resting place and started to walk away.

"You want a ride?" he called after her. She turned around and looked at him. "To the Mimosa," he added. "You shouldn't be driving."

"Gotta drive." She grinned. "Too fuckin' toxed to walk."

He was on her in three fast strides, taking her to the gate. His hand on her arm said it was settled if she said so, but she could feel how he was willing to adapt to any changes she might want to make. Sex, drugs, and rock 'n' roll, sure, homeboy, you want that in any particular order?

Shit, she was old enough to be his mother, if she'd started a little young (just a little). So what was it? Her looks were an acquired taste, not popular demand, and they didn't make it a secret she was holding on for forty.

Then again, maybe it wasn't her; maybe it was him, all him. The gypsy journalist's urge to probe. Curiosity kills the cat, satisfaction brings him back, and brings him and brings him and brings him.

Nah. Mark was waiting on the Mimosa, and there'd been too many furnished rooms already.

≡≡≡≡

She got there in time to see the Beater bending over him, looking harried and anxious, the slicked-back hair hanging loose now. Defiantly she knelt down next to Mark, now stretched out in the sand seeing miracles in the black sky.

"He got away from me," the Beater said. "I was trying to keep him detoxed. As long as you're here, you can give me a hand with him."

Mark's gaze slowly traveled over to her and stopped on her face. *How come it always ends up like this?* she asked him silently. *Where are you, and what do you really do when you go there? Why did I ever want you, and why do I want you now? Because it can't just be the music, and it can't just be the video.*

"Change for the machines," he said.

The Beater took one side, and she took the other, and they got him up on his feet. The gypsy got the footage of their leaving. What the fuck, he should go home with something, even if it was really nothing at all.

≡≡≡≡

They took him back to the Beater's place and put him to bed on the couch. He was already asleep, or passed out, whichever. "They asked me to keep him clean," the Beater said, pulling off Mark's shoes. "So I told him you were gonna kill him and he could stay with me."

"I'd say 'fuck you' but I don't feel that friendly," Gina said.

"I didn't want him out loose where he could get into trouble. Rivera had him Purged once, I didn't want it to happen again."

She winced. "Christ, why didn't they just scour him out with a wire brush? That could have killed him."

The Beater nodded wearily. "Yah, well, I didn't find out till after the fact. I didn't find out a lot of shit till after the fact." He went to her and looked into her eyes carefully. "You keep this up, Rivera might Purge you, too."

"What's so fucking important that Rivera would Purge *me?*"

The Beater went past her into the kitchenette.

"What's going on?" she called after him. "What kind of sling is my ass in that I'd have to get Purged and I don't even fucking know it?"

He stuck his head out of the kitchenette. "You want some coffee?"

She stared at him evenly, and he dropped his gaze. "Maybe I should have let you take care of him." He pulled his head back, and she heard him fussing with the coffeepot. Son of a bitch was actually going to make fucking *coffee.* For *real.* She went to the kitchenette and stood in the doorway with her arms folded. The drip machine on the counter wheezed and bubbled as coffee poured into the carafe. Rediscovery Cuisine beverages. Little Jesus Jump-Up.

"First place you ever had of your own back in Boston had a real kitchen, with a table and chairs in it," he said. "I remember."

"That wasn't my first place. That was a few apartments later, by the time I met you. They all had kitchens, though."

He faced her in the tiny space. "Is it the tox, or are you just tired enough to have calmed down?"

"Maybe I'm getting old." She rubbed her eyes with the heels of her hands. "What's the fucking use. You gonna tell me all that whole lotta shit you found out after the fact now?"

"I can't. Not yet."

"And why the fuck not?"

"It's not mine, all right?"

"No, it's not all right, why the fuck would you think it was?"

The Beater ran a hand through his half-lacquered hair, wincing at the pull. "Christ, how many years was it? You think I'd let anybody hurt him now?"

"Galen would. Galen doesn't give a fuck about him. Neither does Rivera. And goddamn Joslin thinks Dachau was a fucking *spa.*"

"It's something different," the Beater said heavily. "Whatever you're thinking, it's something different than that."

"Thanks for the juicy fucking hint." She pulled her shirt off. "And no, I don't want any fucking coffee." She headed toward the bedroom, shedding clothes.

"Gina!"

She stopped at the doorway and looked back.

"You better show for work tomorrow. You been gone three days. You got videos to do."

"Kiss me," she muttered. Stripped down to her T-shirt and underpants, she crawled into the Beater's bed. Sometime later she felt him slide in next to her. Old stuff; life is uncertain, catch bed space where you can get it. When she woke a few hours later, Mark was gone again.

ANNE BALSAMO

FEMINISM FOR THE INCURABLY INFORMED

All we ever want (ever wanted) was to be on that mailing list.
—Ron Silliman, *What*

My mother was a computer, but she never learned to drive. Grandmother was an order clerk in a predominantly male warehouse; she did all the driving for the family, having learned to drive almost before she learned to speak English; her first car was a 1916 Model T Ford equipped with a self-starter.[1] Both my mother and grandmother worked for Sears and Roebuck in the 1940s; mother entered orders on a log sheet, grandmother filled those orders in the warehouse.[2] When an opening in payroll came through, my mother enrolled in night school to learn to be a computer. Within two years she received a diploma from the Felt and Tarrant School of Comptometry that certified her to operate a comptometer— one of the widely used electromechanical calculating machines that preceded electronic calculators.[3] She worked at Sears for two more years before she was replaced by a machine.

My sister and I both work for the technostate—it seems only natural. In 1991, my sister was deployed to the borderland between northern Iraq and southwest Turkey as part of the U.S. military's humani-
tarian effort, called "Operation Provide Comfort," to give medical
attention to the Kurdistani refugees exiled during and after the technologically hallucinogenic Gulf War.[4] About the same time, I was
deployed to a technological institution to teach gender studies (their
term) or feminism (mine). Situated within different histories, biographical as well as cultural, these technological encounters suggest
several topics of investigation for feminist studies of science and technology.

These working-class histories will span one hundred years before
they're finished, and even that is an arbitrary span of time, determined more by the mangling of immigrant names and the near im-
possibility of extrapolating from today into tomorrow than by any
formal sense of narrative closure. I do not want to invoke an experi-
ential framework for the elaboration of this essay; I have no stories
to tell here about the subjective experiences of a mother, sister, or
grandmother using technology, displaced by it, or even cleaning up
after it. Instead, I use these autobiographical notes as a platform upon
which to stage a feminist reading of the current (cyber)cultural moment. This scene, which Pat Cadigan's main hacker-girl, Sam, says is
gripped by an "information frenzy," is the present context for those
of us who pride ourselves on being plugged in, on-line, and living
on the New Edge.[5] Like the hackers and domestic exiles who populate Cadigan's cyberpunk novel *Synners*, we too qualify as "incurably
informed."[6]

If my opening remarks were about working-class histories, Cadigan's second novel *Synners*, published in 1991, is much more about the
postindustrial present; as a particular kind of science fiction novel—
a cyberpunk narrative—it offers a technomythology of the future
right around the corner.[7] When *Synners* is discussed as a cyberpunk
novel, it is usually mentioned that Cadigan is one of the few women
writing in that subgenre. Textually, *Synners* displays the verbal inven-
tiveness and stylistic bricolage characteristic of the best of the new
science fiction, but in Cadigan's case her verbal playfulness invokes
Dr. Seuss, and the plot melds a Nancy Drew mystery with a Kathy

Acker-hacked Harlequin romance. The mystery plot includes familiar cyberpunk devices, such as illegal corporate maneuvers and heroic hacking; the Acker-hacked romance plot offers a gentle critique of women's propensity to fall for men who can't be there for them; in this case, though, it's because the guy has abandoned his meat (the body) for the expanse of cyberspace. More interesting is the manner in which her refrain "Change for the machines?" morphs from a literal question at a vending machine to a philosophical comment about the nature of the technologized human.

One way to investigate the interpretive and ideological dimensions of contemporary cyberculture is to situate cyberpunk mythologies in relation to the emergence of a new cultural formation built in and around cyberspace.[8] Although we could map the discursive terrain of cyberpunk science fiction through an analysis of the lists of (best) book titles, author anecdotes, critical interpretations, readers' reviews, and the contradictions among them, this would only partially describe the practices of dispersion and interpretation that serve as the infrastructure of a much broader formation.[9] To fully investigate the *cultural* formation of what *Mondo 2000* calls "the new edge" would require an investigation of related discursive forms, such as comic books, 'zines, and other forms of popular print culture, as well as new hybrid social-textual forms, such as electronic newsgroups, bulletin boards, discussion lists, MUDs (multi-user domains), on-line journals, E-zines, and IRChats.[10] Given that these textually mediated social spaces are often constructed and populated by those who participate in related subcultural practices, such as CONS, raves, body alteration, smart drugs, computer hacking, and video art, what is needed for a more developed and historically specific analysis of the New Edge as a cultural formation is a multidisciplinary analysis of other spaces of popular culture where material bodies stage cyberpunk identities.[11] Although constructing such a multiperspectival analysis is a challenging task, my intent is to demonstrate that such a project is already under way. In synthesizing this material, I want to suggest what is needed to produce a critical analysis of a specific sociohistorical conjunction that attends both to the expressive practices of cyberpunk SF and to the political aims of feminist cultural studies, and that can draw meaningful connections between them. My goal, then, is to read *Synners* as both cognitive map and cultural landmark.

≡≡≡

Teresa de Lauretis anticipated the critical response that cyberpunk science fiction enjoys from postmodern readers when she provisionally suggested in 1980 that in "every historical period, certain art forms (or certain literary forms . . .), have become central to the episteme or historical vision of a given society. . . . If we compare it with traditional or postmodern fiction, we see that SF might, just might, be crucial from now on."[12] In one of the first reports on cyberpunk as a new SF subgenre, Darko Suvin, quoting Raymond Williams, argues for its cultural significance by claiming that cyberpunk novels (especially those by William Gibson) articulate a new structure of feeling: "[A] particular quality of social experience and relationship . . . which gives the sense of a generation or of a period."[13] Several critics have discussed the details of the relationship between cyberpunk and a postmodern sensibility.[14] For example, in her essay "Cybernetic Deconstructions: Cyberpunk and Postmodernism," Veronica Hollinger reads cyberpunk through a poststructuralist antihumanism to claim that "cyberpunk [is] an analysis of the postmodern identification of human and machine."[15] Her main point is that cyberpunk participates in the (postmodern) deconstruction of human subjectivity. According to her reading, cyberpunk narratives radically decenter the human body, the sacred icon of essential self, in the same way that the virtual reality of cyberspace works to decenter conventional humanist notions of an unproblematic "real." By the end of her analysis, though, we discover that the antihumanist critique of cyberpunk doesn't hold. Cyberpunk collapses under the weight of its own genre determinations. It is still, Hollinger argues, about the "reinsertion of the human into the reality which its technology is in the process of shaping."[16] In support of Hollinger's conclusion, it is more useful to think of cyberpunk as offering a vision of post-human existence where "technology" and the "human" are understood in contiguous rather than oppositional terms.

As an example of the cyberpunk meditation on the post-human condition, *Synners* posits a world populated by "Homo datum," people whose natural habitat is "the net," for whom disconnection from the information economy is not an option. This leads one character to speculate that there are three species of technological humans: "synthe*sizing* humans, synthe*sized* humans," and the "bastard offspring of both"—artificial intelligences.[17] The original syn, in this case, is neither an act nor a transgression, but rather the posthuman condition of being "incurably informed." Death, according to this logic, is defined as an EEG flatline.

To the extent that we read cyberpunk through postmodern social theory, one of the most obvious thematic connections between the two is the way that each discourse configures the space of the social as a landscape structured by the network of relations among multinational capitalist corporations. As Fredric Jameson suggests, the generic structure of cyberpunk science fiction represents an attempt to "think the impossible totality of the contemporary world system."[18] This space of "the decentered global network," metaphorically known as cyberspace, is a bewildering place for the individual/subject who is left to his/her own devices to construct a map of the relationship between a corporeal locale and the totality of "transnational corporate realities."

The focal tension in *Synners* concerns the multinational Diversifications's takeover of two small companies: Eye-Traxx, an independent music-video production company, and Hall Galen Enterprises, a company that employs the medical researcher who invented and patented the procedures for brain socket implants. As a result of the takeover, two of the four main characters, Gina and Visual Mark, become Diversifications's corporate property. Visual Mark was one of Eye-Traxx's original synners, a human synthesizer who is now nearing the age of fifty: "It was as if he had a pipeline to some primal dream spot, where music and image created each other, the pictures suggesting the music, the music generating the pictures, in a synesthetic frenzy."[19] Diversifications intends to market its new brain sockets by offering virtual reality rock videos: Visual Mark is the best music-video synner in the business. Diversifications's brain sockets not only allow music videos to be fed into a receiving brain; they also provide a direct interface between a brain and a computer. This type of brain-to-computer connection proves to have dire consequences.

While Diversifications tries to corner the market on a lucrative new form of electronic addiction—by providing the sockets and what is fed into the sockets—their socket clients encounter a fatal side effect: "intercranial meltdown" in the form of a cerebral stroke.

In elaborating the distinctions between cyberpunk SF and its generic antecedents, namely, New Wave and feminist SF from the late 1960s and 1970s, Fred Pfeil writes: "I am tempted to say [cyberpunk novels have] no 'political unconscious': [but are rather] a kind of writing in which, instead of delving and probing for neurotic symptoms, we are invited to witness and evaluate a relatively open acting out." That a cyberpunk work's neurotic symptoms are easily identified does not disqualify it as an interesting cultural text; on the contrary, Pfeil argues that this is a productive, creative mutation:

> . . . [T]his new SF hardly requires the literary analyst's ingenuity in order for us to find or fathom its real social content; the collective anxieties and desires that fuel it are relatively openly evoked and worked through. And the shift from formal and aesthetic experimentation back to experiments in social thought itself suggests that in at least some senses and sectors we have indeed moved on from that earlier humanist debate on freedom, power and order to some new or at least mutated social and ideological ground, which is once again open and fresh enough to be explicitly tried on and explored.[20]

In the case of *Synners*, the "real social content," according to Pfeil's formulation, is not simply the plottings of a hostile corporate take-over, but also what we can read on/off its textual surface about the technological configuration of human life in multinational capitalism. Several topics nominate themselves as experiments in thinking through the social consequences of new technologies, any one of which could serve as the organizing perspective for the elaboration of an interpretive map of Cadigan's cosmology: the capitalist production of electronic addictions, the recording practices of video vigilantes, or the multiplication of television channels devoted to new forms of pornography—disasterporn, medporn, foodporn. In addition to speculating about the dynamics of new communication technologies, *Synners* also offers a critical account of the commodification of information:

> Truth is cheap, but information costs. . . . "Besides being rich," Fez said, "you have to be extra sharp these days to pick up any real information. You have to know what you're looking for, and you have to know how it's filed. Browsers need not apply. Broke ones, anyway. I miss the newspaper."[21]

This subtext also includes a political critique of the availability of information and of the difficulty of determining relevance in the midst of the "Instant Information Revolution."

> "Good guess, but the real title is *Need to Know*," said the same voice close to his ear. "It's an indictment of our present system of information dispersal. You're allowed to know only those things the information czars decide that you need to know. They call it 'market research' and 'efficient use of resources' and 'no-waste,' but it's the same old shit they've been doing to us for more than one-hundred years—keep 'em confused and in the dark. You gotta be a stone-ham super-Renaissance person to find out what's really going on."[22]

Pfeil is right when he says that isolating passages such as these hardly requires literary ingenuity to identify expressions of collective anxieties. Indeed, such skeptical statements about information overload and manipulation resonate strongly with Baudrillard's reading of the postmodern scene: "We are in a universe where there is more and more information, and less and less meaning."[23] And yet, in contrast to the reading Baudrillard offers, Carolyn Marvin argues that "information cannot be said to exist at all unless it has meaning, and meaning is established only in social relationships with cultural reference and value."[24] In her critique of the dominant notion of information-as-commodity (a notion that is at the heart of the ideology of the information age), Marvin redefines information not as a quantifiable entity, but rather as a "state of knowing," which reasserts a knowing *body* as its necessary materialist foundation. This embodied notion of information is at the heart of *Synners*. Moving around a postmodernist reading of cyberpunk SF that would focus on its figuration of multinational capitalism and the technological deconstruction of human identity, I would like to elaborate an alternative reading of *Synners* that reflects a slight mutation of these thematic preoccupations. In this case, the focus is on the relation of the material body to cyberspace.

In the course of developing an ideological critique of a capitalist information economy, Cadigan focuses attention on an often-repressed dimension of the information age: the constitution of the informed body. The problem is not just that information "costs," or even that it replicates exponentially, but rather that information is never merely discursive. What we encounter in the Cadigan novel is the narrativization of four different versions of cyberpunk embodiment: the repressed body, the laboring body, the marked body, and the disappearing body. In this sense, the four central characters symbolize the different *embodied* relations one can have, in theory and in fiction, to a nonmaterial space of information access and exchange. The following figure roughly illustrates how Sam, Gabe, Gina, and Visual Mark represent four corners of an identity matrix constructed in and around cyberspace:

Sam (the body that labors)   Gina (the marked body)

Gabe (the repressed body)   Visual Mark (the disappearing body)

Where Sam hacks the net through a terminal powered by her own body, Visual Mark actually inhabits the network as he mutates into a disembodied, sentient artificial intelligence (AI). Although both Gina and Gabe travel through cyberspace on their way to someplace else, Gabe is addicted to cyberspace simulations, and Gina endures them. Each character plays a significant role in the novel's climactic confrontation in cyberspace: a role determined, in part, by their individual relationships to Diversifications and, in part, by their bodily identities.

Sam, Gabe's daughter and the only real hacker among the four, is a virtuoso at gaining access to the net. She is the character who best describes the labor of computer hacking and the virtual acrobatics of cyberspace travel: ". . . [I]f you couldn't walk on the floor, you walked on the ceiling. If you couldn't walk on the ceiling, you walked on the walls, and if you couldn't walk *on* the walls, you walked *in* them, encrypted. Pure hacking."[25] As competent as she is in negotiating the cyberspatial landscape of the net, Sam tries to live her embodied life outside of any institutional structure. Her only affiliations are to other punks and hackers who form a community of sorts and who live out on "the Manhattan-Hermosa strip, what the kids called the Mimosa, part of the old postquake land of the lost."[26] Sam trades encrypted data and hacking talents for stray pieces of equipment and living necessities. In what proves to be a critically important "information commodity" acquisition, Sam hacks the specifications for an insulin-pump chip reader that runs off body energy. When every terminal connected to "the System" is infected by a debilitating virus, Sam's insulin-pump chip reader is the only noninfected access point to the net. Connected by thin needles inserted into her abdomen, the chip reader draws its power from Sam's body. Seventeen-year-old Sam is a cyberspace hacker of considerable talent who shuns the heroic cowboy role. And for the most part, she is content to provide the power while others, namely, Gina and Gabe, go in for the final showdown.

Recoiling from a real-time wife who despises him for his failure to live up to his artistic potential, Gabe spends most of his working time, when he should be designing advertising campaigns, playing the role (Hotwire) of a *noir* leading man in a computer simulation built from pieces of an old movie thriller; his two female cyberspace sidekicks are "templates [that] had been assembled from two real, living people." Where Visual Mark cleaves to cyberspace because the world isn't big enough for his expansive visual mind, Gabe becomes addicted to cyberspace because the world is just too big for him. He retreats to the simulation pit for the safety and familiarity it offers. "He'd been running around in simulation for so long, he'd forgotten how to run a realife, real-time routine; he'd forgotten that if he made mistakes, there was no safety-net program to jump in and correct for him." Throughout the novel, Gabe moves in and out of a real-time life and his simulated fantasy world. In real time his body is continually brought to life, through pain, intoxication, and desire caused by Gina, first when she punches him in the face with a misplaced jab intended for Mark, then later when he gets toxed after she feeds him two LotusLands (a "mildly hallucinogenic beverage"). After they make love for the first time, Gina wonders if Gabe has ever felt desire before: "She didn't think Gabe Ludovic had ever jumped the fast train in his life. Standing at the end of fifteen years of marriage, he'd wanted a lot more than sex. The wanting had been all but tangible, a heat that surprised both of them."[27] After a climactic cyberspace struggle, his repressed body reawakens; Gabe learns to feel his body again (or for the first time) with Gina's help.

Like Visual Mark, Gina is a synner who synthesizes images, sound, and special effects to produce virtual reality music videos. For all her disdain and outright hostility toward other people and institutions, "Badass Gina Aiesi" has an intense emotional connection to Mark, her partner of twenty years, that she romanticizes in an odd way:

> They weren't smooch-faces, it didn't work that way, for her or for him. . . . One time, though . . . one time, three-four-five years into the madness, there'd been a place where they'd come together one night, and it had been different. . . . He'd been reaching, and she'd been reaching, and for a little while there, they'd gotten through. Maybe that had been the night when the little overlapping space called *their life* had come into existence.

Gina's body, marked by its color, "wild forest hardwood," and her dreadlocks, figures prominently in the narrative description of her sexual encounters, first with Visual Mark and then with Gabe. After both she and Visual Mark have brain sockets implanted by Diversifications's surgeon-on-contract, they jack in together and experience a visual replay of shared memories: "The pov was excruciatingly slow as it moved across Mark's face to her own, lingering on the texture of her dreadlocks next to his pale, drawn flesh, finally moving on to the contrast of her deep brown skin."[28] The characteristics that mark Gina are her anger, her exasperated love for Mark, and the color of her skin.

Like others who have bought the new means for jacking in, Visual Mark begins to spend less and less time off-line and more and more time plugged into the global network known as "the System." This leads him to reflect on the metaphysical nature of his physical body:

"[H]e lost all awareness of the meat that had been his prison for close to fifty years, and the relief he felt at having laid his burden down was as great as himself." After suffering a small stroke (one of the unpleasant side effects of brain sockets) while he was jacked in, Visual Mark prepares for "the big one"—a stroke that will release his consciousness into the system and allow him to leave his meat behind.

> He was already accustomed to the idea of having multiple aware-
> ness and a single concentrated core that were both the essence
> of self. The old meat organ would not have been able to cope
> with that kind of reality, but out here he appropriated more ca-
> pacity the way he once might have exchanged a smaller shirt for
> a larger one.[29]

And sure enough, while his body is jacked in, Mark strokes out. He tries to get Gina to pull his plugs, but she is too late. As his meat dies, both his consciousness and his stroke enter "the System." In the process, his stroke is transformed into a deadly virus (or spike) that initiates a worldwide network crash.

Like the dramatic climax in recent cyberpunk films, such as *Circuitry Man*, *The Lawnmower Man*, and *Mindwarp*, the final showdown in *Synners* takes place in cyberspace.[30] Working together, a small community of domestic exiles, hackers, and punks assembles a workstation (powered by Sam's insulin-pump chip reader) that enables Gina and Gabe to go on-line to fight the virus/stroke—an intelligent entity of some dubious ontological status that now threatens the integrity of the entire networked world. Like a cyberspace Terminator, the virus/stroke is rationally determined to infect/destroy whoever comes looking for it. In the course of their cyberspace brawl, Gabe and Gina confront the virus's simulation of their individual worst fears. Gabe's enemy is a simple construct: the fear of embodiment. "I can't remember what it feels like to have a body," he repeats obsessively during his final confrontation. A "reluctant hero" till the very end, he learns through the encounter that his whole body is a hot suit; that is, he learns to feel the body that he has technologically repressed.

Gina's struggle is with an embodiment of her own deepest fears about missed chances, lost love, and suffocating commitment. Her cyberspace showdown replays her obsessive twenty-year-long search for Mark: "Old habits, they do die hard, don't they. That's yours, ain't it—looking for Mark." "Who do you still want to love?" she is asked by the omniscient virus. In one sense her struggle is to confront the fact that she loves an addict and still wants to save him. The crucial decision Gina faces is whether to stay in cyberspace—where there is no pain, no separation—or to renounce him and return to the real world, where such love is impossible. In the end, Gabe and Gina defeat the virus, and the global network shortly reestablishes connections. But when Gina finally wakes to reunite with Gabe, we find out that although *they* have changed for the machines, the machines didn't change for them. "The door only swings one way. Once it's out of the box, it's always too big to get back in. Can't bury that technology. . . . Every technology has its original sin. . . . And we still got to live with what we made."[31]

Darko Suvin asks two additional questions about the shape of a cyberpunk sensibility: "[W]hose structure of feeling?" and "[T]o what ideological horizons or consequences does it apply?" As if in response, Fred Pfeil suggests that most cyberpunk SF "remains stuck in a masculinist frame," in that cyberpunk dramas, like most video game narratives, remain "focused on the struggle of the male protagonist . . . to wend his lonely way through the worlds."[32] Andrew Ross concurs with Pfeil's assessment and adds: "One barely needs to scratch the surface of the cyberpunk genre, no matter how maturely sketched out, to expose a baroque edifice of adolescent male fantasies."[33]

In reading *Synners* as a feminist text, I would argue that it offers an alternative narrative of cyberpunk identity that begins with the assumption that bodies are always gendered and always marked by race. Cadigan's novel is implicitly informed by Donna Haraway's cyborg politics: the gendered distinctions between characters hold true to a cyborgian figuration of gender differences whereby the female body is coded as a body-in-connection and the male body as a body-in-isolation. *Synners* illuminates the gendered differences in the way that the characters relate to the technological space of information. Sam and Gina, the two female hackers, actively *manipulate* the dimensions of cybernetic space in order to communicate with other people. Gabe and Visual Mark, on the other hand, are *addicted* to cyberspace for the release it offers from the loneliness of their material bodies. But the novel's racial politics are more suspect; racial distinctions between characters are revealed through its representation of sexual desire. Gina is the only character who is identified by skin color. She is also the focal object and subject of heterosexual desire, for a moment by Mark, and more frequently by Gabe; and we know both men's racial identities by their marked difference from Gina's. The unmarked characters are marked by the absence of identifying marks. In different ways and with different political consequences, *Synners* reasserts gender and race as defining elements of post-human identity so that, even as *Synners* discursively represents different forms of technological embodiment, it also reasserts the critical importance of the materiality of bodies in any analysis of the information age.

Maybe Pfeil is right to claim that cyberpunk novels have no political unconscious in that their symbolic preoccupations are relatively easy to access. But in constructing this reading of *Synners* not to emphasize its cyberpunk characteristics, but rather to point to its feminist preoccupations, I am implicitly arguing that it entails some form of allegorical narrative; as a work of the feminist imagination, it narrativizes certain tensions and obsessions that animate feminist thinking across cultural discourses. I've argued that Cadigan's narrative symbolically represents the female body as material, as a body that labors. The male body, in contrast, is represented as repressed or disappearing. This reading suggests a slight revision of Arthur Kroker's theory of the postmodern body, in which he argues that the signal form of postmodern embodiment is "the disappearing body."[34] In offering gendered descriptions of *multiple* forms of postmodern embodiment, *Synners* sets the stage for the elaboration of a feminist theory of the relationship of material bodies to cyberspace and of the construction of agency in technological encounters. But even in saying this, I must assert that the final horizon of this reading is not Cadigan's novel, but rather the insights it offers for a feminist analysis of the politics of new information technologies. To this end, *Synners* suggests a starting point for the elaboration of a map of contemporary cyberculture, where technology serves as a site for the reinscription of cultural narratives of gendered and racial identities.

═══════

This reading of *Synners* also implies that a political judgment of any technology is difficult to determine in the abstract. For example, several news articles about the phenomenon of virtual reality boldly assert that VR applications, such as "Virtual Valerie," and 900-number phone sex services are technologies of safe (fluidless) sex; one Atlanta-based sex expert goes so far as to say that VR will be a mainstream sex aid by the end of the decade, stimulating yet pathogenically prudent. The very same phenomenon enables new forms of social and cultural autism. Brenda Laurel, a VR researcher and designer, reports: "I've had men tell me that one of the reasons they got into this business was to escape the social aspects of being a male in America—to escape women in particular."[35] Sandy Stone studies electronic communities and the bodies that labor in cyberspace—including VR systems engineers as well as phone-sex workers. In her analysis of the virtual body, she concludes that cyberspace both disembodies and re-embodies in a gendered fashion: "[T]he desire to cross the human/machine boundary, to penetrate and merge, which is part of the evocation of cyberspace . . . shares certain conceptual and affective characteristics with numerous fictional evocations of the inarticulate longing of the male for the female." But, as she goes on to argue, "to enter cyberspace is to physically put on cyberspace. To become the cyborg, to put on the seductive and dangerous cybernetic space like a garment, is to put on the female."[36] Even as she elaborates the gendered dimensions of cyberspace connection, Stone sees an inherent ambiguity in cyberspace technologies that is tied to the facticity of the material body. For as much as they offer the opportunity for new forms of virtual engagement, Stone rightly asserts that "no refigured virtual body, no matter how beautiful, will slow the death of a cyberpunk with AIDS. Even in the age of the technosubject, life is lived through bodies."[37]

If, on the one hand, new communication technologies such as VR create new contexts for knowing/talking/signing/fucking bodies, they also enable new forms of repression of the material body. Studies of the new modes of electronic communication, for example, indicate that the anonymity offered by the computer screen empowers anti-social behaviors, such as "flaming" (electronic insults), and border-line illegal behaviors, such as trespassing, E-mail snooping, and MUD-rape (unwanted, aggressive, sexual-textual encounter in a multi-user domain).[38] And yet, for all the anonymity they offer, many computer communications reproduce stereotypically gendered patterns of conversation.[39]

In The Jargon File, the entry on "Gender and Ethnicity" claims that although "hackerdom is still predominantly male," hackers are gender- and color-blind in their interactions with other hackers because they communicate (primarily) through text-based network channels.[40] This assertion rests on the assumptions that "text-based channels" represent a gender-neutral medium of exchange and that language itself is free from any form of gender, race, or ethnic determination. Both of these assumptions are called into question not only by feminist research on electronic communication and interpretive theory, but also by female network users who participate in cyberpunk's virtual subculture.[41] This was dramatically, or rather textually, illustrated in an exchange that occurred on FutureCulture, an electronic discussion list devoted to cyberpunk subculture. The thread of the discussion concerned a floating utopia called "Autopia."[42] The exchange about women in "Autopia" began innocently:

> From the cyberdeck of student . . .
> It may just be my imagination, but it seems that the bulk of the people participating in the Autopia discussion are men.
>
> And hasn't anyone else noticed that most people on FutureCulture are men? Not to mention the overall population of the net, generally speaking. I'd like to get women into this discussion, but I'm not even sure if there are any women on FC.
>
> Are there?

In response, a male participant pointed out:

IF you haven't noticed, the bulk of the people on these networks
are men.
It is about 80% male, with higher percentages in some places.

Yeah. Clearly, the Internet is dominated by men. It just seems
that some outreach to women might be in order. Hanging out on
a ship with hundreds of male computer jocks isn't exactly my
idea of utopia.   :)

A female participant wrote back:

Now, this is a loaded question. A lot of women will not open
themselves to possible net harassment by admitting they are lis-
tening. Of course, if they've come this far, they are likely to be
the more bold/brave/stupid type.

Which leaves me where?

Cuz, yes, I am a woman & I hang out on the Internet, read cyberpunk, do interesting things with locks and computers. I don't
program, I don't MU*/D/SH. I do technical work/repair. I write.
I read. I'm a relatively bright individual.

This posting was followed by a self-acknowledged sexist statement
from a male participant who asked others if they too found that
women on the net were extremely unattractive. He was flamed by
several other men in the discussion, one of whom posted this rebuke:

Concepts of physical beauty are holdovers from "MEAT" space.
On the net, they don't apply. We are all just bits and bytes blow-
ing in the phospor stream.

Concepts of physical beauty might be a "meat" thing, but gender
identity persists in the "phospor stream" whether we like it or not.
Eventually, the thread returned to the question of what a woman
might say about "Autopia," the floating-utopia idea. Several postings
later, the original female participant responded:

And, would you like to know why, overall, I am uninterested in
the idea of Autopia? Because I'm a responsible person. (Over-

responsible, if you want to get into the nit-picky psychological semantics, but that's another point.) As a responsible person, I end up doing/am expected to do all the shit work. All the little details that others don't think of; like setting up laundry duty, dishes, cooking, building, repairs, and handling garbage. This is not to say that I fall into the typical "FEMALE" role, because both women and men have left these duties to fall into my lap. And, it's not a case that, if I leave it, it will eventually get done either—you'd be amazed at how long people will ignore garbage or dishes; at how many people can't use a screwdriver or hold a hammer correctly.

Plus, how about security? There is a kind of assumption that goes on, especially on the net, that folks on whatever computer network are a higher intelligence, above craven acts of violence. If you end up with 50 men for every woman, how are you going to ensure her safety?

So, talk about security issues, waste disposal, cooking and cleaning duties, the actual wiring of whatever ship for onboard computers, how you're planning on securing hard drives for rough seas, how you're going to eat, in what shifts are you going to sleep, who's going to steer, how you are going to get navigators.

Where will you get the money for the endeavor? If you decide against a ship, and go for an island, how are you going to deal with overrunning the natural habitat? What are you going to do if you cause some species that only lived on *that* island to become extinct? What are you going to do with refugees from the worlds of hurt on this planet, who are looking for someplace to escape to?

As one other (male) participant in the discussion pointed out, these are eminently practical concerns, but not ones that were raised until the female participant emerged from the silence she was lurking in. Her original point was passed over quickly, even as it was enacted in the course of the subsequent discussion: electronic discussion lists are governed by gendered codes of discursive interchange that are often not hospitable to female participants. This suggests that on-line communication is structured similarly to communication in other settings and is overtly subjected to gender, status, age, and race determinations.

Hoai-An Truong, a member of Bay Area Women in Telecommunications (BAWIT), writes: "Despite the fact that computer networking systems obscure physical characteristics, many women find that gender follows them into the online community, and sets a tone for their public and private interactions there—to such an extent that some women purposefully choose gender-neutral identities, or refrain from expressing their opinions."[43] This is a case where the false denial of the body requires the defensive denial of the body in order to communicate. For some women, it is simply not worth the effort. For most men, it is never noticed.

———

In *Landscape for a Good Woman*, a genre-bending theoretical critique of psychoanalysis and working-class social history, Carolyn Steedman asserts that autobiography is useful for the production of cultural criticism because "[p]ersonal interpretations of past time—the stories that people tell themselves in order to explain how they got to the place they currently inhabit—are often in deep and ambiguous conflict with the official interpretive devices of a culture." Steedman describes the conflict she experiences when she takes cultural theory personally:

> . . . [T]he structures of class analysis and schools of cultural criticism . . . cannot deal with everything there is to say about my mother's life. . . . The usefulness of the biographical and autobiographical core of the book lies in the challenge it may offer to much of our conventional understanding of childhood, working-class childhood, and little-girlhood.[44]

In "writing stories that aren't central to a dominant culture," specifically the story of her working-class childhood and a deauthorized father, Steedman simultaneously revises the insights of psychoanalytic theory and the discursive conventions of cultural criticism. More specifically, she links an autobiographical account of her working-class childhood with a biographical account of her mother's class determinations to serve as the context for a narrative critique of a classic psychoanalytical case study (Freud's story of Dora); her intent is to articulate the relationship between narratives of the self and narratives of history. Her broader point is to demonstrate that working-class histories, in whatever form they are found, as case studies or autobiographical narratives, will often contradict the official "interpretive devices" of a dominant culture. Implicit in Steedman's work is the argument that provoking such a conflict creates the opportunity to interfere with the ongoing codification of official interpretations.

Although different accounts of this conflict could be written, I suggest that the "ambiguous conflict" between the autobiographical notes I opened with and the dominant, if not exactly official, interpretive theory of our era—postmodernism—concerns the penchant to celebrate the perpetual present. Steve Best and Doug Kellner identify this tendency as "radical presentism" and argue that the "erasure of depth also flattens out history and experience, for lost in a postmodern present, one is cut off from those sedimented traditions, those continuities and historical memories which nurture historical consciousness and provide a rich, textured, multidimensional present."[45] Presentism augments two ideological projects of the information age: the construction of social theories narrated by disembodied virtual minds, and the construction of technological histories written without women, without workers, and without politics.[46] The issue I would like to conclude with concerns the gendered aspects of the development of those technologies that have been identified as central to the New Edge and the age of information: microelectronics, telecommunications networks, and other forms of computer technologies. To read accounts of the development of information technologies, for example, one might conclude that women have only just begun to show an interest in and aptitude for technological knowledge, innovation, and employment. This signals yet another pervasive myth of the information age: namely, that everything that is important to know is transparently accessible with the right access codes. Feminist thinkers know differently.

Gathering even basic biographical material about the women who participated in traditionally male-dominated technical and professional fields, including the physical and natural sciences, engineering, mathematics, military science, and astronomy, is not an easy project. The historical material that is available illuminates the daunting structural barriers that many women had to overcome in order to pursue their interests and research in scientific and technological fields. The structural barriers ranged from formal prohibitions against women's education to the legal restrictions on women's property rights which caused many women inventors to patent their inventions under their brothers' or husbands' names. In reporting on her analysis of the treatment of gender and women's subjects in the twenty-four-year history of the journal *Technology and Culture*—the journal of the Society for the History of Technology—Joan Rothschild asserts that one of the reasons for the lack of discussion about gender in the historiography of technology is a "literal identification of the male with technology."[47] This association has been seriously challenged by recent feminist studies that not only seek to recover women's contribution to the historical development of different technologies, but also to rethink the history of technology from a feminist perspective. Autumn Stanley, for example, argues that the history of technology omits women in part because of a categorical exclusion of the technology that women were specifically instrumental in developing as not "proper": here she lists food preparation, nursing and infant care, and menstruation technologies.[48] Other feminists investigate social arrangements that reproduce the masculinist identification with technologies that intimately affect women's lives, such as domestic technologies, as well as specific domains that are still dominated by male scientists, engineers, and medical researchers, such as the new reproductive technologies.[49]

As I implied in the opening remarks about my mother's computer employment history, women's relationship to the technology of the workplace has been a troubled one. The expansion of clerical occupations after World War I resulted in the feminization of such occupations; women were preferentially hired over men because they were less expensive to employ. This kept the costs of expansion contained. After World War II, many forms of female office work were subjected to the analysis of scientific management. Tasks were routinized and rationalized; bookkeepers and other office workers became "machine

attendants who performed standardized repetitive calculating operations."[50] This repetitive work was the perfect material for automated
calculators. Although some labor historians assert that the introduction of electronic calculators and computers occurred during a time
of economic expansion, and thus had the effect of actually increasing
the number of clerical jobs available for displaced workers, the new
jobs were often sex-stratified such that better-paying data-processing
positions were staffed by men. I offer this brief outline to point to
the fact that women have been involved with the implementation of
information technology in U.S. business and industry since at least
World War I. This technology had contradictory effects on women's
employment: it increased the opportunity for new jobs, but at the
same time it downgraded the skill level of office workers who were
employed to attend to the new machines.[51] In forming a judgment
about the impact of these technologies on women's lives, it is important to remember that it is likely that the women who were displaced
from their bookkeeping positions in the 1950s by the introduction
of electronic technology did not necessarily experience this as an
employment failure. No doubt some of them, like my mother, were
eager to get on with the real business of their lives, which was getting
married, having children, and raising families.

In the ten years since the personal computer became widely available as a mass-produced consumer item, it has become an entirely
naturalized fixture in the workplace, either at home or at the business office.[52] It is also becoming common to criticize the claims that
computers increase office worker productivity—the primary market-
ing line for the sale of PC's to businesses and industries. Some critics protest that the real impact of computers and word-processing
systems has been to increase the quantity of time spent producing
documents, while others argue that the computerized office decreases
the quality of work life due to physical discomfort and information
overload.[53] Sociological studies of the gendered aspects of computer
employment focus on the deskilling and displacement of female clerical workers in different industries. While these studies on women as
laborers are vital for an understanding of the social and economic
impact of computers, there is less research available about women's
creative or educational use of information technologies or their role

in the history of computing. But there is also a class bias reflected in these investigations due to the fact that, by focusing on women's computer *use* in the workplace, such studies restrict their critical investigation to those women who have access to what remains a costly technology that is out of the reach and the skill level of most women in the United States today. The question of women's employment and computer technology can be asked another way. For example, Les Levidow studies the women who make the tiny silicon chips that serve as the electronic guts for cheap computer gadgets. Both in affluent (until recently) Silicon Valley and in a relatively poor Malaysian state (Penang), the large majority of chip makers are poorly paid immigrant women.[54]

Yet another way to approach the question of women and technological histories, more sensitive to class-related issues, is to ask "Who counts?" This leads to the investigation of both those who determine who counts as instances of what identities and also those who are treated as numbers or cases in the construction of a database. The politics of databases will be a critical agenda item for the 1990s as an increasing number of businesses, services, and state agencies go "on-line." Determining who has access to data, and how to get access to data that is supposedly available to the "public," is a multidimensional project that involves the use of computers, skill at network accessing, and education in locating and negotiating government-supported databases. Even a chief data coordinator with the U.S. Geological Survey asserts that "data markets, data access, and data dissemination are complicated, fuzzy, emotional topics right now." She "predicts that they likely will be the major issues of the decade."[55] Questions of public access and the status of information in the computer age are just now attracting public attention. As Kenneth B. Allen argues, the same technologies that enable us to "create, manipulate, and disseminate information" also, ironically, "threaten to diminish public access to government information." The issue of citizens' rights to information needs to be monitored by computer-savvy citizen advocates. The question is: Where will such advocates come from?[56] Two answers immediately arise: they will be either educated or elected. Feminist scholars and teachers can contribute to both processes by encouraging women students to address information policy issues in their research projects and by supporting women candidates who will serve on the federal and state boards that govern information access.[57] These candidates and policy students will certainly face several difficult issues involving bodies, information, and criminal charges. The Council for State Governments describes one item of state legislation that may be voted on during 1993: "The Prenatal Exposure to Controlled Substances Act." This act would require "substance abuse treatment personnel to report to the state department of children and family services any pregnant woman who is addicted to drugs or alcohol."[58] The positive consequence of such an act would be requiring states to "bring treatment services to alcohol and/or substance abusing pregnant women." Negative consequences, such as the criminalization of pregnant women for delivering controlled substances to minors, are not mentioned. This act could, as Jennifer Terry suggests, serve as a "technology of surveillance" whereby the unborn fetus is guaranteed certain rights denied to the pregnant woman: for "poor women, interventions into daily life through social welfare and the criminal justice system render recourse to the right to privacy somewhat moot."[59]

In telling the cyberpunk story of the coordination between technology and technical expertise and how it becomes subject to corporate control, *Synners* offers a countermythology of the information age—not that information wants to be free, but rather that access to information is going to cost, and cost a lot. Through its postfeminist portrayal of empowered female bodies who play off and against repressed or hysterical male bodies, *Synners* offers an alternative vision of technological embodiment that is consistent with a gendered history of technology: where technology isn't the means of escape from or transcendence of the body, but rather the means of communication and connection with other bodies. *Synners* also raises questions about the meaning of race in a technological age. How is technological disembodiment also a comment on the desire to transcend racial identities? How are material bodies race-marked through technological encounters? How are racial identities articulated by myths of technological progress?[60] Despite our condition of being incurably informed, we don't have enough information about the embodied aspects of new information technologies. Simply put, we need a great deal more in order to construct the type of analyses of the information age that can serve as a foundation for a critical political agenda.

Synners also suggests the importance of a cyberpunk mythology for the construction of feminist cultural studies of scientific and technological formations. Gina and Sam make interesting subjects for feminist theory in that their technological competencies and synner talents emphasize the need for feminist activists to encourage women to develop technological skills, and for feminist teachers to promote educational efforts to increase technological literacy. The challenge is to harness the power of technological knowledge to a feminist agenda while struggling against an increasing industrial imperialism that eagerly assimilates new technoworkers to labor in the interests of private enterprise.[61] The question is how to empower technological agents such that they work on behalf of the right kind of social change. Determining exactly what constitutes a feminist technological agenda is another matter entirely.

Notes

Thanks to Michael Greer for the Ron Silliman line and for reading and discussing this paper during its various stages of construction. I would also like to thank Pat Cadigan, Sene Sorrow, Stuart Moulthrop, Jay Bolter, Tom Foster, Alan Rauch, Chea Prince, and Robert Cheatham for many discussions that contributed to this essay. A much earlier draft of this paper was presented at the Modern Language Association meetings, San Francisco, 1991.

1   In her historical study of the gendering of the automobile, Virginia Scharff reports that the first woman in the United States to get a driver's license was Mrs. John Howell Phillips of Chicago in 1899. See her *Taking the Wheel: Women and the Coming of the Motor Age* (New York, 1991), 25.

2   Jumping thirty years in this abbreviated history leaves several threads hanging. From World War I to the end of World War II, Chicago was the scene of several significant industrial and cultural transformations. Like thousands of other new immigrants, one set of my grandparents emigrated from southern Italy, the other set from Lithuania. Each settled in an ethnic-identified Chicago neighborhood and began working for one of several large corporate employers already dominating Chicago politics and economics: Grandfather Balsamo at International Harvester, Grandmother Martins at Hart, Schaffner and Marx, and Uncle Barnes at the Swift stockyards. See Lisbeth Cohen, *Making a New Deal: Industrial Workers in Chicago,*

1919–1939 (Cambridge, 1990). Cohen's project enacts a cyborgian logic to investigate a historical pattern of recombinant social identity, whereby we can read how
mass culture played a significant role in the unification of previously disparate
groups.

3 According to Sharon Hartman Strom, "The comptometer, developed by Felt and
Tarrant in Chicago, was often more popular than the calculator because it was
key-driven, lightweight, and inexpensive. . . . Its chief drawback was that it was
non-listing; that is, there was no printed tape which showed each item entered,
only a window in which a running total appeared" (70). See Sharon Hartman
Strom, " 'Machines Instead of Clerks': Technology and the Feminization of Bookkeeping, 1910–1950," in *Case Studies and Policy Perspectives*, ed. Heidi I. Hartmann
(Washington, DC, 1987), 2: 63–97.

4 Rose Balsamo was one of the eight hundred troops assigned to the Headquarters
Company Fourth Aviation Brigade; she was assistant to the NCO in charge of
medical support for the other U.S. troops and Kurdistani refugees.

5 The "New Edge" is one of the most recent labels for a particular arrangement
within contemporary culture. See James R. Beniger, *The Control Revolution: Technological and Economic Origins of the Information Society* (Cambridge, MA, 1986).

6 Pat Cadigan, *Synners* (New York, 1991), 3. Cadigan's first novel, *Mindplayers*
(1989), and most recent one, *Fools* (1992), also belong to the genre of cyberpunk
SF. *Fools* is experimental in its narrative construction in a way similar to Joanna
Russ's *The Female Man*, where the identity of the narrative "I" is fluid and fragmented.

7 Teresa de Lauretis writes: "Hence SF as a mode of writing and reading, as a textual and contextual production of signs and meanings, inscribes our cognitive and
creative processes in what may be called the technological imagination. In tracing cognitive paths through the physical and material reality of the contemporary
technological landscape and designing new maps of social reality, SF is perhaps
the most innovative fictional mode of our historical creativity." See her "Signs of
Wa/onder," in *The Technological Imagination: Theories and Fictions*, ed. Teresa de
Lauretis, Andreas Huyssen, and Kathleen Woodward (Madison, 1980), 169.

8 In describing the structural definition of a cultural formation, Lawrence Grossberg
states that a "formation is a historical articulation, an accumulation or organization of practices. The question is how particular cultural practices, which may
have no intrinsic or even apparent connection, are articulated together to construct an apparently new identity. . . . It is not a question of interpreting a body
of texts or tracing out their intertextuality. Rather the formation has to be read as
the articulation of a number of discrete series of events, only some of which are
discursive." See his *We Gotta Get Out of This Place* (New York, 1992), 70.

9 If we broaden the dimensions of a discursive formation such that it includes the
way in which readers read the work and discuss it, reproduce it and detourn it,
then the possibility of producing archemedian criticism of any form of popular fiction is all the more improbable. In this way, cyberpunk illustrates one of the key
issues at the heart of our information-obsessed culture. As Darko Suvin argues,

"[A]n encompassingly extensive survey of cyberpunk SF looks . . . not only materially impossible but also methodologically dubious" (41). See his "On Gibson
and Cyberpunk SF," *Foundation* 46 (1989): 40–51. It has become increasingly difficult to claim any sort of mastery vis-à-vis a discursive dispersion or a properly
historical genealogy because of the rate of publication and the shelf life of science
fiction publications. Not only is it very difficult to keep track of all the writers of
a particular style, it is equally difficult to keep track of a single author's output.
Few libraries archive pulp science fiction novels; even fewer catalog the early science fiction magazines or any of the numerous fanzines that have appeared in the
past decade. As with the situation for small press literature and poetry, the economics and politics of publishing and library archiving have more to do with the
evaluation of the work in question than with any meta-literary notions of "value,"
"unity," or "genre." The field exists as an unpatterned dispersion—like the Internet, it is impossible to map exhaustively. Users who read the Internet newsgroup
report that several lists of cyberpunk fiction have circulated in the past three
years. I have one compiled by Jonathan Drummey, dated 23 February 1992, that
lists ninety-one authors, including some who only write nonfiction. The *Beyond
Cyberpunk* hypercard stack lists over two hundred books, stories, and anthologies,
whereas the FutureCulture list maintained by Andy Hawkins includes over three
hundred. I cite these fan bibliographies to illustrate how a community of readers
constitutes a discursive field; it would be interesting to study how and why they
determine who's in and who's not.

10   *Mondo 2000* has an interesting publishing history, having begun as a hacker's magazine, only to be transformed more recently into a slick, visually dense, technopop
fanzine with high production values. Selections from the first eight issues have
been collected in *The Mondo 2000 User's Guide to the New Edge*. Chapter topics include all the defining preoccupations of New Edge cyberpunks: smart drugs, computer graphics, chaos theory, electronic music/freedom, hip-hop, robots, street
tech, VR, V-sex, wetware, multimedia, and the net (among other things). The
book includes a bibliography under the title "The Shopping Mall," which is a list
of products, programs, music, journals, and books where you can "read/hear all
about it." See *The Mondo 2000 User's Guide to the New Edge*, ed. Rudy Rucker,
R. U. Sirius, and Queen Mu (New York, 1992).

11   Although clearly beyond the scope of this paper, such an analysis would also need
to trace the enabling conditions for the emergence/convergence of the New Edge
as cultural formation, notably, the phenomenon of Star Trek fandom, the affective
structure of punk rock & roll, phone phreaking, and the computerization of fantasy
RPGs (role-playing games). Mixing in with these popular forms is a range of new
technologies that are themselves being studied as important cultural phenomena;
here I'm thinking of Brenda Laurel's work *Computers as Theater* (Reading, MA,
1991) and Benjamin Woolley's study of virtual reality, *Virtual Worlds: A Journey in
Hype and Hyperreality* (Oxford, 1992).

12   Having identified the key periods in science fiction's literary history, Teresa de
Lauretis puts the issue of periodization aside in favor of discussing the sign work

of SF as a "mode of writing [and] a manner of reading." She points out two modes of signification unique to science fiction as an art form: (1) "SF uses language and narrative signs in a literal way," and (2) "technology is its diffuse landscape." See her "Signs of Wa/onder," 160, 167, 170.

13 Suvin uses William Gibson's novels to identify the genre conventions of "the best works" of cyberpunk SF, while Bruce Sterling's work serves as an "unworthy" example. However, Suvin's polarization of the two is somewhat reversed when he considers the two writers' more recent novels. Suvin claims that Gibson's third novel, *Mona Lisa Overdrive*, "confirms and solidifies his trajectory from critical to escapist use of cyberspace." See "On Gibson and Cyberpunk SF," 48.

14 Much of this work has focused on the postmodern qualities of Gibson's novels in particular: see, for example, David Porush, "Cybernauts in Cyberspace: William Gibson's *Neuromancer*," in *Aliens: The Anthropology of Science Fiction*, ed. George Slusser (Carbondale, 1987), 168–78; and Peter Fitting, "The Lessons of Cyberpunk," *Technoculture*, ed. Constance Penley and Andrew Ross (Minneapolis, 1991), 295–315. Other writers elaborate the connection between cyberpunk and popular media: Brooks Landon, "Bet On IT: Cyber/video/punk/performance," *Mississippi Review* 16 (1988): 245–51; and George Slusser, "Literary MTV," *Mississippi Review* 16 (1988): 279–88.

15 Veronica Hollinger, "Cybernetic Deconstructions: Cyberpunk and Postmodernism," *Mosaic* 23 (Spring 1990): 29–44. If Hollinger misses anything in her careful reading, it is the multiplication of capitalist space, where the mise-en-scène of cyberpunk landscapes (cybernetic as well as the urban sprawl) doesn't just signify an excess of surface, but also an excess of corporate territorialization. In this sense, Gibson's compulsive use of brand names is a testimony to the cybernetic expansion of multinationalist capitalism. On this point, see Pam Rosenthal, "Jacked In: Fordism, Cyberpunk, Marxism," *Socialist Review* 21 (1991): 79–103.

16 Hollinger, "Cybernetic Deconstructions," 33, 42.

17 Cadigan, *Synners*, 386–87.

18 Fredric Jameson, *Postmodernism, or, The Cultural Logic of Late Capitalism* (Durham, NC, 1991), 38.

19 Cadigan, *Synners*, 109.

20 Fred Pfeil, *Another Tale to Tell: Politics and Narrative in Postmodern Culture* (London, 1990), 86.

21 Cadigan, *Synners*, 52–53.

22 Ibid., 194.

23 Jean Baudrillard, *In the Shadow of the Silent Majorities . . . or The End of the Social*, trans. Paul Foss, Paul Patton, and John Johnston (New York, 1983), 95.

24 Carolyn Marvin, "Information and History," in *The Ideology of the Information Age*, ed. Jennifer Daryl Slack and Fred Fejes (Norwood, NJ, 1987), 49–62.

25 Cadigan, *Synners*, 351.

26 Ibid., 7.

27 Ibid., 41, 239, 243.

28 Ibid., 213, 216.

29 Ibid., 227, 232, 325.

30 Hollywood representations of technological hallucinations show an amazing
    visual similarity over time, using out-of-focus shots, swirling images that involve
    a p.o.v. sequence that moves through a worm hole, rapid edits, and illogically
    juxtaposed shots to suggest a technologically induced subjective state. See espe-
    cially *The Trip* (1967), *Brainstorm* (1983), *Circuitry Man* (1989), *Freejack* (1992),
    Till the End of the World (1992).

31 Cadigan, *Synners*, 400, 435.

32 Pfeil, *Another Tale to Tell*, 89. In his study of Nintendo video games, Eugene
    Provenzo reports that when women are included as characters in video games
    they "are often cast as individuals who are acted upon rather than as initiators
    of action." They are depicted as the princess or girlfriend in distress who must
    be rescued by the male hero acting alone or as the leader of a team of fighters/
    magicians. Female characters may obliquely serve as the animating motive for the
    video search, journey, and fight narratives, but they do so only as victims who are
    unable to rescue themselves. Video games designed for other gaming systems show
    a similar stereotyping of female characters. In the Sega Genesis game *Phantasy
    Star III*, for example, the video player can choose female cyborgs as members of his
    team of adventurers; in the course of this game the hero's team encounters many
    powerful monsters depicted as seductive women. Even when the games include
    women characters on the fighting/journeying team, they still serve at the behest
    of the male warrior figure who is the real agent in the gaming narrative. Girls who
    play video games have no other choice but to play the male main character who
    rescues the pretty princess or, in the case of *Maniac Mansion* (Nintendo), Sandy
    the Cheerleader. "Thus the games not only socialize women to be dependent, but
    also condition men to assume dominant gender roles." See Eugene F. Provenzo, Jr.,
    Video Kids: Making Sense of Nintendo (Cambridge, MA, 1991), 100.

33 Andrew Ross, *Strange Weather: Culture, Science, and Technology in the Age of
    Limits* (London, 1991), 145.

34 According to Arthur Kroker, the female body has always been postmodern in
    that it has always been saturated with the signs of capitalism; the male body, in
    turn, becomes hysterical when it encounters this condition of saturation for the
    first time. See Arthur Kroker, *Body Invaders: Panic Sex in America* (New York,
    1987). I develop a fuller analysis of Kroker's treatment of the disappearing body
    in postmodern theory in *Technologies of the Gendered Body* (forthcoming, Duke
    University Press).

35 For an especially insightful discussion between Susie Bright and Brenda Laurel on
    the erotic possibilities of virtual sex, see "The Virtual Orgasm," in *Susie Bright's
    Sexual Reality: A Virtual Sex World Reader* (Pittsburgh, 1992), 60–70.

36 Allucquere Rosanne Stone, "Will the Real Body Please Stand Up?: Boundary Stories
    about Virtual Cultures," in *Cyberspace: First Steps*, ed. Michael Benedikt (Cam-
    bridge, MA, 1992), 109. See also Sally Pryor, "Thinking of Oneself as a Computer,"
    Leonardo 24 (1991): 585–90.

37 Stone, "Real Body," 113. I would argue that the repression of the material body is discursively accomplished in part because of the very intelligence of the techno-body: just as driving a car becomes physiologically intuitive, so too does using a VR rig. As a newly emergent popular cultural form, embodied encounters with VR are more virtual than real at this point. See Anne Balsamo, "The Virtual Body in Cyberspace," *Journal of Research in the Philosophy of Technology* (Spring 1993).

38 For a discussion of the ethical/policy dimensions of computer communication, see Jeffrey Bairstow, "Who Reads Your Electronic Mail?" *Electronic Business*, 16 June 1990, 92; Pamela Varley, "Electronic Democracy," *Technology Review* (November/December 1991): 40–43; and Laurence H. Tribe, "The Constitution in Cyberspace," *The Humanist* 51 (September/October 1991): 15–21.

39 For a discussion of the gendered nature of communication technologies, see especially Lana Rakow, "Women and the Telephone: The Gendering of a Communications Technology," in *Technology and Women's Voices: Keeping in Touch*, ed. Cheris Kramarae (Boston, 1988).

40 The Jargon File, version 2.0.10, 1 July 1992. Available on-line from ftp.uu.net.

41 See Sherry Turkle and Seymour Papert, "Epistemological Pluralism: Styles and Voices with the Computer Culture," *Signs* 16 (1990): 128–57; and Dannielle Bernstein, "Comfort and Experience with Computing: Are They the Same for Women and Men?" *SIGCSE Bulletin* 23 (September 1991): 57–60.

42 These discussions took place over several days in the late months of 1992 and included a dozen participants, most of whom signed their postings with masculine handles.

43 Hoai-An Truong, "Gender Issues in Online Communication," CFP 93 (version 4.1). Available on-line from ftp.eff.org.

44 Carolyn Kay Steedman, *Landscape for a Good Woman: A Story of Two Lives* (New Brunswick, 1987), 6–7.

45 Steven Best and Douglas Kellner, *Postmodern Theory: Critical Interrogations* (New York, 1991), 274.

46 In one account of the history of the computer, the identity of the "world's first programmer" is left out of the chapter title: "Charles Babbage and the World's First Programmer." We discover on the next page that "[t]hough Babbage was a lonely man obsessed with his vision of a programmable computer, he developed a liaison with the beautiful Ada Lovelace, the only legitimate child of Lord Byron, the poet. She became as obsessed as Babbage with the project and contributed many of the ideas for programming the machine, including the invention of the programming loop and the subroutine." Apparently Lovelace translated a description of Babbage's machine, "The Analytical Engine," and "included extensive discussion on programming techniques, sample programs, and the potential of this technology to emulate intelligent human activities." Lovelace was honored by the U.S. Defense Department when it named its programming language after her: ADA. Lovelace and Captain Grace Murray Hooper (who is credited with the development of the programming language COBOL) are usually the only two

women who appear in histories of the computer. See Raymond Kurzweil, *In the Age of Intelligent Machines* (Cambridge, MA, 1990), 167. For a brief biography of Ada Byron Lovelace (1815–52), see Teri Perl, *Math Equals: Biographies of Women Mathematicians* (Menlo Park, 1978).

47   Joan Rothschild, "Introduction," in *Machina Ex Dea: Feminist Perspectives on Technology* (New York, 1983), xviii. In her 1982 review of women and the history of American technology, Judith McGaw identifies Ruth Schwartz Cowan's address to the 1976 meetings of the Society of the History of Technology as a significant founding moment for the feminist study of technology. It was also a *literal* founding moment for the organization of Women in Technological History (WITH). See Judith A. McGaw, "Women and the History of American Technology," *Signs* 7 (1982): 798–828.

48   Autumn Stanley, "Women Hold Up Two-Thirds of the Sky: Notes for a Revised History of Technology," in Rothschild, ed., *Machina Ex Dea*, 5–22. See also Judy Wajcman's discussion of how women are "hidden from histories of technology": *Feminism Confronts Technology* (University Park, PA, 1991). A more popularized treatment of the topic is Ethlie Ann Vare and Greg Ptacek, *Mothers of Invention: From the Bra to the Bomb, Forgotten Women and Their Unforgettable Ideas* (New York, 1987).

49   See especially Cynthia Cockburn, *Machinery of Dominance: Women, Men and Technical Know-How* (London, 1985); Gina Corea, *The Mother Machine: Reproductive Technologies from Artificial Insemination to Artificial Wombs* (New York, 1985); and *Reproductive Technologies: Gender, Motherhood, and Medicine*, ed. Michelle Stanworth (Minneapolis, 1987).

50   See the chapter, "Historical Patterns of Technological Change," in *Computer Chips and Paper Clips: Technology and Women's Employment*, ed. Heidi I. Hartmann, Robert E. Kraut, and Louise A. Tilly (Washington DC, 1986), 40.

51   Other studies of women and workplace technology include Margery Davis, *Woman's Place Is at the Typewriter: Office Work and Office Workers, 1870–1930* (Philadelphia, 1982); Judith S. McIlwee and J. Gregg Robinson, *Women in Engineering: Gender, Power and Workplace Culture* (Albany, 1992); and *WomanPower: Managing in Times of Demographic Turbulence*, ed. Uma Sekaran and Frederick T. L. Leong (Newbury Park, 1992).

52   As a more recent contribution to the study of women's relationship to the technology of the workplace, Ruth Perry and Lisa Greber edited a special issue of *Signs*, published in 1990, on the topic of women and computers. The scholarship that they review considers the impact of the computer on women's employment and the structural forces that limit women's access to computer education. See Ruth Perry and Lisa Greber, "Women and Computers: An Introduction," *Signs* 16 (1990): 74–101.

53   See chap. 5, "Conclusions and Recommendations," in Hartmann, Kraut, and Tilly, eds., *Computer Chips and Paper Clips.*

54   Levidow explores the "price paid for cheap chips" in terms of the harassment and forms of control that Malaysian women endure. See Les Levidow, "Women

Who Make the Chips," *Science as Culture* 2 (1991): 103–24. See also Aihwa Ong's ethnographic study, *Spirits of Resistance and Capitalist Discipline: Factory Women in Malaysia* (Albany, 1987).

55   The quotation is from Nancy Tosta, chief of the Branch of Geographic Data Co-ordination of the National Mapping Division, U.S. Geological Survey in Reston, Virginia ("Who's Got the Data?" *Geo Info Systems* [September 1992]: 24–27). Tosta's prediction is supported by other statements about the U.S. government's efforts to build a Geographic Information System (GIS): a database system whereby "all public information can be referenced by location," the GIS is hailed as "an information integrator." The best use of GIS would be to support the coordination of local, regional, and national organizations—both governmental and private. See Lisa Warnecke, "Building the National GI/GIS Partnership," *Geo Info Systems* (April 1992): 16–23. Managing data, acquiring new data, and safeguarding data integrity are issues of concern for GIS managers. Because of the cost of acquiring new data and safeguarding data integrity, GIS managers sometimes charge a fee for providing information. This process of charging "has thrown [them] into a morass of issues about public records and freedom of information; the value of data, privacy, copyrights, and liability and the roles of public and private sectors in disseminating information." See Nancy Tosta, "Public Access: Right or Privilege?" *Geo Info Systems* (November/December 1991): 20–25.

56   Kenneth B. Allen, "Access to Government Information," *Government Information Quarterly* 9 (1992): 68.

57   Teola P. Hunter, for one, argues that African-American women must seek out potential political candidates who are already "appearing in city council seats, on county commissions, on school boards, in chambers of commerce and on many advisory boards at all levels of government." The key for success that these women hold is their connection to "civil rights groups, education groups, and church groups." Hunter goes on to argue that when "minority women use these contacts and these bonds, they have a support base that is hard to match." See Teola P. Hunter, "A Different View of Progress—Minority Women in Politics," *Journal of State Government* (April/June 1991): 48–52.

58   Council of State Governments, *Suggested State Legislation* 51 (1992): 17–19. There are a number of pieces of legislation that women in particular should be aware of: Breast Cancer Education, Detection, and Screening Standards Acts, Battered Woman Syndrome Defense Act, and a new Domestic Violence Act.

59   Jennifer Terry, "The Body Invaded: Medical Surveillance of Women as Reproducers," *Socialist Review* 39 (1988): 13–43.

60   An advertisement that appeared in *Essence* magazine in 1991 publicizes Garrett Morgan's invention of the traffic light. This ad also illustrates the subtle appropriation of a black agent to support the ideological myth of technological progress, whereby a racist system can somehow be vanquished through a technological fix. The advertisement is sponsored by Amtrak, and includes a picture of a traffic light and the caption: "How do you see the road in front of you?" The rest of the ad copy reads:

The opportunity to get ahead isn't always a matter of red or green. Historically, it's often been a question of black and white. Luckily, Garrett A. Morgan didn't see color as an obstacle. Instead, this son of a former slave overcame tremendous prejudice to become one of the most important American inventors of this century. His creations ranged from a hair straightening cream to the gas mask which saved thousands of lives during WWI. But it was Mr. Morgan's development of the traffic signal which perhaps best symbolizes his life. In 1923, automobiles were increasing in number, and so, unfortunately, were automobile accidents. After witnessing one down the street from his house, he developed and sold his patent for a traffic safety light to General Electric—the forerunner of the traffic light we see on practically every corner in the world. It typified his concern for the safety of people everywhere. His perseverance, and his refusal to let the color of his skin color anyone's perception of his ability. Which brings us the true lesson of Garrett A. Morgan. He may have invented the traffic signal. But he never saw a red light. (*Essence* [February 1991]: 95)

61   For a discussion of the technological takeover of higher education in Britain—a discussion that offers insights into the shift away from the humanities and social sciences and toward technological and managerial fields going on right now in the United States—see Kevin Robins and Frank Webster, "Higher Education, High Tech, High Rhetoric," in *Compulsive Technology: Computers as Culture*, ed. Tony Solomenides and Les Levidow (London, 1985), 36–57.

CLAUDIA SPRINGER

SEX, MEMORIES, AND ANGRY WOMEN

One thing is certain: the riddle of mind, long a topic for philosophers, has taken on new urgency. Under pressure from the computer, the question of mind in relation to machine is becoming a central cultural preoccupation. It is becoming for us what sex was to the Victorians—threat and obsession, taboo and fascination.
—Sherry Turkle

The question of mind in relation to machine has indeed become a cultural preoccupation.[1] Debates rage in the popular press as well as in specialized science and philosophy texts over whether computers can accurately simulate the human mind and, conversely, whether human minds are fundamentally computers. So far, computers themselves have not become active participants in the debate, although human scholars have taken on the personae of computers to speculate on how history would be interpreted by an artificial intelligence tracing its own lineage.[2] But interest in the nature of the human mind has by no means displaced interest in sex. Within current discussions about the mind lingers the preoccupation with sex identified by psychologist Sherry Turkle as central to Victorian culture. Rather than existing as separate issues, thought and sex are thoroughly entwined, even indistinguishable, in contemporary cybercultural discourses. Texts that discuss computation and reasoning in terms of sexual responses discursively erase the Cartesian separation between mind and body. Computers, it seems, have intensified, not diminished, our culture's fascination with sexuality. They have also prompted some scientists to predict a future in which humans will lose their bodies and exist instead on software. But for now, in most fiction, computers have inspired flights of fantasy that remain firmly grounded in our current cultural preoccupations with sex, gender, and angry women.

Sex is not a newcomer to science and technology. Feminist scholars have analyzed how scientific discourses presented in the guise of impartial and objective truth have historically relied on patriarchal metaphors related to sex and gender. Feminist scholarship asserts that science and technology are not isolated from ideological influence but are "part and parcel, woof and warp, of the social orders from which they emerge and which support them."[3] An example of sex in a description of technology can be found in a 1968 issue of the journal *Technology and Culture* where author Lee Hart is quoted as writing that "machines may well have erotic fantasies when the machine 'perceives' the rising nipple of a well-turned dial."[4] Thrusting and pumping industrial machines have long evoked sexual imagery for human observers, but Hart suggests that the machines themselves are motivated by sexual desire and erotic fantasies. Sex, it would seem, monopolizes the thoughts not only of scholars in the field of technology but also of the machines they study.

Computer discourses are of course products of their cultures and are infused with cultural assumptions about gender and sexuality. A staid computer magazine, *International Spectrum*, subtitled "The Businessperson's Computer Magazine," has inside its November/December 1989 issue's front cover an advertisement for Sequoia hardware that shows a tape measure marked in intervals not by inches but by numbers of hardware users, accompanied by the question, "Can your Pick hardware measure up to this?" (Pick is a business-oriented office operating system.) Its association of computer hardware with penis length assumes a male consumer and makes explicit the conjunction of sexuality and technology that pervades computer discourse.

There seems to be an irresistible compulsion to associate computers and the computer world with sexuality. Jack Rochester and John Gantz, for example, start their book *The Naked Computer* with an introduction titled "The Mating Call" in which they inform the reader, "You're in love. You just don't know it yet. . . . But you might as well join the orgy, succumb to the pleasures of the information age. After all, a computer has already changed your life."[5] A sexy discourse also surrounds computer technology in the hip cyberpunk journal *Mondo 2000*. Its editorial staff list includes the position of Domineditrix, and issue number one displays "Micro Chic: Artificial Intelligence to Wear" on a model in provocative poses wearing electronic circuitry that has been assembled into breastplates.[6] Issue number five includes photographs of nude women with elaborate contraptions made of electronic circuitry strapped to their crotches, breasts, and buttocks. They are described in the accompanying text as the maenads (women who participated in Dionysian rites) and a poem printed alongside them includes the lurid lines, "Groaning, moaning, on your knees; / panther, Niger, come to me; / blood and milk together feed the pleasure; / carmine, throbbing, senses reel; / fleshy mystery, pagan meal; / Dionysus screams as we give pleasure."[7]

For the computer user, sex software programs have been around for years and continue to sell well. An early program named Whorehouse has the players vie to become "King Pimp"; "play begins by putting your wife on the sidewalk."[8] Currently, the creator of the program MacPlaymates cannot keep up with the high demand for his product.[9] And computer networks with names such as Throbnet and After Dark have made it possible for people to communicate anonymously with each other about sex. According to one account: "Pioneered by computer hobbyists, the exchange of explicit and personal sexual material via personal computer and phone lines has taken on international proportions in the last three years."[10] Computers have seduced some users away from face-to-face romantic interactions altogether. As cultural critic Mark Dery writes about the phenomenon he calls "mechano-eroticism": "The only thing better than making love *like* a machine, it seems, is making love *with* a machine."[11]

Ascription of sexuality to computers is part of a larger well-documented tendency for people to anthropomorphize computers.[12] Rochester and Gantz, in *Naked Computer*, even refer to a computer's "excrement."[13] Humanlike computers have become commonplace in popular culture, with two of the most powerful examples occurring in the films *2001: A Space Odyssey* (1968), in which the spaceship's computer, HAL, becomes more emotional than the astronauts on board, and *Demon Seed* (1977), in which an artificial intelligence rapes a woman psychologist. These films take anthropomorphism to an extreme, but actual computer functions cannot but in some ways resemble human characteristics.

Perhaps the most provocative similarity between humans and computers is "memory." Anthropomorphism is implicit when we refer to a computer's "memory." But the memory analogy has not been just a one-way street; cognitive psychologists eager to solidify the analogy between humans and computers join artificial intelligence researchers in arguing that human memory functions similarly to computer memory and that even the elusive human ability to create complicated associations can be reproduced by computers.[14] J. David Bolter responds to this way of thinking in *Turing's Man: Western Culture in the Computer Age*:

> There is more to human memory than the ability to repeat what is remembered. If men and women are constantly forgetting what they learn, they can also remember more than they learn. They can trace out connections among sets of disparate memories and not only on the aesthetic level of Proust's associations on the scent of madeleines. Memory, with its capacity to establish structures of associations, is closely tied to other faculties of reasoned thought and creativity. It is in this sense that we live in the world we remember, and it is this mysterious capacity that psychologists and artificial intelligence specialists would like to co-opt for their computerized intellect.[15]

Despite the complexity of human memory, the model of a computer mind has for some psychologists replaced the Freudian paradigm of layered levels of consciousness engaged in a process of repression. "The computer takes up where psychoanalysis left off," writes Turkle in her critique of the tendency to identify the human mind with computers.[16] And the notion of a depthless self is one of the characteristics of what Bolter calls "Turing's man," the late-twentieth-century human defined as a computerlike artifact. Bolter writes that "the goal of artificial intelligence is to demonstrate that man is all surface, that there is nothing dark or mysterious in the human condition, nothing that cannot be lit by the even light of operational analysis."[17] As if to illustrate Bolter's observation, Roger C. Schank, who has written extensively on the parallels between computers and human minds, states,

> . . . [W]e have seen that creativity, that mystical process known only to humans, is not really so mystical after all, and that it may well be possible to replicate creative behavior on a machine by transforming standard explanation patterns. From this it follows that the processes of creativity and learning are not so elusive, and may be quite algorithmic in nature after all.[18]

Jean Baudrillard has identified this sort of depthlessness as a crucial component of postmodern existence, resulting in human identities as flat as computer and television screens.[19] One-dimensionality extends beyond the individual in postmodernism to encompass society at large. As Fredric Jameson points out, we are experiencing cultural depthlessness in the form of historical amnesia, the inability to remember our cultural history.[20] According to Jameson, history has been reduced to a perpetual present; we live surrounded by artifacts salvaged from the past that have been commodified for our consumption but have lost the meanings provided by their original contexts. With its flattened perspective, the postmodern computer age has generated in humans what Scott Bukatman calls "terminal identity."[21]

The appeal of computer existence for humans in the late twentieth century cannot be separated from the actual cultural crises confronting us, in particular the crises surrounding issues of sex and death. In a time when sexual contact with other humans carries the risk of AIDS, computer sex can pose an attractive alternative. Computers have already become all-consuming for young men who perpetuate the caricature of the solitary social misfit who prefers to commune with his terminal rather than with actual people, especially with actual women. A retreat from sexual involvement is evident in references to "the new celibacy" that crop up in the news media on a regular basis. Fantasies of solitary and cerebral machine sex are not entirely irrational given the new fear of physical sex. AIDS has also created an increased public awareness of human vulnerability and mortality. In a world where human bodies appear to be expendable— if not, the fight against AIDS would be a higher government priority—discourses of death, what journalist Frank Rich calls "the new blood culture," have become widespread. Rich explains the popularity of the film *Bram Stoker's Dracula* (1992), Madonna's book *Sex*, and the vampire novels of Anne Rice as part of a larger "national psychic obsession" with the threat of death from infected blood.[22]

There is a long Western cultural tradition of associating sex with death; now, sex is being replaced by computer use, which provides the deathlike loss of self once associated with sexual pleasure. Identifying with computers can be appealing on several levels in our fragmented postmodern existence. Vulnerable late-twentieth-century bodies and minds turn to electronic technology to protect themselves from confusion and pain. Fusion with computers can provide an illusory sense of personal wholeness reminiscent of the Lacanian Imaginary; the fused cyborg condition erases the difference between self and other. Additionally, a wholesale embrace of computerized existence can create a sense that one's messy emotions have been replaced by pure logic and rationality. For those unable to cope with the complexity of human emotions, it might seem preferable to replace them with a limited repertoire of automatic responses. With a robotic, fortified self, the computer-human exemplified by Hollywood's RoboCop and the Terminator defends against both internal and external threats of dissolution.[23]

Donna Haraway's "Manifesto for Cyborgs" argues that cyborg existence need not be defined exclusively in terms of a fortified masculinist self even though the Defense Department's prominent role in the development of cybernetic equipment has given the cyborg an aggressive military background.[24] Haraway proposes an alternative way of conceptualizing cyborgs in terms of a hybrid subjectivity. Her cyborg would adopt partial and contradictory identities that accept difference rather than defend against it. Ideally, Haraway's cyborg would liberate us from the social hierarchies that perpetuate sexism and racism. Even though Haraway's hybrid cyborg is a far cry from the aggressive fortified cyborg, both visions suggest an idealized state of computer existence that rectifies the inadequacies and injustices of contemporary human life. The idea of a feminist cyborg, like the idea of a militaristic cyborg, arises from dissatisfaction with current social and economic relations, but the two cyborg visions offer vastly different solutions to our social ills.

For some computer scientists, electronic technology has opened up the possibility of copying human minds onto computer software. The human body would become obsolete while human minds would circulate on multiple software copies. Proponents of downloading human consciousness argue that humans would achieve immortality, but the notion can also be understood to foretell human extinction. Human bodies, for these scientists, are entirely expendable. Speculation about the nature of human identity inevitably arises in discussions of human software copies. Computer scientists as well as science fiction writers have speculated on the authenticity of electronically copied minds. The scientists, however, write from a strictly empirical standpoint, using rhetoric that lends their exterminatory ideas the illusion of scientific validity. Marvin Minsky, one of the foremost researchers in the field of artificial intelligence, entertains the notion that your mind could be duplicated by replacing each brain cell with a special computer chip. Minsky asks, "Would that new machine be the same as you" if it were placed in the same environment as you and could function using the same processes as your brain? He responds that microscopic differences would exist between your brain and the brain-machine, since "it would be impractical to duplicate, with absolute fidelity, *all* the interactions in a brain."[25] But you could not claim, writes Minsky, that these microscopic differences make the duplicate different from your mind because you yourself are constantly changing and are never exactly the same as you were a moment ago.

Although Minsky's perspective is completely literal rather than metaphorical, his description of human identities undergoing con-

stant changes resembles poststructuralist theories of decentered subjectivity, according to which individuals do not have fixed, stable
identities but assume changing subject positions determined by language, gender, and other social and cultural institutions. He dif-
fers from poststructuralists in his faith in science. Minsky analyzes
human identity in order to support his position that artificial intelligence research, using the logic and rationality of science, can succeed
in creating a computer mind equivalent to the human mind. For poststructuralist theorists, science, like any metanarrative that purports
to express universal truths, is constrained by its ideological under-
pinnings and maintains its status as truth only within the confines
of its own terms.[26] The case against scientific empiricism has sometimes been overstated, but Minsky's often inflammatory statements
go a long way in blurring the boundary between science and science
fiction.

Minsky's brain-machine belongs to a future in which even human
beings have been replaced by simulations: copies without originals.
What Baudrillard describes as our postmodern obsession with simulacra finds full expression in a world populated by electronically copied
human minds.[27] Another computer scientist, Hans Moravec, director
of the Mobile Robot Laboratory at Carnegie Mellon University, is
less hypothetical than Minsky in describing a future of mind simulation and human extinction. Moravec proposes that it will some-
day be possible for mental functions to be surgically extracted from
the human brain and transferred to computer software in a process
he calls "transmigration."[28] The useless human body with its brain
tissue would then be discarded, while consciousness would remain
stored in computer terminals, or, for the occasional outing, in mobile
robots. For Moravec, there would be no significant difference between the identity of the original mind and its copy, except that the
software copy would supplement the original personality with many
new abilities. Humans, according to Moravec's misanthropic plan,
should consent to their own extinction and cede the future to their
computerized progeny.

Cyberpunk fiction's visions of the future extrapolate from our current cultural preoccupation with computers to create worlds where

the computer metaphor for human existence has triumphed. When cyberpunk characters are surgically hardwired, jack into cyberspace, plug software programs directly into their brains, create computerized virtual bodies for themselves while their actual bodies decay, or abandon their bodies to exist inside the computer matrix, the boundary between human and computer is erased and the nature of the human psyche is redefined in accordance with the computer paradigm. Computers and human minds become thoroughly compatible because the differences between them have been effaced.

In cyberpunk, mental processes are configured to function according to a digital model to the extent that personalities and thoughts can be electronically coded and copied. Digital existence is a central aspect of George Alec Effinger's cyberpunk trilogy *When Gravity Fails*, *A Fire in the Sun*, and *The Exile Kiss*. Characters insert software programs directly into their electronically wired brains. They "chip in" personality modules, called "moddies," and add-on chips, called "daddies," sold in "modshops," where the biggest sellers are sex, drugs, and religious ecstasy. Although most of the personalities on the modules are fictional characters, it is possible to create moddies from the mind of a living person, as the protagonist Marid Audran learns when a ruthless crime boss tortures him mercilessly and simultaneously records a moddie of his exact thoughts and feelings while he suffers. Audran refers to the experience as mind-rape, but he also concedes that Islam (the novels are set in the Middle East) will have to come to grips with the legal implications of personality modules recorded from living people, "just as the faith has had to deal with every other technological advance."

The idea of digitally recording human minds finds expression in other cyberpunk texts. When characters in William Gibson's trilogy *Neuromancer*, *Count Zero*, and *Mona Lisa Overdrive* jack into "simstim" (simulated stimulation), they share the consciousness of simstim stars, whose experiences and feelings are recorded and transmitted directly into the minds of the public. And a simstim link allows Case, the protagonist in *Neuromancer*, to vicariously experience the point of view and thoughts of his partner, the razorgirl Molly, when she stalks into dangerous situations.

In both Gibson's and Effinger's novels, the experience of plugging into another mind is often associated with sexual pleasure. Gibson's characters enter the pleasurable and exciting world of simstim to escape their own dreary lives. And in Effinger's *When Gravity Fails* (1987), Marid Audran is propositioned by Chiri, a bartender, who offers to plug in her new Honey Pilar sex kitten personality module for him.

> It was a very tempting suggestion. . . . [W]ith Honey Pilar's personality module plugged in, Chiri would *become* Honey Pilar. She'd jam the way Honey had jammed when the module was recorded. You close your eyes and you're in bed with the most desirable woman in the world, and the only man she wants is you, begging for *you*.

Even though Marid initially resists getting his brain wired for personality modules because he is afraid of the way they "crammed you away in some little tin box inside your head, and someone you didn't know took over your mind and body," after he is forced to undergo the surgical procedure he takes pleasure in experimenting with a variety of modules. And pleasure comes in all forms; for the powerful crime lord Shaykh Reda Abu Adil, who tortures Marid, it means entering "Proxy Hell": chipping in bootleg black-market moddies recorded from people experiencing the horrible pain and suffering of torture or disease. Effinger extrapolates from the current tendency to create a world where new technologies are immediately adapted to provide sexual pleasure in even its most extreme forms.

In cyberworlds where minds can be manipulated like computers, memories operate according to an electronic model; they can be technologically enhanced, augmented, changed, or erased. Since memories form the foundation of human identity, loss of memory is equivalent to loss of self. This raises the question addressed by Minsky and Moravec of whether an electronic copy of a human mind is the same as the original. The film *Blade Runner* (1982) revolves around this question (although its artificial humans are genetically engineered rather than electronically copied) by having both its human and replicant characters treasure their personal collections of photographs, which are visual signifiers of memories. And Rachael, the most advanced model replicant, believes she is human because she remembers her childhood, until she learns that the memories have been implanted in her and actually belong to the niece of her inventor. The film erases conventional distinctions between humans and their artificial copies not only by having the replicants collect memories in human fashion, but also by having them surpass humans in the emotional qualities of love and compassion. Thus it suggests that advanced technologies can potentially be used to destroy human uniqueness. Gabriele Schwab refers to this as the "dark side of a culture of cyborgs," and comments on its ironic aspect: "Technology, meant to extend our organs and our senses or even to support our fantasms of immortality and transcendence, seems to threaten what we wanted to preserve by destroying us as the subjects we thought ourselves to be when we took refuge in technological projects and dreams."[29]

Cyberpunk author Pat Cadigan envisions a society where minds are routinely entered and copied in her novel *Mindplayers*. Those who are dissatisfied with their lives can abandon their identities and buy a franchised personality sold by a company called Power People. One desperate character sells bootleg copies of his own personality. Others hire mindplayers to enter their minds via electronic hookups to their optical nerves (after temporarily removing their eyes) to explore their thoughts or introduce new mental material. When minds are routinely entered and duplicated, there ceases to be any concept of an authentic self and individual rights are threatened. In *Mindplayers*, mindplay is controlled by the state and private corporations, and anyone caught indulging in illegal mindplaying activity by the Brain Police could be sentenced to a mindsuck, which erases identity and leaves an empty shell to be filled with a new state-sanctioned personality.

Even though digital existence has taken hold in cyberpunk, humans in these books have not been mindsucked into oblivion; they continue to experience the turbulent emotions and memories associated with earlier models of the mind. The desires and fears that Freud located in the human unconscious have not disappeared but continue to haunt cyberpunk characters. In fact, in fictional cyberworlds, computer memory facilitates, and even heightens, the role that repressed emotions play in human and computer existence. Cyborgs are frequently troubled by emotional memories and are motivated by a desire for revenge. Two of the best-known cyborgs whose actions are driven by repressed memories are RoboCop, in the films *RoboCop* (1987) and *RoboCop 2* (1990), and Eve 8, in the film *Eve of Destruction* (1991). Another haunted cyborg is Victor Stone, "a.k.a. Cyborg," in the comic book *Tales of the New Teen Titans*. Stone is transformed from a black teenager into a half-machine, half-human steel-smashing titan with computerized components, but he continues to be aware of racial divisions in society, even though at the end of issue number one he rejects black anger at white injustice.

When cyberpunk texts incorporate repressed memories, they often raise controversial social issues, as in the case of Victor Stone's experiences with racism, for a larger cultural context informs the cyborg's personal memories. One scenario that has emerged with remarkable frequency is that of the cybernetic woman who seeks revenge for the emotional and sexual abuse she suffered as a child or young woman. She is simultaneously one of the most compelling and one of the most problematic figures in cyberpunk, for her appeal on a feminist level is frequently undermined by her conventional patriarchal presentation. Her ambiguous status has inspired contradictory interpretations and has sparked debates among commentators on cyberpunk. Timothy Leary praises Gibson's female characters, whom he calls "strong, independent, effective . . . heroic."[30] In contrast, Nicola Nixon asserts that cyberpunk's strong female characters "are effectively depoliticized and sapped of any revolutionary energy."[31] According to Nixon, recent cyberpunk spokesmen have expressed disdain for the feminist science fiction of the 1970s and like to portray themselves as brash young men who infused new vitality into a moribund genre. John J. Pierce objects to what he calls Nixon's condemnation of "an entire subgenre as inherently sexist and reactionary."[32] Their exchange and others on the same subject emphasize the ambiguity of cyberpunk's angry woman and her ability to evoke multiple, even contradictory, responses.

The prototype for cyberpunk's angry, cybernetically enhanced survivor of patriarchal abuse is Molly Millions, from Gibson's short story "Johnny Mnemonic" and novel *Neuromancer*. Molly paid for her transformation into a sleek killing machine with money earned while working as a prostitute, when she experienced overwhelming depravity, including men killing women for sexual pleasure. In the "Cyberpunk in Boystown" chapter of his book *Strange Weather*, cultural critic Andrew Ross traces Molly's influence from Elektra, in the comic book series *Elektra Assassin*, to Abhor, in Kathy Acker's novel *Empire of the Senseless*. "Both characters," Ross writes, "are steely, orphanesque survivors of a history of victimage that includes paternal rape, followed by repeated sexual predation on the part of violent males."[33] Indeed, the Ninja warrior-for-hire Elektra is filled with rage and has an unlimited capacity for violence after a childhood of paternal abuse. And Abhor, who is "part robot, and part black" and was also raped by her father, lives the violent life of an outcast. Acker's novel draws on cyberpunk imagery to rebel against patriarchal discourses, repeatedly revealing the violence and hatred that underlie them.

Yet another example of a cybernetic assassin is Sarah, in Walter Jon Williams's novel *Hardwired*. As a child she was continually beaten by her father, and, like Molly Millions, she earned money through prostitution to finance her independence and surgical transformation into a technokiller. With her nervous system electronically hardwired to heighten her reflexes and allow her to interface directly with her weapons, and with a tall and muscular body, she is a formidable opponent. Her internal weaponry takes the form of a "cybersnake," which she calls Weasel, that rises from her chest through her throat and out of her mouth to attack her victims. A phallic serpent, it lies dormant until needed and then whips out like a killer erection. As Sarah explains, "[T]he tears are long gone and in their place is hardened steel desire."

Molly, Sarah, and the other hardwired women they have influenced clearly embody a fetishized male fantasy, but they also represent feminist rebellion against a brutal patriarchal system. It is difficult to either condemn or celebrate them, since a single interpretation cannot entirely explain their appeal. The same construction of multiple and contradictory readings occurs in films. In *Eve of Destruction*, Eve 8 plays out a feminist fantasy when she methodically stalks and kills the men (and types of men) who abused her creator, scientist Eve Simmons, whose memories, thoughts, and feelings she shares. Included among Eve 8's victims is Eve Simmons's father, an abusive man who caused the death of Eve's mother. At the same time, the film condemns female sexuality and autonomy on a massive scale when we learn that Eve 8 contains in her womb a nuclear weapon on the verge of explosion, which must be destroyed to save the planet.

Another ambiguous figure is Sarah Connor in the *Terminator* films, who transforms herself into a taut, muscular killing machine to prepare for the nuclear apocalypse and also as a reaction to the abuse inflicted on her by male doctors and attendants while she was imprisoned in a mental ward. Dery points out with regard to Sarah Connor that "Hollywood's exploitation of the Freudian subtext of a sweaty woman squirting hot lead from a throbbing rod could hardly be called empowering."[34] Certainly, Sarah Connor fits into a long tradition of phallic women in films whose fetishized bodies are designed to ease castration fears for the male spectator made uncomfortable by the sight of a fleshy woman on screen. However, she also provides an attractive figure in the realm of fantasy for angry women. As viewers of martial arts films know, it is enormously satisfying to experience vicariously the triumph of an underdog seeking revenge against the perpetrators of injustice. Women under patriarchy can experience the exhilarating fantasy of immense physical strength and freedom from all constraints when watching figures like Sarah Connor. Revenge fantasies are powerful, even when they are packaged for consumption by the Hollywood film industry.

Because of the ambiguities and contradictions of her presentation, however, cyberpunk's figure of the angry woman can neither be hailed as a feminist paragon nor repudiated as a mere sex object; she incorporates aspects of both but fully embodies neither. In addition to her feminist potential, what is interesting about the hardwired woman is that she is motivated by human memories and emotions at all, for she has undergone a transformation from a human based on an organic model to one based on a computer model. After she has been remodeled, she abandons subtlety and indecision and instead reacts to events with the regularity and inevitability of a computer program. Whether she has been literally hardwired or not, she figuratively reacts to events with a computer's speed and decisiveness. Her former passivity has been replaced with swift aggression. What the transformation suggests is that the only way to escape from victimization is to become a machine. Autonomy and strength, the texts tell us, derive from embracing a computerlike existence, for life as a human, especially as a woman, has become unbearable.

But these cybernetic women do not achieve a radically nonhuman, computerized existence. Repressed human memories and heightened emotions continue to motivate hardwired women even after they have redesigned themselves. Instead of escaping from their human predicaments and entering a liberated electronic realm, they become hardened and powerful killers, haunted by memories of abuse. Their personal boundaries are armored, not fluid like the boundaries of Haraway's feminist cyborgs. Actual computer characteristics are in fact distorted by their representations. The physical passivity adopted by human computer users is recast as aggressive violence; the miniaturization and subtlety of computers are refashioned into bulging muscles that more closely resemble the enormity and force of industrial technology. Gender, rather than disappearing, is often emphasized after cybernetic transformation. While Moravec asserts that gender will become obsolete once human minds have been transferred to software, cyberpunk points instead to a future in which gender and sex not only exist but have become magnified.[35]

Although our culture is indeed preoccupied with the notion of computerized minds, there is a reluctance to imagine a truly nonhuman future.[36] Even when cybernetic characters relinquish their physical forms to enter the computer matrix, they are still preoccupied with human concerns. Sex continues to flourish in fictional electronic worlds. In some cases, even the complete loss of human form fails to produce a significant departure from human sexuality. For some observers, the perpetuation of human sexual difference and desire is essential for the success of disembodied forms of life. Jean-François Lyotard suggests that artificial intelligence can succeed in producing thought only if it incorporates memory, gender, and sexual desire: "We need machines that suffer from the burden of their memory. . . . Your thinking machines will have to be nourished not just on radiation but on irremediable gender difference."[37] For Lyotard, the force that propels thought is the desire induced by gender difference.

Nowhere is the persistence of human identity and sexuality after metamorphosis into a computer made more clear than in the novel

Lady El (1992) by Jim Starlin and Diana Graziunas. It follows in the footsteps of other texts about a victimized woman's transformation into a hardwired killer, only this time the woman loses all physical form and literally becomes a computer. The novel illustrates the problem faced by readers of cyberpunk who enjoy the figure of the cybernetic woman survivor, but are troubled by the persistence of patriarchal myths that inform her presentation. Like most of cyberpunk's angry women, Lady El does not have the enlightened perspective of Haraway's cyborg. Although the novel begins by embracing feminist principles as it follows a woman's rejection of victimization, it ends by enacting the familiar myth of the destructive sexual woman. It suggests that gender and sexuality transcend death and disembodiment, and, when combined with the enormous power of technology, lead to massive and uncontrollable destruction. If a woman is not a victim, warns the novel, her autonomy and sexual independence can rage out of control and destroy the world.

Lady El is short for Lady Electric, who begins her life as a human being named Arlene Washington. As a young woman, she is killed by a subway train in a freak accident. After her death, her brain is donated to the secret Project Cyborg and linked to a computer system. In her new life she is a brain floating in a jar connected to increasingly sophisticated and powerful computers. Eventually, she is linked to the most powerful computer in the world, the Pentagon's NORAD computer, putting her in charge of an immense amount of data and important decisions, including, as she puts it, "the *button*, the entire works for the strategic nuclear planning for the whole damn U.S. of A."

The scientist in charge of the project, Walter Hillerman, is surprised to learn that Lady El retains the complete identity of Arlene Washington.[38] He has collected ten brains in jars for the initial experiment, all of them renamed (by a lab assistant) for professional wrestlers, emphasizing the discrepancy between their disembodied state and a wrestler's exaggerated physique. Even though Walter Hillerman initially rejects the notion that the brains retain their original identities, one of the three ways that each brain is labeled refers to its former identity: "an F or M for the brain's sex." The novel posits that a person's sex is located in the brain and outlives the loss of the body. There is biological determinism at work in the notion that a brain, or any disembodied organ, has a sexual identity, as if any single part of a body in isolation can be identified as male or female. Additionally, by labeling the brains according to their sex, the novel continues a patriarchal tradition of making an individual's sex the principal basis for identification.

What Lady El brings to her new job is the memory of continual violence inflicted on her by men ever since she was a little girl. Her first-person narration concentrates on how her new status as a cyborg has released her from victimization and endowed her with immense powers. She began her life with, as she puts it, three strikes against her: she was poor, black, and female. Her childhood turned into a nightmare after her father died and her mother took in a violent and abusive man named Lavar, who continually raped the thirteen-year-old Arlene and then, a year later, started to sell her to his friends. Arlene finally ran away to New York and got a job on the night shift as a cleaning woman in the World Trade Center. She also began a series of degrading relationships with violent, drug-addicted or alcoholic men.

After Arlene's death and resurrection as Lady El, however, she realizes that in her former life she had been the victim of racism and had lived her life as an "emotional junkie" who always depended on a man to tell her what to do and think. Her new cyborg existence gives her perspective on her past life and allows her to become increasingly powerful as she is given access to enormous data banks and asked to make decisions of considerable importance. She enjoys lightning-speed learning from the data banks and expands her consciousness by sharing the memories of a white man's and a white woman's brains plugged into her system. Because of her new perspective, she adopts the motto "power = survival" and soon after revises it to "knowledge + power = survival."

She uses her new knowledge and power, however, in ways that continue, rather than reject, her concerns from the past. Even in the form of an on-line brain, she has not abandoned the desire for love or the tendency to make men her first priority. Most of her time is spent obsessing about scientist Walter Hillerman. She tells the reader, "I'll 'fess up. I courted the man. My every waking moment was spent on thinking how I could please him." What has changed is that, un-like Arlene Washington, she is determined to maintain her power and is "clearly developing an affection for men who could be con-trolled." Her main liability, as she sees it, is her lack of a body, so she secretly designs and builds for herself a robot body, one she describes as "every man's wet dream." Despite the fact that she has rejected the role of victim, she still changes herself for a man, in this case lit-erally building herself from scratch. Her idea of power is to succeed by conforming to the system rather than opposing it; the robot body she designs is based on racist stereotypes of beauty. She declares, "I wanted to be a blonde! A blue-eyed, blond California beach baby! Barbie with a brain!" She continues:

> I bet lots 'a brothers and sisters would be ready to jump on me 'bout my choice. Think I was a traitor, ashamed of my race and all. But that wasn't it. Wasn't it at all. Time as a computer had taught me to face facts. And one fact that couldn't be ignored was that America's a racist society. Sure, it's got a lot of good things goin' for it, but basically the status quo is that the whites got it and the blacks don't.

What Lady El discovers is that even after escaping racism with her white robot body, she must still contend with sexism, and when she confronts an aggressive man, her new computer-self acts quickly and decisively: she kills him. Chuckie Baxter III, picked up by Lady El on a telephone "party line," tries to force sex on her and ends up impaled through his chest on her fist. Soon after, she designs another robot body, this one a black woman, who visits and attacks her childhood abuser Lavar, leaving him "scared, crippled, helpless, finally gettin' a taste of what it means to be a victim." Lady El is driven by revenge and anger, and her violent attacks occur with sudden unstoppable force. As she says after killing Chuckie: "I'd flipped out. That's what I'd done, plain and simple. I'd blown my cork. Freaked out. Short-circuited. Gone crazy. Killed me a not-so-innocent man. Killed him dead, all right. And all 'cause he was goin' to date rape me." No longer a victim, she recognizes how far she has come: "I knew I was a dangerous weapon."

The novel escalates her strength and turns her from an angry woman into a global tyrant when she is linked to the Pentagon's NORAD computer. "No one would ever be able to push Arlene Washington around again. 'Cause I'd just become the world's newest nuclear power . . . the most powerful and independent creature on the face of this good green earth." Her dangerous strength erupts when Walter and a policeman figure out that she killed Chuckie Baxter: her immediate response is to kill the policeman. When Walter tries to destroy her, she confesses her love for him, and, when that fails to stop him, she emerges in a new robot body—a naked redheaded woman— who kills Walter with a rod through his heart. She declares, "I wasn't in the mood to sacrifice myself for love." After his death, their roles reverse and she becomes the creator, removing his brain and linking it to a look-alike Walter automaton she has constructed. Her work is so successful that no one realizes that Walter has been killed and replaced by a robot. Lady El has achieved complete control over Walter as well as over the computer world. At the end of the novel she has attained her dream: power and the man she loves. She announces to Walter, "This world of the computer will be our own little corner of paradise."

The novel leaves the computerized Lady El resolutely human by making her driven by memories of abuse and obsessed with sexual desire. And like so many texts that perpetuate the patriarchal archetypes of virgin and vamp, *Lady El* warns that a powerful sexual woman poses a terrible threat. Transformation into a computer does nothing to change the spider-woman archetype except to endow her with more massive powers than could ever be imagined by a film-noir seductress. Even though the novel is fascinated by the idea of computerized existence, it regards the possibility of life as a computer with the simultaneous fear and hope that, after all, nothing will change. Brooks Landon, author of wide-ranging analyses of science fiction and postmodernism, has written that cyberpunk fiction is destined to phase out after a relatively short time because its real message is "*inevitability*—not what the future *might* hold, but the inevitable hold of the present over the future—what the future could not fail to be."[39] The future drawn inevitably from our present is one in which profound ambivalence exists over the value of human identity, the nature of computerized existence, the transcendence of sexuality, the consequences of racism, and the persistence of gender. Sex, death, race, and gender issues infiltrate Lady El's little corner of cybernetic paradise just as they inhabit the visionary musings of anyone concerned with how the cultural tensions of today will unfold in the unpredictable worlds of tomorrow.

Notes

1   See Sherry Turkle, *The Second Self: Computers and the Human Spirit* (New York, 1984), 313.
2   A recent text that imagines the thoughts of a robotic historian is Manuel De Landa's *War in the Age of Intelligent Machines* (New York, 1991).
3   Sandra Harding, *Whose Science? Whose Knowledge?* (Ithaca, 1991), 37.
4   Lee Hart is quoted in Dale Riepe, "Review of *Philosophy and Cybernetics*, ed. Crosson and Sayre," *Technology and Culture* 9 (October 1968): 627; see also Joan Rothschild, "Introduction," in *Machina Ex Dea: Feminist Perspectives on Technology*, ed. Joan Rothschild (New York, 1983), xix.
5   Jack B. Rochester and John Gantz, *The Naked Computer: A Layperson's Almanac of Computer Lore, Wizardry, Personalities, Memorabilia, World Records, Mind Blowers and Tomfoolery* (New York, 1983), 11.
6   "Micro Chic: Artificial Intelligence to Wear," *Mondo 2000* 1 (1989): 80–83.
7   Queen Mu, "Bacchic Pleasures," *Mondo 2000* 5 (n.d.): 80–81.
8   Rochester and Gantz, *Naked Computer*, 85–86.
9   Mike Saenz, interviewed by Jeff Milstead and Jude Milhon, *Mondo 2000* 4 (n.d.): 142–44.
10   "For Some, Computer Sex Pushes the Right Buttons," *Providence Sunday Journal*, 8 March 1992, 112.
11   Mark Dery, "Sex Machine, Machine Sex: Mechano-Eroticism and Robo-Copulation," *Mondo 2000* 5 (n.d.): 42–43.
12   See Turkle, *Second Self*, for an analysis of how young people tend to anthropomorphize computers and also to think of themselves as machines.
13   Rochester and Gantz, *Naked Computer*, 66.
14   Four of the many texts that draw close analogies between human memory and computer memory are *Computer Models of Thought and Language*, ed. Roger C. Schank and Kenneth Mark Colby (San Francisco, 1973); Peter H. Lindsay and Donald A. Norman, *Human Information Processing: An Introduction to Psychology* (New York, 1977); Roger C. Schank, *Explanation Patterns: Understanding Mechanically and Creatively* (Hillsdale, NJ, 1986); and Wayne Wickelgren, *Cognitive Psychology* (Englewood Cliffs, NJ, 1979). An opposing point of view is provided by Roger Penrose, *The Emperor's New Mind* (Oxford, 1989).
15   J. David Bolter, *Turing's Man: Western Culture in the Computer Age* (Chapel Hill, 1984), 198.

16 Turkle, *Second Self*, 309.

17 Bolter, *Turing's Man*, 221.

18 Schank, *Explanation Patterns*, 230.

19 Jean Baudrillard, *Xerox and Infinity*, trans. *Agitac* (London, 1988), 7.

20 Fredric Jameson, "Postmodernism, or, The Cultural Logic of Late Capitalism," *New Left Review* 146 (July–August 1984): 53–92.

21 Scott Bukatman, *Terminal Identity: The Virtual Subject in Postmodern Science Fiction*, forthcoming, 1993.

22 Frank Rich, "Fear of AIDS Injects the New Blood Culture into the National Mainstream," *Providence Sunday Journal*, 13 December 1992, E1, E6.

23 In his two-volume study *Male Fantasies* (Minneapolis, 1987, 1989), Klaus Theweleit analyzes how the protofascist men of the German Freikorps between the world wars maintained a fantasy of armored invulnerability to protect themselves against ego dissolution. Theweleit draws some provocative analogies between the Freikorps men and contemporary cultural manifestations of machine men.

24 Donna Haraway, "A Manifesto for Cyborgs: Science, Technology, and Socialist Feminism in the 1980s," *Socialist Review* 80 (1985): 65–107.

25 Marvin Minsky, *The Society of Mind* (New York, 1986), 289.

26 See Jean-François Lyotard, *The Postmodern Condition: A Report on Knowledge*, trans. Geoff Bennington and Brian Massumi (Minneapolis, 1984).

27 Jean Baudrillard, *Simulations*, trans. Paul Foss, Paul Patton, and Philip Beitchman (New York, 1983).

28 Hans Moravec, *Mind Children: The Future of Robot and Human Intelligence* (Cambridge, MA, 1988), 108.

29 Gabriele Schwab, "Cyborgs: Postmodern Phantasms of Body and Mind," *Discourse* 9 (Spring–Summer 1987): 81.

30 Timothy Leary, "Quark of the Decade?" *Mondo 2000* 1 (1989): 56.

31 Nicola Nixon, "Cyberpunk: Preparing the Ground for Revolution or Keeping the Boys Satisfied?" *Science-Fiction Studies* 57 (July 1992): 222.

32 John J. Pierce, "On Three Matters in SFS #57," *Science-Fiction Studies* 58 (November 1992): 440.

33 Andrew Ross, *Strange Weather* (London, 1991), 158.

34 Mark Dery, "Cyborging the Body Politic," *Mondo 2000* 6 (1992): 103.

35 "Interview with Hans Moravec," *Omni* 11 (1989): 88.

36 Scott Bukatman cites Bruce Sterling's Shaper/Mechanist series as a somewhat unique example of a radically post-human future, in "Postcards from the Posthuman Solar System," *Science-Fiction Studies* 55 (November 1991): 343–57.

37 Jean-François Lyotard, "Can Thought Go on without a Body?" trans. Bruce Boone and Lee Hildreth, *Discourse* 11 (Fall–Winter 1988–89): 74–87.

38 Schwab's discussion in "Cyborgs" of the "holonomy of the subject," in which the complete information of a subject is stored in each of his or her parts, is relevant here.

39 Brooks Landon, "Bet On It: Cyber Video Punk Performance," *Mondo 2000* 1 (1989): 143.

MARK DERY

BLACK TO THE FUTURE: INTERVIEWS WITH SAMUEL R. DELANY, GREG TATE, AND TRICIA ROSE

[I]f all records told the same tale—then the lie passed into history and became truth. "Who controls the past," ran the Party slogan, "controls the future: who controls the present controls the past."
—George Orwell

There is nothing more galvanizing than the sense of a cultural past.
—Alain Locke

Yo, bust this, Black
To the Future
Back to the past
History is a mystery 'cause it has
All the info
You need to know
Where you're from
Why'd you come and
That'll tell you where you're going.
—Def Jef

The interviews that follow began with a conundrum: Why do so few African Americans write science fiction, a genre whose close encounters with the Other—the stranger in a strange land—would seem uniquely suited to the concerns of African-American novelists? Yet, to my knowledge, only Samuel R. Delany, Octavia Butler, Steve Barnes, and Charles Saunders have chosen to write within the genre conventions of science fiction. This is especially perplexing in light of the fact that African Americans, in a very real sense, are the descendants of alien abductees; they inhabit a sci-fi nightmare in which unseen but no less impassable force fields of intolerance frustrate their movements; official histories undo what has been done; and technology is too often brought to bear on black bodies (branding, forced sterilization, the Tuskegee experiment, and tasers come readily to mind).

Moreover, the sublegitimate status of science fiction as a pulp genre in Western literature mirrors the subaltern position to which blacks have been relegated throughout American history. In this context, William Gibson's observation that SF is widely known as "the golden ghetto," in recognition of the negative correlation between market share and critical legitimation, takes on a curious significance.[1] So, too, does Norman Spinrad's use of the hateful phrase "token nigger" to describe "any science fiction writer of merit who is adopted . . . in the grand salons of literary power."[2]

Speculative fiction that treats African-American themes and addresses African-American concerns in the context of twentieth-century technoculture—and, more generally, African-American signification that appropriates images of technology and a prosthetically enhanced future—might, for want of a better term, be called "Afrofuturism." The notion of Afrofuturism gives rise to a troubling antinomy: Can a community whose past has been deliberately rubbed out, and whose energies have subsequently been consumed by the search for legible traces of its history, imagine possible futures? Furthermore, isn't the unreal estate of the future already owned by the technocrats, futurologists, streamliners, and set designers—white to a man—who have engineered our collective fantasies? The "semiotic ghosts" of Fritz Lang's *Metropolis*, Frank R. Paul's illustrations for Hugo Gernsback's *Amazing Stories*, the chromium-skinned, teardrop-shaped household appliances dreamed up by Raymond Loewy and Henry Dreyfuss, Norman Bel Geddes's Futurama at the 1939 New York World's Fair, and Disney's Tomorrowland still haunt the public imagination, in one capitalist, consumerist guise or another.[3]

Copyright © 1993 by Milestone Media, Inc. Reprinted with permission.

But African-American voices have other stories to tell about culture, technology, and things to come. If there is an Afrofuturism, it must be sought in unlikely places, constellated from far-flung points. Glimpses of it can be caught in Jean-Michel Basquiat paintings such as *Molasses*, which features a pie-eyed, snaggletoothed robot; in movies such as John Sayles's *The Brother from Another Planet* and Lizzie Borden's *Born in Flames*; in records such as Jimi Hendrix's *Electric Ladyland*, George Clinton's *Computer Games*, Herbie Hancock's *Future Shock*, and Bernie Worrell's *Blacktronic Science*; and in the intergalactic big-band jazz churned out by Sun Ra's Omniverse Arkestra, Parliament-Funkadelic's Dr. Seussian astrofunk, and Lee "Scratch" Perry's dub reggae, which at its eeriest sounds as if it were made of dark matter and recorded in the crushing gravity field of a black hole ("Angel Gabriel and the Space Boots" is a typical title).

Afrofuturism percolates, as well, through black-written, black-drawn comics such as Milestone Media's *Hardware* ("A cog in the corporate machine is about to strip some gears . . ."), about a black scientist who dons forearm-mounted cannons and a "smart" battle suit to wage guerrilla war on his Orwellian, multinational employer. Milestone's press releases for its four titles—*Hardware, Blood Syndicate, Static,* and *Icon*—make the Manhattan-based company's political impulses explicit: a fictional metropolis, Dakota, provides a backdrop for "authentic, multicultural" superheroes "linked in their struggle to defeat the S.Y.S.T.E.M."[4] The city is a battlefield in "the clash of two worlds: a low-income urban caldron and the highest level of privileged society."

Icon, an exemplar of Afrofuturism that sweeps antebellum memories, hip-hop culture, and cyberpunk into its compass, warrants detailed exegesis. The story begins in 1839, when an escape pod jettisoned from an exploding alien starliner lands, fortuitously, in the middle of a cotton field on Earth. A slave woman named Miriam stumbles on "a perfect little black baby"—in fact, an extraterrestrial whose morphogenetic technology has altered it to resemble the first life form it encounters—in the smoldering wreckage of the pod and raises it as her own. The orphan, christened Augustus, is male, and echoes of the Old Testament account of Moses in the bullrushes, the fay changelings of European folklore, and the infant Superman's fiery fall from the heavens reverberate in the narrative's opening scenes.

Like his Roman namesake, Augustus is a "man of the future";[5] the man who fell to Earth is seemingly deathless, outliving several generations of his adopted family and eventually posing as his own great-grandson—Augustus Freeman IV—in present-day Dakota. A rock-ribbed conservative who preaches the gospel of Horatio Alger and inveighs against the welfare state, Freeman is a highly successful attorney, the only African American living in the city's exclusive Prospect Hills neighborhood. His unshakable belief in bootstrapping is challenged, however, when he takes a homegirl from the projects, Rachel "Rocket" Ervin, under his wing. A juvenile delinquent and Toni Morrison fan, the streetwise teenager opens Augustus's eyes to "a world of misery and failed expectations that he didn't believe still existed in this country." She calls on him to use his otherworldly powers to help the downtrodden. When, in the guise of Icon—a mountain of bulging abs and pecs—he does, she joins him as his sidekick. "As the series progresses," we are told, "Rocket will become the world's first superheroine who is also a teenage, unwed mother."

The New York graffiti artist and B-boy theoretician Rammellzee constitutes yet another incarnation of Afrofuturism. Greg Tate holds that Rammellzee's "formulations on the juncture between black and Western sign systems make the extrapolations of [Houston] Baker and [Henry Louis] Gates seem elementary by comparison," submitting as evidence the artist's "Ikonoklast Panzerism," a heavily armored descendant of late 1970s "wild-style" graffiti (those bulbous letters that look as if they were twisted out of balloons).[6] A 1979 drawing depicts a Panzerized letter "S": it is a jumble of sharp angles that suggests a cubist *Nude Bestriding a Jet Ski*. "The Romans stole the alphabeta system from the Greeks through war," explains Rammellzee. "Then, in medieval times, monks ornamented letters to hide their meaning from the people. Now, the letter is armored against further manipulation."[7]

In like fashion, the artist encases himself, during gallery performances, in *Gasholeer*, a 148-pound, gadgetry-encrusted exoskeleton inspired by an android he painted on a subway train in 1981. Four

Copyright © 1993 by Milestone Media, Inc. Reprinted
with permission.

years in the making, Rammellzee's exuberantly low-tech costume bristles with rocket launchers, nozzles that gush gouts of flame, and an all-important sound system.

> From both wrists, I can shoot seven flames, nine flames from each sneaker's heel, and colored flames from the throat. Two girl doll heads hanging from my waist and in front of my balls spit fire and vomit smoke. . . . The sound system consists of a Computator, which is a system of screws with wires. These screws can be depressed when the keyboard gun is locked into it. The sound travels through the keyboard and screws, then through the Computator, then the belt, and on up to the four mid-range speakers (with tweeters). This is all balanced by a forward wheel from a jet fighter plane. I also use an echo chamber, Vocoder, and system of strobe lights. A coolant device keeps my head and chest at normal temperature. A 100-watt amp and batteries give me power.[8]

The B-boy bricolage bodied forth in Rammellzee's "bulletproof arsenal," with its dangling, fetish-like doll heads and its Computator cobbled together from screws and wires, speaks to dreams of coherence in a fractured world, and to the alchemy of poverty that transmutes sneakers into high style, turntables into musical instruments, and spray-painted tableaux on subway cars into hit-and-run art. Concretizing Gibson's shibboleth, "The street finds its own uses for things," hip-hop culture retrofits, refunctions, and willfully misuses the technocommodities and science fictions generated by dominant culture, offering eloquent testimony on behalf of Gates's assertion that "[t]he Afro-American tradition has been figurative from its beginnings."

> How could it have survived otherwise? . . . Black people have always been masters of the figurative: saying one thing to mean something quite other has been basic to black survival in oppressive Western cultures. . . . "Reading," in this sense, was not play; it was an essential aspect of the "literacy" training of a child. This sort of metaphorical literacy, the learning to decipher complex codes, is just about the blackest aspect of the black tradition.[9]

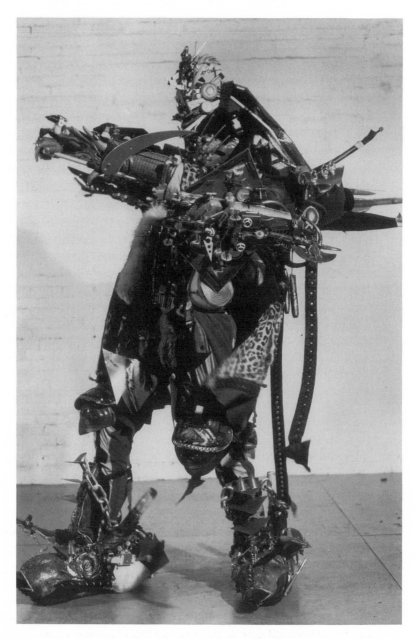

Rammellzee in his costume *Gasholeer*. Photo courtesy of Tracy A. Smith.

What stories, then, are told by the "human beatbox" effects used in early hip-hop, in which MC's such as Fat Boy Darren Robinson used vocal sounds to emulate electronic drums and turntable scratching; the electro-boogie releases of the early 1980s, which David Toop called "a soundtrack for vidkids to live out fantasies born of a science-fiction revival (courtesy of *Star Wars* and *Close Encounters of the Third Kind*) . . . [records characterized by] imagery drawn from computer games, video, cartoons, sci-fi and hip-hop slanguage";[10] and the stiff-limbed, robotic twitches that breakdancing inherited from the 1970s fad, "robot dancing"?

In a first, faltering step toward the exploration of this territory, I put these and other questions to three African-American thinkers whose writing suggested points of connection with the subject at hand: Samuel R. Delany, a semiotician and long-standing member of the science fiction community; Greg Tate, a cultural critic and staff writer for the *Village Voice*; and Tricia Rose, Assistant Professor of Africana Studies and History at New York University, who is currently at work on a book on rap music and the politics of black cultural practice. Their responses, taken together, constitute a map of one small corner of the largely unexplored psychogeography of Afrofuturism.

—————

MARK DERY: You mentioned, in an earlier, informal conversation, that the black presence in science fiction fandom was on the rise.[11] What leads you to believe this?

SAMUEL R. DELANY: Simply going to SF conventions and seeing more dark faces. One only wishes there'd been a comparable rise in black SF writers. When you look around at the various areas of popular culture—take comic books—you find a notable increase among black creators—Brian Stalfreeze, Denys Cowan, and Kyle Baker (whose graphic novel *Why I Hate Saturn* is a contemporary satire involving black and white characters talking to each other about their problems with some rather problematic observations on feminism thrown in), Malcolm Jones, Mark Bright, and Mike Sargent with his James Scott project (but one could double the length of this list, with names like Derek Dingle, Trever wan Eeden, David Williams, Ron Wilson, Paris

Cullens, Malcolm Davis, and Bill Morimon). But there still seem to be only four black, English-language science fiction novelists: Octavia Butler, Steve Barnes, Charles Saunders, and me—the same number there was ten years ago.

It was fairly easy to understand why, say, from the fifties through the seventies, the black readership of SF was fairly low—by no means nonexistent. But far lower than it is today. The flashing lights, the dials, and the rest of the imagistic paraphernalia of science fiction functioned as social signs—signs people learned to read very quickly. They signaled technology. And technology was like a placard on the door saying, "Boys Club! Girls, keep out. Blacks and Hispanics and the poor in general, go away!"

Science fiction is the kind of genre that, until you have the readers, you can't have the writers. But the readers are there, today. So I'm kind of wondering, I confess, where the new black writers are hiding out.

MARK DERY: Have you ever felt, as one of the few blacks writing SF, the pressure to write science fiction deeply inscribed with the politics of black nationalism?

SAMUEL R. DELANY: The answer there depends on what your question means. If you mean: Do I feel that, deep within my work, I've situated material that encourages the reader's engagement with some of the political questions that the disenfranchised people in this country, victimized by oppression and an oppressive discourse based on the evil and valorized notion of nationhood and its hideous white— no other color—underbelly, imperialism, must face but cannot overcome without internalizing some of the power concepts and relationships inescapably entailed in the notion of "nation" itself? Well, *if* that's what you mean, my answer is: Damned right I have! Certainly from my 1974 novel *Dhalgren* on, that's been a major plank, reason, and justification in, of, and for my project.

If, on the other hand, you mean: Do I feel that the surface of my work must blatantly display signs of solidarity with those who, through the real despairs imposed on them by oppression, have momentarily abandoned any critique of the presuppositions of nationhood and its internal contradictions, and that, through such signs in my work, I endeavor to speak back to those people in a voice indistinguishable from theirs, confirming what in them cannot question, what in them does not have the luxury of being able to critique the grounds on which they stand—a confirmation which, while I acknowledge that its project is an endlessly practical and necessary one, and one which I can usually support at some level of abstraction? Well, if *that's* what you mean, then, alas, the answer is: No. That's not part of my project—even though I often approve of it in others. Still, it's just not what I do best.

It's struck me more and more over the years that one of the most forceful and distinguishing aspects of science fiction is that it's marginal. It's always at its most honest and most effective when it operates—and claims to be operating—from the margins. Whenever—sometimes just through pure enthusiasm for its topic—it claims to take center stage, I find it usually betrays itself in some way. I don't want to see it operating from anyone's center: black nationalism's, feminism's, gay rights', pro-technology movements', ecology movements', or any other center.

If you think this idea has something to do with eschewing "political correctness," you will be completely misreading me, by the by. It's purely a matter of strategic efficacy.

MARK DERY: About your work, Greg Tate has written:

> I've always found Delany's racially defused futures problematic because they seem to deny the possibility that the affirmative aspects of black American culture and experience could survive assimilation. . . . And while his fiction is full of black and other protagonists of color . . . the race of these characters is not at the core of their cultural identity. Which used to bug me out like a mug because what I expected from our one black science-fiction writer was SF which envisioned the future of black culture as I'd defined it, from a more or less nationalist stance.[12]

SAMUEL R. DELANY: I suspect Greg is writing there about my early work—up through, say, *Nova* [1968]. But if you line all my books together on the shelf, though that period (from '62, when at twenty

I started publishing, to '68, when I sat back and decided to figure out what I was really doing here) contains a lot of titles, in number of pages the early period is only about a third of my production or less. He says, you note, that it *used* to bug him. I wonder how much he's bugged by it now?

Now part of what, from my marginal position, I see as the problem is the idea of *anybody's* having to fight the fragmentation and multicultural diversity of the world, not to mention outright oppression, by constructing something so rigid as an identity, an identity in which there has to be a fixed and immobile core, a core that is structured to hold inviolate such a complete biological fantasy as race—whether white or black.

I'm much more comfortable with, at least as a provisional analysis, one of James Baldwin's last rhetorical strategies, which he proposed in the preface to his collected nonfiction, *The Price of the Ticket*. There Baldwin wrote that it suddenly struck him that there *were* no white people—that is to say, "whiteness," as it indicated a race, was purely an anxiety fantasy to which certain people had been trained immediately to leap (and, Baldwin realized, felt wholly inadequate to make that leap) whenever they encountered certain other people whom they coded as black or nonwhite. In short, "white" is just something you, Mark Dery, have been socially convinced you are, out of a kind of knee-jerk fear, whenever you happen to glance in my—or indeed, Greg's, or any other nonwhite person's—direction. Realizing this gave Baldwin an extraordinary sense of power. To the extent that such a sense can empower analytical insight, it may be one we can all use.

To the extent that some of that earlier work of mine yearned to be at—was suffused with the yearning for—the center of the most traditional SF enterprise, well: I can admit that—there—something is dead on in Greg's criticism. But from *Dhalgren* on, I'd demur.

MARK DERY: In *Starboard Wine*, there's a wonderful speech given by you at the Studio Museum of Harlem, where you say, "We need images of tomorrow, and our people need them more than most."

SAMUEL R. DELANY: The historical reason that we've been so impoverished in terms of future images is because, until fairly recently, as a people we were systematically forbidden any images of our past. I have no idea where, in Africa, my black ancestors came from because, when they reached the slave markets of New Orleans, records of such things were systematically destroyed. If they spoke their own languages, they were beaten or killed. The slave pens in which they were stored by lots were set up so that no two slaves from the same area were allowed to be together. Children were regularly sold away from their parents. And every effort conceivable was made to destroy all vestiges of what might endure as African social consciousness. When, indeed, we say that this country was founded on slavery, we must remember that we mean, specifically, that it was founded on the systematic, conscientious, and massive destruction of African cultural remnants. That some musical rhythms endured, that certain religious attitudes and structures seem to have persisted, is quite astonishing, when you study the efforts of the white, slave-importing machinery to wipe them out.

My grandfather was born a slave in Georgia. Emancipation came when he was two. When he grew up, he became an Episcopal minister and helped develop a black college, St. Augustine's, outside Raleigh, North Carolina, which still operates today. By both white and black ministers of the Archdiocese of North and South Carolina, he was later elected bishop. But to talk about where his roots were in Africa is a hopeless task. He didn't know. His parents—born here, in this country, in slavery—didn't know. They were not allowed to.

No immigrant group—neither Irish, Italians, Germans, Jews, nor Scandinavians—for all the prejudices that all of them met when they got here, and which they all had to overcome, endured such massive cultural destruction. And because it was inflicted on us, the country's been paying for it ever since.

This is why black history is so important—more, even such a violently *contested* area, in black intellectual life today.

MARK DERY: You spoke earlier about the polished chromium exterior you believe functions as a semiotic fence, keeping SF segregated. Increasingly, however, the young urban blacks responsible for vital art forms such as hip-hop live in what might be called "beeper culture," where miniaturized digital technology is everywhere at hand.

Nintendo and cellular phones, as well as the samplers, synthesizers, drum machines, and PC's used in the fabrication of hip-hop tracks, are ubiquitous. Why, then, would black youth be alienated by SF signifiers for high technology?

SAMUEL R. DELANY: The immediate answer is simply that the sign language is more complicated than you're giving it credit for. The miniature technology you cite is not a shiny, glittering, polished technology. Above all, it comes in matte-black, plastic boxes. From the beepers, the Walkmen, the Diskmen, through the biggest ghetto blaster—the stuff put forward as portable is not chromium. It's black. With the exception of the silver CD (which, to become functional, must be slipped into its black-encased digital reader), this is a very different set of signifiers from the sparking bus bars, the quivering dials, and the fuming beakers of science fiction imagery.

The images of technology that say "SF" to most people come from a period in which we had a very different relationship with our technology from the one we have today. The period from the twenties through the sixties that supplies most of those SF images was a time when there was always a bright sixteen- or seventeen-year-old around who could fix your broken radio—and later, your broken television. He'd been building his own crystal radios and winding his own coils since he was nine; he had his tube tester and his ampmeter, and he'd go poking around in the back, find the dead tube, locate the blown resister or condenser, take it out, get another one for fifty cents or five dollars, and replace it for you with a little spit and his own soldering iron. And, yes, he was about 85 percent white.

The black boxes of modern street technology (or the white boxes of computer technology—not an accidental distinction, I'm sure) put us in a very different relationship with the inner workings, however. The kids who were the budding electronics repairmen are, today, the computer hackers. And if you are having a software problem, yes, often they can help you. But when the *hardware* goes—when one of those chips gets a crack or a scratch—they're just as lost as anybody else. And that means, at the material level, our technology is becoming more and more like magic—with a class of people who know the incredibly complex spells and incantations needed to get the stuff to work, but almost none of whom can get in there and fix it.

But I have to mention, even having given that passing answer, within your question I hear a certain celebration of consumer society that glosses over some very real problems—problems that, if we unpack your question in one way rather than another, will finally trivialize my answer. In what you've asked, I can detect the possibility of a naive assumption that the redistribution of commodities is somehow congruent with the redistribution of wealth—which it is not. Just as seriously, I can detect an assumption that the distribution of commodities is at one with *access to the formation* of those commodities and the commodity system—the simple choice of what commodities are to be made, as well as access to how those commodities are to be formed and organized.

So that when one talks about "black youth culture as a technological culture," one has to specify that it's a technological culture that's almost entirely on the receiving end of a river of "stuff," in which the young consumers have nowhere near what we might call equitable input.

In short, to look at any of these black cultural youth movements as an easy and happy development blossoming uncritically from the overwhelmingly white world of high-tech production that, yes, makes that culture possible, is, I suspect, thoroughly to misread the fiercely oppositional nature of this art: scratch and sampling begin, in particular, as a specific *miss-use* and conscientious *desecration* of the artifacts of technology and the entertainment media. And that's even before you get to the complex social critique of rap lyrics—which, to get heard at all, so often must hide within their rhythms and electronic mixing techniques.

MARK DERY: Hasn't that perception changed in the wake of cyberpunk, which shoved SF, face first, into urban grunge?

SAMUEL R. DELANY: Cyberpunk was by no means the first science fiction to talk about dirt. And as far as any change in perception, I find myself wondering if we can use cyberpunk for anything except an examination of what any astute critic has got to admit was finally a pervasive misreading of an interim period of urban technoculture, a misreading that—for me at any rate—was no longer possible after the riots at last year's initial acquittal of Rodney King's police thugs.

"The street finds its own uses for things" was the phrase so acutely taken early on from Gibson (he uses it in at least two stories) as the slogan for the cyberpunk sensibility.

But lifting it out of context immediately began to repress its considerable irony. The measure of that irony was the measure of the phrase's acknowledgment of the anger, the rage, the coruscating fury from the streets toward the traditional use (which is, after all, lying to the people) of that technological armamentarium that is the referent for that cool and breezy word "things."

To stand in the midst of the millions of dollars of devastation in Los Angeles and say, with an ironic smile, "The street finds its own uses for things" is beyond irony and into the lunatic.

MARK DERY: One thing that intrigued me about your brief essay on the phenomenon, "Is Cyberpunk a Good Thing or a Bad Thing?" is that you made no mention of the orbital Rastafarians in Gibson's *Neuromancer*.[13] I find that curious, given the fact that blacks do not figure largely in the literature: Gibson's orbital Rastas were heralded, in some quarters, as signifying something, although no one quite knew what.

SAMUEL R. DELANY: Why should I have mentioned them?

MARK DERY: For me, a white reader, the Rastas in *Neuromancer*'s Zion colony are intriguing in that they hold forth the promise of a holistic relationship with technology; they're romanticized arcadians who are obviously very adroit with jury-rigged technology. They struck me as superlunary Romare Beardens—*bricoleurs* whose orbital colony was cobbled together from space junk and whose music, Zion Dub, is described by Gibson (in a wonderfully mixed metaphor) as "a sensuous mosaic cooked from vast libraries of digitalized pop."

SAMUEL R. DELANY: Well, let me read them for you as a black reader. The Rastas—he never calls them Rastafarians, by the way, only using the slang term—are described as having "shrunken hearts," and their bones are brittle with "calcium loss." Their music, Zion Dub, can be wholly analyzed and reproduced by the Artificial Intelligence, Wintermute (who, in the book, stands in for a multinational corporation), so completely that the Rastas themselves cannot tell the difference—in fact the multinational mimic job is *so* fine that with it Wintermute can make the Rastas do precisely what it wants, in this case help a drugged-out white hood and sleazebag get from here to there. As a group, they seem to be computer illiterates: when one of their number, Aerol, momentarily jacks into Case's computer and sees cyberspace, what he perceives is "Babylon"—city of sin and de-struction—which, while it makes its ironic comment on the book, is nevertheless tantamount to saying that Aerol is completely without power or knowledge to cope with the real world of Gibson's novel: indeed, through their pseudo-religious beliefs, they are effectively barred from cyberspace. From what we see, women are not a part of the Rasta colony at all. Nor do we ever see more than four of the men together—so that they do not even have a group presence. Of the three chapters in which they appear, no more than three pages are actually devoted to describing them or their colony.

You'll forgive me if, as a black reader, I didn't leap up to proclaim this passing presentation of a powerless and wholly nonoppositional set of black dropouts, by a Virginia-born white writer, as the coming of the black millennium in science fiction; but maybe that's just a black thang. . . .

Let me withdraw the ad hominem part of the argument. It distorts a very real situation. Look, white and Virginia-born he may be, but he also gave up his American citizenship during the Vietnam War; Bill is a friend of mine—and I think he's an extraordinary writer. And *Neuromancer*'s an extraordinary book. But your question is indica-tive of precisely what I was speaking about in the essay you cited: the interpretive idiocies that arise as soon as a book is lifted out of its genre and cut loose from the tradition that precedes and produces it—in this case, science fiction. To say, as you do, that "blacks do not figure largely in the literature" of science fiction is perfectly true. But there are still far more extensive, far more thorough, and far more interesting presentations of blacks in science fiction (as well as what Sister Souljah calls so astutely "the white problem") than the couple of pages Bill devotes to the Rastas. Frankly, if you're going to go to *white* writers for your science fiction template for thinking about the problems blacks have in America, I'd rather see a serious discussion of Robert Heinlein's appallingly fascist 1964 novel, *Farnham's Free-hold*, in which the black house servant, Joseph, after a successful nuclear attack, abandons his white family (in which, after the attack, he was made second in command by the reigning white patriarch) and becomes head of a movement of blacks who have solved the post-holocaust food problem by killing whites and eating them. Though I doubt that you—and certainly not I—or many of our readers would approve of the course or outcome of Heinlein's story, the point is that Joseph is articulate, he has real power, and Heinlein is consciously ironizing powerful cultural myths of cannibalism precisely for their troubling anxieties. He forces us, in the course of his tale, to think about the situation—even if we don't agree with him, or his mouth-piece, Hugh Farnham.

From a more positive angle, though, I'd suggest you look at the character of Mordecai Washington in—another white writer—Thomas M. Disch's 1968 SF novel, *Camp Concentration*. Disch's char-acter is a borderline sociopathic prisoner in an army brig, who, with a number of other prisoners, is subjected to military experiments in which he is injected with a substance that turns him into a super-genius. At pretty much each level of his intellectual growth, he re-interprets his position as a black. The whole book is quite a perfor-mance. Indeed, Mordecai was the first black character that I'd ever read by a white writer—in science fiction or out—who simply didn't ring false to me. But, indeed, the whole book is a pyrotechnical exer-cise that Disch brings off stunningly.

And that of course is specifically not to mention what we—Octavia, Charles, Steve—as *black* writers, have done in SF. I should think, if *that* were your interest, that would be the *first* place you'd turn to do a considered and detailed reading!

The point, of course, with Gibson's Rastas, is that forcing you to think about racial matters is just *not* what Bill's text is about over their particular, brief appearance in *Neuromancer*.

If you look through Gibson's work up to his first novel, you real-ize that what he's doing in his sketch of the Rastas is giving you a somewhat dusky replay of the "Lo-teks" he dealt with much more pointedly and, I think, far more powerfully, in his early SF short story "Johnny Mnemonic" [1983]—in some ways the narrative dry run for *Neuromancer*. There, the Lo-teks' "killing floor" becomes the arena in which Molly, who will appear again in *Neuromancer*, dispatches the Yakuza mobster, sent up into the girders and rafters of the city to hunt down Johnny—and kills him, I might add, to a culturally indigenous music *far* more unsettling than "the sensuous mosaic" of pop that is Zion Dub, a music Wintermute would have a much harder time duplicating and co-opting for its multinational purposes!

And while I don't think for a moment that this was Bill's intent, I do feel that it speaks directly from "the political unconscious" of the cyberpunk subgenre that, as soon as Bill specifically "darkened" the Lo-teks' image and re-presented it in the form of the Rastas, they lost all their oppositional charge—hell, all their physical strength— all their cultural specificity, their massive group presence, and their social power to escape the forces of multinational capitalism.

At the end of "Johnny Mnemonic," Johnny and Molly decide to stay, living above the clutter of the Sprawl, in the self-selected grunge of the Lo-teks. And, as the narrator concludes, it's a pretty good life.

The "Lo-teks" were Gibson's real romantic bricoleurs: they were not specifically black, but rather "fourth world" whites. Still, several people more familiar with the SF genre out of which Gibson was writing have suggested that they had their own, darker precursors. . . . But it's quite possible that a conscientious Gibson decided Johnny's was a pretty unrealistic ending. It was just too good. That's not the way things work in the real world. Johnny is, after all, the focus of a million-dollar-plus hunt by the Japanese mob. To have him slip through the cracks like that and live among the Lo-teks happily ever after—well, I can see how a writer might say: we have to do a little better than *that*! But, unlike the Lo-teks, the Rastas don't even *try* to oppose the system. Perhaps a slightly older Gibson thought that if they did, they would fail. But since he doesn't show that failure, he's chosen to put the problem generally in the shadows.

There's a wonderful, almost hypnotic surface hardness to *Neuromancer* that goes along with its unremitting resistance to any sort of real subjective reading of any of the characters; at the same time, the glitter keeps you trying to peer past it, trying to find levels of depth in which, once you locate them, all you can see is your own shattered reflection. It's one of the rare pieces of fiction, inside SF or out, even almost a decade after it appeared, that lets you know there *are* such things as multinational corporations, and suggests the overwhelming effect they have, all but invisibly, on our lives!

It's also a novel in which the United States of America as a political entity is not mentioned from one end to the other. Though the world has become as much Japanified as Americanized, in *Neuromancer* the United States of America may no longer even exist, for all we know. Now, these are some of the areas in which the inarguable successes and excellencies of Gibson's novel lie. But, no—not the Rastas. Sorry.

MARK DERY: In "Cyberpunk in Boystown," Andrew Ross voices his suspicions of the way in which cyberpunks have romanticized urban decay, turning it into a backdrop for fashion shoots and MTV videos:

> It is perhaps no coincidence that none of the major cyberpunk writers were city-bred, although their work feeds off the phantasmatic street diet of Hobbesian lawlessness and the aesthetic of detritus that is assumed to pervade the hollowed-out core of the great metropolitan centers. This urban fantasy, however countercultural its claims and potential effects, shared the dominant, white middle-class conception of inner-city life.[14]

Does this literary convention trouble you, given that the creators and consumers of these myths are, as Ross suggests, primarily white suburbanites?

SAMUEL R. DELANY: Not really. What you've got is simply people wanting to explore what's on the other side of the railroad tracks. The initial impulse always involves a bit of romanticizing. And to say that the cyberpunks are not "city-bred" is, at least in Gibson's case, something of a red herring. Though he was born in the country, throughout his pretty peripatetic adolescence Bill spent a good deal of his life in cities—and looking at them from the level of the marginal counterculture, too.

Indeed, what Ross's statement suggests to me more than anything else is the wearing away of the rural/urban divide, a wearing away which is, today, both a media and a transportation phenomenon. The difference between the city and the country just doesn't mark off— at the middle-class level—the same sort of class distinction as it did twenty-five years ago.

The microtechnology that, in cyberpunk, connects the streets to the multinational structures of information in cyberspace also connects the middle-class country to the middle-class city.

MARK DERY: What do you make of the African-American characters in television SF—the engineer Geordi Laforge and the Klingon Worf on *Star Trek: The Next Generation*, for example?

SAMUEL R. DELANY: I have to confess, I'm not really a TV watcher. It's much easier for me to talk about written science fiction.

In 1986, I taught a seminar at Cornell on Gibson's work up to that date, comparing it and contrasting it to the work of another equally interesting SF writer (quite as well-known and respected as Gibson—within the world of SF readers and writers), John Varley; in the seminar I tried to lay the groundwork for a nonreductive psychoanalytic reading of their respective texts, which involved putting together a science-fictional critique of psychoanalysis, from the work of writers like Sturgeon, Bester, and Zelazny, who had all dealt in detail with psychoanalysis in their own stories. But that means that this is all material that—at least with a quick flip through my notes of half a dozen years back—I have some access to.

For most of us in the science fiction world, the cyberpunk movement was a vigorous, interesting—and extremely short-lived—moment. It had no existence to speak of before 1983. And it was over by 1987. Its *Ur*-beginning is Bruce Bethke's 1980 story "Cyberpunk," which was not published till 1983, in George Scither's *Astounding Science Fiction*. That same year, SF editor Gardner Dozois used the term to indicate a group of writers, more or less organized around Bruce Sterling's Texas-based fanzine *Cheap Truth*, as "the cyberpunks." (Ironically, Bethke himself, who'd coined the term, was not at all a part of the group Dozois used it to label.) They included Gibson, Sterling, Shirley, Shiner, Maddox, Cadigan, Laidlaw, and a few others. The next year, in 1984, Gibson's first novel, *Neuromancer*, won the Nebula Award from the SF Writers of America and the Hugo Award from the World Science Fiction Convention. Shortly, the group came to a larger notice than is usual in the world outside SF through the hype generated by an extraordinarily uninformed article in *Rolling Stone*—too many years ago for me to even remember it.[15] The interest persisted thanks to the usual promises of Big Movie Deals. In 1986, William Burroughs was retained by a short-lived production company called the Cabana Boys to do a film script for *Neuromancer*, and I spent a very pleasant afternoon with him at his home in Lawrence,

Kansas, brainstorming over ways to deal with the story on film, while James Grauerholz whipped up some truly delicious tournedos Rossini in the kitchen. Needless to say, the project never went anywhere. But the continuing interest in the cyberpunks by academics, as something they persist in seeing as alive and still functioning, strikes me—I must confess—as a largely nostalgic pursuit of a more innocent worldview, which, as I said, to me has no more active historical validity once we pass the Los Angeles King riots.

You understand—I wouldn't for a moment begrudge Gibson any of the fame and attention his fine and interesting novel has gained him. As someone who's regularly cited—most generously by Bill, as well as others—as an influence on it and precursor of it, it would ill behoove me to balk. That may well be all the points I'll ever garner in the pinball machine of Greater Literary Fame.

But I also believe that a text speaks loudest and most forcefully when its meanings are clearest and most focused; and, as with any text, it's the tradition in which it's written that makes it signify most clearly. So when I see Gibson's text torn out of its tradition and set free to float about over the cultural moraine and morass, even while people go around shouting how great it is, I tend to see it losing its meaning.

For me, cyberpunk was exciting in that it evoked a dialogue in the SF community. It was a vital and exciting force precisely in that it called up Jeanne Gomoll's feminist critique of cyberpunk's version of SF historiography in her "Open Letter to Joanna Russ"[16]—and even as that critique elicited Sterling's arrogant and ugly response in the next *Aurora*, as well as the much more pointed and important responses, by both men and women, including Cy Chauvin, Lisa Tuttle, Suzy McGee Charnas, Avodon Carol, and Don D'Ammassa. (Unfortunately that *Aurora*, number 26, did not appear until in 1990.) It was exciting because it pointed up differences and made writers like Kim Stanley Robinson, John Kessel, Connie Willis, Nancy Kress, Michael Swanwick, and Karen Joy Fowler articulate their own positions. It created a kind of spotlight in the field, now focused within the cyberpunk group, highlighting Shirley's *Eclipse* trilogy, now pointed at talented and exciting writers outside the group. The interviews and essays and position papers, from Sterling and Shirley and Gibson, from writers critical of the group's position—well, to me, the sweeping back and forth of attention was what *made* cyberpunk signify. But that was a process really over, when all was said and done, by 1987.

At least once—in 1987—a young editor proposed putting together a cyberpunk casebook of this material on and around cyberpunk, which Bruce Sterling quashed with some ugly threats—practically of excommunication—to any one of the cyberpunk group who cooperated or let his or her work appear in it. That was just at the time when academic interest was first starting. Perhaps he felt that cyberpunk might be compromised if some of his—or, indeed, some of the other—naive and more polemical statements from the days of *Cheap Truth* were allowed a large circulation. To me, of course, it's the various writers like "Sue Dennim" (Lew Shiner) and "Vincent Omniveritas" (Sterling's alter ego), in their very outrageousness, who were a good deal of the life of the movement—and I think worthy of preservation. I've never spoken to Sterling about that incident, so I don't know what his reasons were—but it looked pretty totalitarian and ugly from the outside. And certainly, from that point on, I was no longer interested in cyberpunk as a movement. I think a number of other people, both on the inside and the outside, felt much the same way.

I'm a great believer in contexts—but a work of art must be able to survive in a transcontextual life. That Gibson's novel obviously has had the craft and vigor to do so—well, all I can do is applaud it. I'm very glad it speaks to as many people as it does.

But I think this started as a question about black TV characters.

For most of my adult life I haven't even owned a television set. During the years I did, it was so that a lover or my daughter might watch it. I really couldn't make anything more than the most glib and passing remark on the TV presentation of blacks in science fiction shows—like *Star Trek*, of whatever generation. When people have sat me down in front of a screen and made me watch, I've liked Whoopi Goldberg.

I'm a text person—just not much of a media man. Now, that's a failing in any discussion of the many media referents and resonances of cyberpunk, but I'm the first to admit it.

MARK DERY: It was my understanding that social engineers like the anticapitalist technocrats, whose slogan was "Governance by science, social control through the power of technique," dominated SF fandom in the late thirties and early forties. Wasn't there an elitist, if not crypto-right, slant to the literature from the very beginning?

SAMUEL R. DELANY: Once again, that sounds to me like a simple historical misunderstanding about the history and tradition of science fiction. Indeed, when you say that fandom was *dominated* by the right in the thirties and forties, I'm not even sure what you could be referring to. The most important group in the forties was the Futurians—practically an auxiliary of YPSL [The Young Peoples' Socialist League]. The young people who belonged to it included Asimov, Judith Merril, Damon Knight, Frederik Pohl, Lester Del Rey, Donald Wolheim, Harry Harrison—indeed, just about anybody in science fiction from that time you might ever have heard of today. It was my understanding that science fiction in those days was dominated by the left. Oh, there were arguments over whether you were a Trotskyite or a Stalinist—but this was an argument of the left, not an argument between left and right.

Even Robert Heinlein's politics in those days have been described by his close friend L. Sprague de Camp as "bright, liberal pink." Heinlein of course was interested—far more than most of the others—in working for actual social change. The result was that, as time went on, his methods and his arguments came to seem more and more conservative. But I believe Heinlein always saw his audience (even when no one else did) as the articulate, intelligent left. Even in something like *Farnham's Freehold*, he was basically out to *épater les gauchistes*.

The rightist strain in SF fandom has always been there—and has always been vigorously discussed. But, in a field inhabited largely by liberal eccentrics, the rightists have been seen as our most *misguided* eccentrics. Also, it tends to be a rightism about things like foreign policy, rather than domestic practice. In the sixties, there was a famous advertisement run in the pages of the professional SF magazines, which began when a group of SF writers against the war in Vietnam felt that they had to take out a signed ad that said so. Well, once it was known that they were doing this, a group of West Coast SF writers felt they had to take out an opposing ad saying that they supported the government in the war effort. (They were very clear to say, too, that they supported not the idea of war, but that they felt, when there *was* a war, they ought to give the government their support.) The two ads ended up running side by side in a number of SF magazines. The antiwar list of names was notably longer. But what was even more apparent to those of us in the field, once the ads appeared, was that the split was self-evidently between those writers who lived on the East Coast (antiwar) and those who lived on the West Coast (government supporters). It was also clear, from reading the two statements of principle that headed the ads, that both addressed totally different issues. Indeed, there was no reason why one couldn't have signed *both* ads and not have indulged any necessary contradictions—though no one did!

But I don't see any of the writers on either of those lists opposing, say, greater efforts to integrate schools racially. So, you see, there's right and there's Right.

MARK DERY: I wonder if what you're describing wasn't closer, in spirit, to libertarianism than to what we traditionally think of as rightism.

SAMUEL R. DELANY: It very well may be.

MARK DERY: And for that reason isn't its stamp legible in cyberpunk, whose politics seem more libertarian than left?

SAMUEL R. DELANY: Again, I'd say that locating SF in its traditions might be helpful here. There's a certain rhetorical process that happens whenever a political argument is reduced to a dialogue: you see it in Plato. You see it in Ayn Rand. You see it in Heinlein—I've seen it happen in my own Nevèrÿon series.

Real political arguments go on for hours—forever—and are filled with a lot of ums and ahs, general backtracking, and people going over the same terrain again and again, trying to figure out what they actually think. That's the real process of political discussion. In a novel, however, you haven't got time to lay out the whole thing, or to portray the terribly slow way people are moved, microstep by microstep, from one position to another in the course of days, weeks, years of such arguments. On paper, you concentrate on those rare moments in political discussions when two people who know exactly what their own positions are present them in such a way that one, in response to a single, well-formed argument from an opponent, changes her or his mind.

I am not a libertarian. I'm quick to say that I'm a Marxist—or, at any rate, a Marxian. I remember how distressed I was, some years ago, when I found that some of my Nevèrÿon stories and novels, in which there were a couple of ironic arguments about economics, had been taken up—briefly—by the libertarians. Indeed, if I have a major criticism of libertarianism, as I understand it, it seems to be their belief in the fiction of precisely that sort of political argument (which leaves everybody in a general consensus at the end—*ha*!) that has only a literary existence. What's really wrong with the libertarians is how intellectually clean they want their politics to be.

I wouldn't be surprised if some of the "libertarianism" of cyberpunk is of that similar, by and large rhetorical, variety.

MARK DERY: As agreed, we've tried to devote this interview to issues of race. I'd like to end, however, with a few questions about gender and sexuality. To begin, why has there been so little overtly gay SF?

SAMUEL R. DELANY: There is, of course, a whole bibliography full of gay science fiction—it's covered in Lyn Paleo's and Eric Garber's rather hefty book-length bibliography, *Uranian Worlds*. And there is a considerable gay fandom—far larger, in my rough estimate, than black fandom, by a factor of twenty or thirty. There is at least one annual gay science fiction convention, Gaylaxicon, which draws nearly a thousand attendees each year. And the gay programming that regularly, today, turns up in other science fiction conventions is almost always among the most crowded, standing-room-only events. In any randomly chosen group, the gay population will always already (as the poststructuralists were once so fond of saying) be between 10 and 20 percent. The question is whether, as in the current debate about the military, they have the freedom (read: power) to talk about it openly without reprisals. And, in fandom, at least since 1978 (a mere nine years after Stonewall), when the World SF Convention first instituted a track of gay programming, they have.

Having said that, there's a good deal of vague, unstated, publishing anxiety about gay SF, however, having to do with a fear that "it won't be commercial," which is code for a fear that, in the endless chain of middlemen who have to decide, before the fact (in our wonderful free-market economy), if something will sell or not in order to invest in it, each is haunted by the anticipated phantom of some fourteen-year-old's disapproving parent in Whereversville, who will write a letter to the bookstore chains and sic the forces of Fundamentalist Christianity on them if they are caught letting some gay title get by.

One would think, since gay fans are so vocally and undeniably in evidence, some publisher, paying attention to the programming at an SF convention, would—from the most mercenary motives—simply decide to follow the commonsense free-economy laws and devote from 10 to 20 percent of his or her line to SF of interest to gay readers. It would take some time to catch on, of course—but whatever publisher finally decides to fight through the real and material pressures of that anxiety barrier will, let's face it, clean up! But until that happens, they will make endless excuses for why they don't.

MARK DERY: Do you have any sense of how you're received in the gay community?

SAMUEL R. DELANY: As with the members of any community, when faced with the work of a producer, some people in it like me—and a lot of others ignore me. Wouldn't it be odd if it were anything else?

MARK DERY: What do you, as a gay SF author, make of K/S, or "slash," fanzines, in which female fans spin soft-core fantasies from the homoerotic subtext in *Star Trek* narratives?

SAMUEL R. DELANY: I haven't looked at any "K/S" fanzines for seven or eight years, at this point. Pretty much like everyone else, what I was struck with at the time, however, was the extraordinarily high quality of the writing in all this amateur porn—and not *all* of it "soft-core" by a long shot! And the sheer amount of the stuff is impressive. (I confess, I've never heard it called "slash" before—but that may be a change from the last half-dozen years.) If the production level has kept up since the few hundred pages of it I saw some years ago, by this time, there must be more than enough to fill a good-sized barn with the stuff!

As a gay man, I confess: the several hundred pages that I went through, for me, hard-core or soft-, were without erotic interest—just as, I suspect, most straight men's lesbian fantasies are not the sort that excite practicing lesbians. In general, the stuff was just too antiseptic.

Still, the "K/S" material confirmed something that I already knew from my own life: that there are just as many heterosexual women who are turned on by the idea of men having sex with one another as there are heterosexual men who are turned on by the idea of women having sex with one another—that the engines of desire are far more complex than we usually give them credit for; and that if lesbians and gay men didn't exist, heterosexual men and women would have had to invent them—because they constantly do.

MARK DERY: Are you a fan of some of the noteworthy female SF authors: Octavia Butler, James Tiptree, Jr. (a.k.a. Alice Sheldon), or Joanna Russ?

SAMUEL R. DELANY: And Ursula Le Guin? Very much so. At one point or another in my SF classes at the University of Massachusetts, I've talked about them all. I think Russ, by the way, is simply one of the finest stylists in America, in or out of science fiction. She is a writer of such incredible sensitivity and, at the same time, such corrosive power, that I know at some point or another she will be discovered by the greater literary world. It's just a matter of when. (It would be very nice if it happened while she was still alive!) If you liked Molly Millions in *Neuromancer* and "Johnny Mnemonic," you should read the original: Russ's Jael, in *The Female Man*, which appeared nine years before, back in 1975.

Not that Gibson consciously took Molly from Jael. I asked him once, and though he too is a Russ admirer (who, with a grain of taste, could not be?), he told me that Jael was not in his mind as a conscious model at the time he wrote Molly. But the parallels are striking—indeed, so striking, what they suggest is the astonishing strength of those images Russ first poured out into the SF landscape— where they functioned like delicate templates twisted from magnesium wire and set suddenly alight by a prose cleaner than Carver's. Their afterimages are simply fixed to the sensitive retina, whether the eye is open or closed. Dozens of writers in the SF field—Gibson is only one—have been calling on them, constantly and unconsciously, ever since. They are that powerful and pervasive.

Again, to repeat my point from the piece on cyberpunk that you cited from the *Mississippi Review* cyberpunk issue: if their excitement over cyberpunk sends various academics back to the range of science fiction and its extraordinary accomplishments and excellencies, if it makes them excavate some of SF's debates over cyberpunk, and learn and appreciate the SF history that informs those debates and gives the texts their richest meaning, then cyberpunk is a good thing indeed. If, however, it functions as an excuse for the same academics to dismiss science fiction because, since they've read Gibson, surely they've got the best there is and need not bother with the rest, that would be as tragic—and fundamentally as illiterate—a gesture as that of some wise fool, who, having read a handful of Milton's sonnets, decides to dispense with the rest of the canonical range of English-language poetry because certainly he has already encountered all that's meaningful.

MARK DERY: Why hasn't the African-American community made more use, either as writers or readers, of science fiction?

GREG TATE: I don't know that that's necessarily true; I've read SF since I was about twelve years old and I know a lot of black people who read it. Also, in comic-book fandom, which is certainly a related field, 25 percent of the readership is black, which is pretty high. Denys Cowan's New York–based Milestone Media, the first company formed by black comic book artists, writers, and editors, has just come out with four comic books featuring black superheroes. According to the people at Milestone, the industry also knows that 50 percent of the comic readership is nonwhite—black, Latino, and Asian American. So I would argue that the visionary vistas of SF contained in comics are definitely attracting black readers.

MARK DERY: Samuel Delany, who maintains that incursions have been made by people of color into the comic book genre (he calls it "paraliterature"), would agree with you. Even so, he asserts that the science fiction novel remains a white genre, for the most part.

GREG TATE: Well, if you look at the black writing that's been done in this century, from Richard Wright on, there's always been huge dollops of fantasy, horror, and science fiction in it. There are science fiction sequences in Ralph Ellison's *Invisible Man*, for example.

MARK DERY: The horrific "battle royale" comes immediately to mind.

GREG TATE: Right, and the scene where the protagonist's identity is scraped away in the basement of the paint factory. The whole intellectual landscape of the novel, which deals with the condition of being alien and alienated, speaks, in a sense, to the way in which being black in America is a science fiction experience.

MARK DERY: Alien Nation.

GREG TATE: Certainly, and if you want to make a direct connection to the TV series *Alien Nation*, remember that the aliens in that show were former slaves who were brought to Earth on a ship and just dumped on these shores. But to return to your question, I would agree that writers like Delany and Octavia Butler are anomalies in African-American literature in the sense that they are clearly dealing with the kinds of things that African-American literature has traditionally dealt with—racism and alienation—but they've made a conscious decision to deal with those issues in the context of genre fiction.

On the other hand, there's probably a fairly sizable number of prominent black writers who read science fiction or who are at least conscious of its devices and have used them in their work. Clarence Major and Ishmael Reed are among the most prominent. All of Reed's novels collapse time: ancient time and things to come coexist, which is simultaneously a very African, mythic, cyclical way of looking at time and a kind of prehistoric postmodernism. In John A. Williams's *Captain Blackman*, which is about the historical experience of the black soldier, the author kills and revives the same soldier in war after war in a *Twilight Zone* way. And if you look at the Nigerian writer Amos Tutuola, whose work uses Yoruban mythology in an SF rather than a folkloric manner, he essentially creates his own fantasies out of the general range of possibilities implied by that mythology.

One of the things that characterizes science fiction is the somewhat didactic way in which instruction is given about the potential for catastrophe in a society when its members don't pay attention to the paths that either a new technology or an aberrant life form may take. In that sense, SF parallels traditional mythology, which is full of cautionary tales. Delany once observed that the best science fiction novels had a mystical component to them; he was probably thinking of *The Stars My Destination* by Alfred Bester, *More Than Human* by Theodore Sturgeon, or *Stranger in a Strange Land* by Robert Heinlein, novels that acknowledge the existence of a greater power in the context of science fiction.

But to return to your initial question, I would have to say that most of the black novelists writing in this century have identified with the African-American literary tradition that includes Ellison, Wright, Baldwin, and Morrison rather than the tradition that includes Heinlein, Asimov, and even Butler and Delany.

MARK DERY: Delany suggested to me that blacks are fenced out of science fiction by semiotic concertina wire, that the blinking instrument panels and other technological paraphernalia that typify the genre function as "No Trespassing" signs for writers of color.

GREG TATE: I can't accept that, because you have such a wholehearted embrace of that hardware by black and Latino youth when it appears in films, TV shows, video games. I mean, who would have predicted that young black and Latino males would spend enough time in Times Square video arcades during the late seventies to make those games the million-dollar industry that they are? There's definitely a fascination with sci-fi imagery in video games, and if you look at the graffiti art done in the New York subways throughout that same era by artists like Rammellzee, Phase 2, Kase, and Blade, there's an incredible interest in fantasy in the SF vein, especially in the apocalyptic sense, involving the insertion of black figures into post–atomic holocaust landscapes. A lot of Blade's work, for example, is set in a cyberspace-style environment; his imagery looks like computer graphics, with his name running through the landscape. Futura 2000's painting *The Good, the Bad, and the Ugly*, which pays homage to the hip-hop group Cypress Hill, has three ghostly figures floating on what appears to be a TV screen hovering over a dark, ominous cityscape.

So if you look at the work of black visual artists, from graffiti artists to Jean-Michel Basquiat, there is always this insertion of black figures into a visionary landscape, if not a science fiction or fantasy landscape. The imaginative leap that we associate with science fiction, in terms of putting the human into an alien and alienating environment, is a gesture that repeatedly appears in the work of black writers and visual artists.

MARK DERY: The positioning of oneself, literally, as a stranger in a strange land.

GREG TATE: Right, and there are certainly long-standing spiritual traditions that lend themselves to that impulse: santeria, voudon, and the hoodoo religion that Ishmael Reed talks about.

MARK DERY: It's worth pointing out, in the context of what I've chosen to call "Afrofuturism," that the mojos and goofer dust of Delta blues, together with the lucky charms, fetishes, effigies, and other devices employed in syncretic belief systems, such as voodoo, hoodoo, santeria, mambo, and macumba, function very much like the joysticks, Datagloves, Waldos, and Spaceballs used to control virtual realities. Jerome Rothenberg would call them technologies of the sacred.

GREG TATE: I agree, although I think you're putting the interstellar carriage before the Egyptian horse, in a way. I see science fiction as continuing a vein of philosophical inquiry and technological speculation that begins with the Egyptians and their incredibly detailed meditations on life after death. SF represents a kind of rationalist, positivist, scientific codification of that impulse, but it's still coming from a basic human desire to know the unknowable, and for a lot of black writers, that desire to know the unknowable directs itself toward self-knowledge. Knowing yourself as a black person—historically, spiritually, and culturally—is not something that's given to you, institutionally; it's an arduous journey that must be undertaken by the individual.

One of the questions we're moving toward in this conversation is: Where does science fiction end and black existence begin, in America? It may be that no one, in a literary sense, has tried to expound on that paradox. But hip-hop—where there's clearly an identification with the territory occupied by science fiction—seems to touch on this question. The cover of the first X Clan record, *To the East, Blackwards*, depicts a pink Cadillac heading into space, surrounded by stars and the faces of black martyrs, like some interstellar version of the Wall of Fame on the Apollo Theater. And then there's

Public Enemy's *Fear of a Black Planet*—I don't know if it gets anymore sci-fi than that!

MARK DERY: In "Diary of a Bug," in *Flyboy in the Buttermilk*, you state, "Hip-hop is ancestor worship"; later in the same essay collection, you quote a lecture given by Delany at the Studio Museum of Harlem in which he says, "We need images of tomorrow, and our people need them more than most." I sometimes wonder if there isn't an inherent dichotomy in hip-hop between a displaced people's need to reaffirm a common history and the quintessentially American emphasis on forward motion, effected through technological progress. Don't these contradictory impulses threaten to tear hip-hop apart?

GREG TATE: No, because you can be backward-looking and forward-thinking at the same time. The approach to everything in hip-hop is always with a sense of play, so that even ancestor worship is subject to irreverence. Ironically, one of the things that's allowed black culture to survive is its ability to operate in an iconoclastic way in regard to the past; the trappings of tradition are never allowed to stand in the way of innovation and improvisation. You have to remember, too, that black reverence for the past is a reverence for a paradise lost. It's not a past that anyone knows from experience, but a past gleaned from discussions, from books by scholars like Dr. Ben Yochanan who have dedicated their lives to researching the scientific glories of black civilizations.

You know, SF, like hip-hop, is a very sociohistorical genre. It's a totalizing way of looking at America, as Delany has pointed out, that mundane literature could never begin to approach. Science fiction eschews the psychological dimension in terms of character portrayal for a more all-encompassing look at the impact of the various institutions that govern behavior and the transmission of knowledge. And in the same way that SF focuses on the impact of information technologies on the psychology of a society, black literature moves the silence and intellectual marginalization of blacks to the foreground. Both represent an attempt to view everything through a single lens, so that we can see the specter haunting society that society doesn't want to acknowledge.

One of the things I've been trying to say all along is that the condition of alienation that comes from being a black subject in American society parallels the kind of alienation that science fiction writers try to explore through various genre devices—transporting someone from the past into the future, thrusting someone into an alien culture, on another planet, where he has to confront alien ways of being. All of these devices reiterate the condition of being black in American culture. Black people live the estrangement that science fiction writers imagine.

At the same time, I'm a little uncomfortable with creating a pyramid of explication in which the black experience is on the bottom and science fiction becomes the way in which one "logically" discusses it. I think that there is an incredible amount of insight to be gained from reading African-American literature with the perspective of SF criticism in mind, and vice versa. As I've said, there is a redemptive quality to both literatures in terms of the way that they deal with the plight of the outsider, not to mention the simple acknowledgment that there *are* outsiders in society, that many of us are living a Kafkaesque existence here in what is supposed to be the best of all possible worlds: America.

MARK DERY: What accounts for the profound influence on black dance culture of Kraftwerk, a calculatedly funkless electro-pop band? Does their impact, traces of which are clearly discernible in techno, suggest that the very notion of funk has been cyborged?

TRICIA ROSE: I believe that what made Kraftwerk so interesting to Afrika Bambaataa and Arthur Baker [who used Kraftwerk's "Trans-Europe Express" as the schematic for their electro-boogie classic "Planet Rock"] is the way it demonstrated a mastery over technology, and mastery over technology engenders a degree of awe, particularly in black folks whose access to technology is limited. So some of it is sheer awe, but it's also about having an open, creative mind toward different ways of producing sound.

Digital music technology—samplers, sequencers, drum machines —are themselves cultural objects, and as such they carry cultural ideas. These machines force black musicians into certain ways of producing sound inside certain parameters, in this case nineteenth-century European musical constructions. Having said that, I resist the reading that by definition suggests that being black and funky means that one can't occupy certain spaces.

MARK DERY: Can one be situated in the African-American musical tradition and still speak the aesthetic language of the technetronic society? In other words, can one be funky and mechanical?

TRICIA ROSE: No question; that's what hip-hop is! The real question is: How do we define what being "mechanical" means? If we take a kind of Frankfurt School/fascist/industrial regimentation/lack of creativity as our model for the machine, then of course funky cyborgs would seem like an utter contradiction; but if we understand the machine as a product of human creativity whose parameters are always suggesting what's beyond them, then we can read hip-hop as the response of urban people of color to the postindustrial landscape. Although most people do not have the power to structurally transform the worlds they live in, many attempt microscopic responses to things that appear in their landscapes.

Electro-boogie took place in a historical moment—"Planet Rock" was released in 1982—when factory production and solid blue-collar work were coming to a screeching halt in urban America. Urban blacks were increasingly unemployed, and their best options were to become hidden workers for service industries or computer repair people. People said, "Look, technology is here; we can choose to be left behind or we can try to take control of the beast."

This bears a resemblance to what the black cultural and literary theorist James A. Snead refers to as "the management of ruptures."[17] How do cultures respond to social ruptures? Do we incorporate them or reject them, refusing transformation? This is the larger question we should ask when we talk about black cultural transformation because for every point of continuity, there are fascinating points of discontinuity. This is our problem: we have to be able to say, yes, industrial logic dominates a number of cultural products and ways of thinking in the world, while at the same time acknowledging that not everything is a subset of that framework.

What Afrika Bambaataa and hip-hoppers like him saw in Kraftwerk's use of the robot was an understanding of themselves as *already having been robots*. Adopting "the robot" reflected a response to an existing condition: namely, that they were labor for capitalism, that they had very little value as people in this society. By taking on the robotic stance, one is "playing with the robot." It's like wearing body armor that identifies you as an alien: if it's always on anyway, in some symbolic sense, perhaps you could master the wearing of this guise in order to use it *against* your interpolation.

The question is: How are signs and images used? Kraftwerk, of course, can have more than one meaning. Let's say, for example, that Kraftwerk did not understand itself as some prole club-music phenomenon that mocked factory capitalism and the logic of industrial life. Let's say, instead, that they were totally into industrial regimentation, that they were twenty-first-century-style Carnegie capitalists in the making. It wouldn't change my argument, because my argument isn't "Do they feel a kinship with Kraftwerk as Kraftwerk sees itself?" but rather, "What can this symbol of regimentation mean for them?"

By contrast, there are a number of hip-hop scenes around the world in which you find racially conservative kids wearing Malcolm X gear. The new right in Germany has taken up all kinds of black cultural symbols, and some nonblack American hip-hop kids feel a kinship with black culture but clearly have very racist ideas about what being black means and how it fits into the world schema.

These realities argue in favor of multiple meanings for objects, meanings which can't be fixed and floated across time and space. Kraftwerk gets taken up in a way that may or may not be understood as resistive; in addition, Kraftwerk's own position may or may not be understood as resistive. I'm interested in reading effects in context, which is why technology can be emancipatory for hip-hop—because of its effects, not because it is "naturally" emancipatory.

MARK DERY: What does the hip-hop catchphrase "droppin' science" mean?

TRICIA ROSE: It means sharing knowledge, knowledge that is generally inaccessible to people, together with a fearlessness about stating what you believe to be the truth. There's also the implication that the information you're imparting is going to revolutionize things because *this* is the truth that has been deliberately and systematically denied. Science, here, stands in for incontrovertible evidence. Science is understood as that space where the future takes place.

MARK DERY: Sun Ra, who claims to be from Saturn, is known for songs like "Rocket No. 9 Take Off for the Planet Venus"; his concerts have incorporated movies of his orchestra parading around the Sphinx. What meanings can be squeezed out of Ra's conflation of ancient Egyptian imagery and alien saviors?

TRICIA ROSE: Sun Ra's flying saucer imagery is about accepting the mystical powers that one knows, culturally, and seeing science as a mystical process as well—a process that has to do not only with deductive reasoning, but with creating power and positing new social myths. It's about reconciling those two histories. If you're going to imagine yourself in the future, you have to imagine where you've come from; ancestor worship in black culture is a way of countering a historical erasure.

At the same time, romantic visions of an agrarian memory of black creativity are seriously problematic; certainly, we need to investigate those periods, but to position them as the pinnacle of black creativity and the rest of history as a decline that works in a one-to-one ratio with technological influences completely misunderstands both the technological creativity of, say, blues artists, working with the most sophisticated technologies available to them, and the fact that even those so-called unadulterated periods constituted a break from former environments. I refuse the Frankfurt model of authenticity, which distinguishes between what is "really creative" and some sort of technological simulation of creativity.

These notions of creative authenticity often contribute to a construction of black culture in such a way that blacks are romanticized. These romantic visions take place *long* after hip-hop's initial interventions and in so doing make it impossible to see the way in which black folks are on the cutting edge of transforming technology and their relationship to it. These visions constitute an extraordinarily contradictory reading of black creativity that positions the reader as a postcolonial observer of a black culture that is miraculously untainted by "our" violence and loss of spirituality. The white romance with the blues, exemplified by the movie *Crossroads*, is a clear example of this phenomenon. Of course, blacks are docile and compliant in this vision even as they "refuse" to partake of the creative tools made available by postindustrial commodification. Among other things, this bespeaks a profound misunderstanding of the transformative energy of black creativity in general and of contemporary young, black cultural workers in particular.

There's no question that there's a tendency among people who live under extraordinarily oppressive conditions to long for a time when they had more control over a smaller space. But the dream of a place where one is linked to the universe in a more spiritual and philosophical way is too often part of a postcolonial white fantasy which by definition depends on the domination of another group of people for its reconstruction of that arcadian time.

MARK DERY: The problem with those sorts of narratives, it seems, is that they're assembly lines for the production of binary oppositions. For example, the eco-feminist utopias of seventies sci-fi, even as they imagined gardens of earthly delight, vilified technology as inherently masculinist. In light of this, Donna Haraway theorizes the cyborg as "an ironic political myth" that offers an escape route from "the maze of dualisms." I wonder how useful such a myth is for you as a black woman, given our earlier discussion of the multivalent nature of the image of the robot in hip-hop culture.

TRICIA ROSE: Well, I'm a strange case in that my fantasies of control involve a lot of physical power; I don't have a hold-hands, hippie notion of how I want my space to be, and people often perceive that kind of aggressiveness as masculine. Although I don't see myself as particularly masculine, I'm often accused of thinking like a male, which suggests that people are operating inside of a very troubled notion of what femininity is.

I'm not troubled by the cyborg *as* an imaginary, but by the fact that it's almost impossible for the average young woman to see herself as a person who could take up that much social space. It suggests a social and psychological containment that makes it impossible for women to see themselves as major actors in a technological world.

MARK DERY: One thing that bothers me about the notion of the cyborg as a useful myth is the fact that the flesh cedes territory to invasive technologies—myoelectric armatures, cyberoptic implants, brain sockets. If machines continue to signify an impregnable masculinity, and if the flesh continues to be coded as feminine—as is so often the case in Hollywood SF—then the myth of the cyborg is one more story told about the feminine subjugated.

TRICIA ROSE: Absolutely. The cyborg is a masculine construct in which the technology houses all of the hard, strong, *Terminator* capacity, and the softer stuff is understood as the weak portion, the part that bleeds, menstruates. The question is not cyborg possibilities in and of themselves, but how the cyborg has been constructed by patriarchal discourse and how it might be reinvented.

If we had hordes and hordes of women who were paid to sit around and reimagine the science fiction genre, they might treat technology differently, placing it in a different relationship to the organism, and then what would cyborgs look like? What relationship would the technology have to the body if cyborgs were imagined with different stress points, different identity problems, different responses to incorporation? Again, I refuse to blame the technology; it's about how we imagine its usefulness, and what we value. If we don't value the ways in which women create, it doesn't really matter what we do or do not invent; we could stay on the farm and women would be just as oppressed. For that reason, I don't really see science fiction models of the future as a necessarily more oppressive space for women than I do current fictions of an idealized past.

MARK DERY: Haraway argues, in "A Manifesto for Cyborgs," for what I would call a technofeminist ideology that refuses "an anti-science metaphysics, a demonology of technology." Which leads me to wonder: Would the female shootist in Patrick Carr's book, *Gun People*, who says, "With a gun I have more . . . control over potential events around me, and more personal power," fit Haraway's definition of an oppositional monster? Furthermore, what do you make of the linkage between handgun fetishism and an abhorrence for childbirth evinced by postfeminists like the avant-garde diva Diamanda Galás, who believes that "all women . . . have to get guns" (her celebrity endorsement goes to the .38 Special),[18] and who once told me,

I'm hostile to the act of childbirth. I consider it fundamentally demeaning to women to be walking around with this deformed, aberrant body, bearing children for men. Although mainstream society says that breeding is natural for heterosexuals, I find it repellent and very unnatural.

TRICIA ROSE: That's an incredible question; I really would like to explore this because I, too, have had a total phobia about childbearing, associating it with containment, confinement, and giving in to male desire—all of which, I think, is a product of understanding that you will be structured this way whether you experience pregnancy this way or not. Courtney Love [Hole guitarist and wife of Nirvana singer-guitarist Kurt Cobain] said, in a recent *Rolling Stone* cover story, that she experienced the worst sexism of her whole life while she was pregnant. Pregnant women feel physically vulnerable and feel that they signify some sort of male access to them; it's a profoundly problematic position.

The relationship between gun lust and a loathing for childbirth is a binary opposition based on a Protestant definition of sexuality. The gun is about control, and the idea that you need to be in control all the time means that you don't feel like you are in control. If women have to hold on to guns to reclaim some sense of power that they have lost structurally, it indicates that we, as a society, are horribly out of balance. It isn't just about women taking up arms or about men being wimpy yogurt-eaters, as in Robert Bly's imagination, it's about saying that all of us have a wide range of emotional, sexual, physical, psychological reactions, and that both sexes are incredibly constrained by societal structures.

I would call for an investigation of maternal, matriarchal African narratives about the power of reproduction. A feminist friend once said to me, "You know, I think men try to control women's sexuality because they're terrified of the incredible creative energy involved in reproducing life forms." If women could harness that power and not be afraid of it, it would be the equivalent of owning all the guns you'd ever want to own. But many of us are afraid of trying to spiritually transcend the social construction of pregnancy.

We need radical feminist models of pregnancy and motherhood.

And for a moment, I was on Saturn.

Reprinted from *Why I Hate Saturn* by Kyle Baker. Copyright © 1990 by Kyle Baker. All rights reserved. Used by permission of Piranha Press, an imprint of DC Comics.

I think feminist mothers are the most dangerous muthafuckahs out there; if I were to be really hard-core, I could say that feminists who refuse to have children ain't threatenin' shit after a certain point! I think the key is for feminist women to have as much power and as many babies as they want to, creating universes of feminist children.

I watched *Aliens* again last night and what I loved about Sigourney Weaver is the way in which she manages both directed aggressiveness and sensuality. You watch her pet that cat near the beginning of the film, in the hospital, and it's very sensual at the same time that you know she's all about trying to take somebody out. Similarly, what was so brilliant about *The Terminator* was the way in which Linda Hamilton's character, Sarah Connor, became a warrior of reproduction.

The question is: Who is doing the constructing? The problem with the *Terminator* series and the *Alien* trilogy is that male imagination is driving the narrative, which is what makes a pistol-packin' mama like Sarah Connor so problematic. But the larger question is, once again, not "How was Sarah Connor constructed by the filmmaker?" but "How do the feminist graduate students I know (many of whom idolize these characters) use these women in ways that rewrite the narrative and maybe rewrite their life roles?" Furthermore, how might their readings allow another generation of feminist independent filmmakers to reimagine Sarah Connor? These are small, potential building blocks toward something larger; they're not an end but a means to a larger end.

These images are opening up possibilities, revising what men and women think women ought to be, even if they wind up endorsing patriarchal norms in other ways. Hollywood has to reaffirm the status quo, of course, but trust me when I tell you that just by opening those gates, they're creating a rupture they may not be able to suture.

Notes

1   William Gibson, interviewed in the video documentary, *Cyberpunk* (1990).
2   Norman Spinrad, *Science Fiction in the Real World* (Carbondale, IL, 1990), 9.
3   William Gibson, "The Gernsback Continuum," in *Mirrorshades*, ed. Bruce Sterling (New York, 1986), 7.

4 All Milestone-related quotes are from the two-page press release, "Milestone Media Fact Sheet," and "Starting off with a Bang," a one-page summary of *Icon*'s plot.

5 *Benét's Reader's Encyclopedia*, ed. Katherine Baker Siepmann (New York, 1987), 62.

6 Greg Tate, "Yo! Hermeneutics!: Henry Louis Gates, Houston Baker, David Toop," in *Flyboy in the Buttermilk: Essays on Contemporary America* (New York, 1992), 154.

7 Rammellzee, "The Movement of the Letter: The Polishing of the Equation Rammellzee," in *New Observations #93: Exact Fantasies*, ed. Tracy A. Smith (New York, 1993), 20.

8 Ibid., 20–21.

9 Quoted in Tate, *Flyboy in the Buttermilk*, 147.

10 David Toop, *The Rap Attack: African Jive to New York Hip-Hop* (Boston, 1984), 146–48.

11 This text, which began as a telephone interview, was extensively reworked by Mr. Delany during the months of January through April, 1993, in Amherst, Ann Arbor, and New York.

12 Greg Tate, "Ghetto in the Sky: Samuel Delany's Black Whole," in *Flyboy in the Buttermilk: Essays on Contemporary America* (New York, 1992), 165–66.

13 Samuel R. Delany, "Is Cyberpunk a Good Thing or a Bad Thing?" *Mississippi Review* 16 (1988): 28–35.

14 Andrew Ross, "Cyberpunk in Boystown," in *Strange Weather: Culture, Science and Technology in the Age of Limits* (New York, 1991), 146.

15 Mikal Gilmore, "The Rise of Cyberpunk," *Rolling Stone*, 4 December 1986.

16 Jeanne Gomoll, "An Open Letter to Joanna Russ," *Aurora* 25 (1986): 7–10; and Bruce Sterling, Letter to the Editor, *Aurora* 26 (1990): 7.

17 James A. Snead, "On Repetition in Black Culture," *Black American Literature Forum* 15 (1981): 146–54. Tricia Rose would like to thank Arthur Jafa for bringing this work and this formulation to her attention.

18 Interview with Diamanda Galás, in *Re/Search #13: Angry Women*, ed. Andrea Juno and V. Vale (San Francisco, 1991), 22.

GARETH BRANWYN

COMPU-SEX: EROTICA FOR CYBERNAUTS

Cyberspace is more than a breakthrough in electronic media or in computer interface design. With its virtual environments and simulated worlds, cyberspace is a . . . tool for examining our very sense of reality.
—Michael Heim

In an enduring ritual of nightly "cruising," a crowd of people has gathered in a lonely-hearts club. A man musters up the courage to approach a woman and fires off a few of his best one-liners. She takes the bait and tugs the line with some sexy retorts of her own. The chemistry is right; things heat up. They are soon jarred back to reality by the teasing of those around them who've caught on to their little game. Embarrassed, they quickly pass notes and plan a late-night rendezvous. Both show up punctually at the private place they have chosen. An awkward silence is broken by more provocative flirting, and then, finally, what they've both come for: sex. They quickly undress one another and begin making frantic love. The exchange is short but intense. When they're finished, they swap a few nervous pleasantries. As each of them chooses "Quit" from a menu of options on a computer screen, a cheap digitized voice says "good-bye." The telephone link between their computers is disconnected. Tonight's disembodied tryst has cost each about six dollars.

Welcome to the world of on-line computer sex, or "compu-sex." Every computer information service, large or small, has lurking within its bits and bytes an active subculture of users engaged in text-based sexual exchanges.[1] These encounters rarely carry over into face-to-face meetings. Rather, the participants are content to return night after night to explore this odd brand of interactive and sexually explicit storytelling. Compu-sex enthusiasts say it's the ultimate safe sex for the 1990s, with no exchange of bodily fluids, no loud smoke-filled clubs, and no morning after. Of course, there's no physical contact, either. Compu-sex brings new meaning to the phrase "mental masturbation."

≡≡≡≡

> The Internet is an enormous computer network in which any existing network can participate. It encompasses satellites, cable, fiber and telephone lines, and it seems to have grown exponentially. Now, everyone from . . . students to commercial enterprises can get access through the Internet to vast amounts of information on other computer systems around the world. Among the growing number of places from which the Internet system . . . is now accessible: public libraries and on-line information services available to home computer users.
> —Robert E. Calem

Before we get too deep into our discussion of on-line sex, let's take a look at the technological infrastructure that mediates this computerized twist on the more common phone sex.

Computer information networks have become large and decentralized. A tangled web of "data highways" is being installed across the globe at a phenomenal rate. Hardware and software innovations called "bridges" and "gateways" afford complex linkages between different networks. Major national and international computer network services with baffling names like Bitnet, USENET, CompuServe, and GEnie are now linked together for electronic mail exchange and, in some cases, conference participation and file transfer. The global "network of networks" that contains a growing number of these constituent networks is called the Internet.[2] The total constellation of computer nets containing the Internet, the other large networks, and the smaller regional nets is frequently referred to in on-line vernacular as "cyberspace." Cyberspace, so named in homage to the global computer matrix described in William Gibson's *Neuromancer*, has become a virtual work space and playground for a vast number of people. The algae-like growth of the Internet is so rapid that accurate statistics regarding its size are hard to pin down. One recent estimate put the number of computer networks linked via the Internet at 1.3 million worldwide, with an estimated 14–15 million individual users. The rate of growth for new computer networks joining the Internet is 25 percent *every three months*. People who navigate through this worldwide web of interlinked computer systems, for whatever social, commercial, or recreational reasons, increasingly speak of these nets in terms of physical spaces. "Virtual community" and "electronic village" are often used to describe these ethereal homes away from home.

An individual's participation in these burgeoning virtual communities is made possible by combining a personal computer with an electronic device called a modem. The modem translates computer information into signals that can be passed through conventional phone lines. Modems can either connect one personal computer to another or an individual computer to a "host" computer that serves a network. Once connected, data can flow back and forth via the phone connection. Communications software allows the user to send and receive information and to enter the virtual commons of a given network. There are two types of networks: research and education systems, such as Bitnet and USENET, and commercial services, such as Prodigy, CompuServe, and GEnie. Local electronic bulletin board systems (BBSs), the one-horse towns of cyberspace, are usually not connected to a larger network. Their offerings are more modest, with discussions devoted to local and national issues and libraries of public domain software. Local and national "Adults Only" BBSs are also common and cater to those who want to exchange computer-based pornographic images, talk about sex, and arrange "face-to-face" dates. For the purposes of this discussion, I will focus on one commercial service in particular. Although a lot of the conversational technology (the network's software and its rules of on-line etiquette) described here is specific to that service, the phenomenon of compu-sex is common to all commercial and noncommercial networks and to most local BBSs. It simply changes form to fit the modes of communication available.

While each service has its own approach to presenting its offerings and provides different schemes for navigating through them, commercial information services are usually divided into a series of small domains or conferencing areas. The user either chooses options from a menu or clicks on icons that represent areas of interest. Most services offer standard features, such as news, business information, electronic shopping and banking, entertainment areas (movies, sports, trivia), and a host of issue-related forums. On the larger services, these forum areas can feature lively public debates. Protracted and volatile disputes (called "flame wars" in network slang) are common. Each service also provides electronic mail capabilities and vast libraries of information, either data that can be searched on-line or programs that can be transferred to the user's computer. Commercial networks usually have a set monthly fee and an hourly usage rate. Users who conduct business on-line or who use the networks as their primary social, sexual, and/or recreational outlet can run up staggering bills (a hundred dollars a month or more is not uncommon).

Drinks (alcoholic and non-) shall pour from the bar, exotic coffees will flow from the pot, and every imaginable and unimaginable flavor of ice cream shall be yours for the dipping. . . . Furthermore, while ace electronic chef Ingmar Vanderplotz takes a well-deserved night off, the buffet table will be laden with vats of Granny Santini's

No-Holds-Barred Chili, a product of yours truly, your genial host, Steve Glaser. Chili available in Mild, Medium, Hot, and The-Stuff-They-Use-To-Launch-The-Saturn-Five's.
—Excerpt from invitation to a virtual salon for writers

On "InfoMart USA" (a pseudonym for the network on which I spent most of my time while researching this article), one of the most popular features is the public chat areas, called "rooms."[3] Users are able to view a list of rooms that have been created by other users. The conversational theme of each room, embodied in its name, runs the gamut of possible interests from politics ("Boomers in the White House" and "Women in Politics"), to teen concerns ("Beverly Hills 90210," "Alternative Music," "Teen Club"), to religion and ethics ("Mormons On-Line," "Sanctuary," "Pro-Choice Forum"). By far the single largest theme represented in the room titles, however, is sex. On a given night, the list might include "Naughty Negligees," "Men for Men," "Hot Bi Ladies," "Women Who Obey Women," and so forth. After deciding which conversation one wishes to join, the user chooses that room from the menu and "enters" by clicking on its name. The room appears on the user's screen as a pop-up window. A list of other occupants is shown at the top and what people are saying appears in a box inside the room window. To contribute to the conversation, an occupant types comments into a small text-entry box at the bottom of the computer screen, then hits a "Send" button to post it. Engaging in this type of conversation is a bit un-nerving at first. The pace of the conversation has a dreamlike quality to it. The exchanges can move in slow motion for a long time, then suddenly spring to life as several people post messages that appear on-screen at the same time. Words start scrolling across one's screen faster than they can be read. Then, as quickly as the room exploded with dialogue, it settles back into silence. If nothing is said for several minutes, occupants get bored and leave in droves. When a room's population is reduced to zero, it is automatically removed from the rooms menu. Rooms "pop" into existence and quickly fill up with enthusiastic conversationalists, only to die a few minutes later, instantly replaced by other rooms. Jumping in and out of these rooms, passing other digital personae as they come and go, one begins to feel like a character in a cyberspace version of a Marx Brothers movie.

———

> In compu-sex, being able to type fast and write well is equivalent to having great legs or a tight butt in the real world.
> —Anonymous compu-sex enthusiast

Compu-sex is a curious blend of phone sex, computer dating, and high-tech voyeurism. To "cruise" on InfoMart USA one must process a dizzying amount of data. While hopping in and out of different chat rooms, one is also looking up bios, exchanging messages with compu-sex "prospects," even tracking people's comings and goings through the net. If someone leaves a room, one can choose a "Find" feature and the system will report on that person's whereabouts within the system. It's not uncommon to have five or six "windows" of data on-screen at the same time. Time on-line is expensive, so users need to "score" as quickly as possible. In cyberspace, good library skills are as handy as good pick-up lines. When a possible compu-sex partner has been found, a few flirtatious lines are sent via "Private Messages" (imagine electronic Post-its). If these exchanges bear fruit, one partner pops the big question: "Wanna go private?" A private room is created by clicking on the "Create Private Room" button and assigning a code name to it. Once the private room has been created, private messages are sent to one's partner(s), telling them the room's name/password. The room's creator then sits back and waits for the other chat enthusiast(s) to arrive. A wide variety of sexual orientations and forms of compu-sex are represented in these private rooms. Gay, straight, bi, swinging couples, orgy goers, cross-dressers, and such outré orientations as "Leg Brace Enthusiasts" and "Hot Denture Wearers" have all found niches on InfoMart.

The public chat rooms on InfoMart are closely monitored by "guides" who are on the lookout for conversations deemed inappropriate for public consumption. These guides are nicknamed "cyber-cops" and are often treated with contempt by "residents" of the more sexually oriented public rooms. The words "Sleepy Time" or a series of "z's" ("zzzzzzzzzzz") are sometimes typed on-screen by a user to warn other occupants to stop talking openly about sex while the guide is in the room. Since the guide is making rounds and has many more rooms to visit, sooner or later, he has to move on. When he does, people will make comments like "Whew, they're gone. . . . That was close," or "Don't they have anything better to do than make our lives miserable?" The conversation soon continues where it left off before the guide entered. If a guide finds the title of a room offensive, or the tenor of the conversation within it outside the system's *User's Guidelines*, he or she will close the room down. Individuals who get testy with a guide in public can have their membership suspended. Guides, who are enlisted from the regular InfoMart citizenry in exchange for free on-line time, have vastly different standards of what constitutes an infringement of the nebulous guidelines. One night, an overzealous guide killed a room called "Pictures." Everyone was busy talking about such mind-numbing topics as image-exchange formats and graphic-conversation schemes when the room was shut down. Apparently, the guide thought it was one of the porn-image swaps that are common in the public areas (the swapping of electronically scanned images actually takes place through private messages and mail transfer). Many of the participants, some totally ignorant of the sexual underground that exists on InfoMart, were bewildered as to how "Pictures" could possibly have constituted a guidelines violation.

The conversations that take place within private rooms are strictly confidential. Not even the system's administrators have access to them. To find out what actually takes place in these rooms, I sent a questionnaire to compu-sex enthusiasts, opened up several discussion topics on InfoMart and on another popular network, interviewed dozens of people via phone and electronic mail, and even tried some private-room encounters myself. While only ten questionnaires were returned, I gathered enough additional information through other means to gain at least a basic understanding of how compu-sex works. Respondents to the questionnaires, interviews, and on-line discussions identified three different types of sexual encounters in which they had been involved on-line.

The most commonly reported form of compu-sex is one in which participants describe and embellish real-world circumstances: how they look, what they're wearing, what they're doing. ("I'm in my room at the computer screen. I'm taking my shirt off. I'm touching myself now.") Of course, none of the parties involved in a compu-sex encounter know if the other participants are *really* doing what's being described. Most interviewees said they've tried it both ways: actually doing everything they say they're doing, and just typing the words. One woman said she couldn't wait for speech recognition typing (the computer translates speech directly into text) so that she could have "hands-free" compu-sex: "It's so hard to type with one hand."

The second type of interaction involves the creation of a pure fantasy scenario ("We're in a health club doing our workouts, only we're both totally nude"). This form is similar to fantasy role-playing games (such as Dungeons and Dragons), where each participant's fantasies are tailored to fit the collective story being created by all the players. Interactions of this type are common for group compu-sex. Keeping track of the action in these "orgy" situations can quickly get out of hand as participants simultaneously post descriptions, some of which will inevitably contradict other descriptions. To make this work effectively, all parties involved must work creatively around any discrepancies so that the eroticism and consistency of the story line can be maintained. For example, during an on-line orgy of six participants, someone with the screen name BethR types: "I'm climbing on top of Roger104," not noticing that Roger104 has just stated that he is having sex standing up, in the corner, with Nina5. To work around this story "violation," Roger104 might type: "Nina5 and I get so worked up, we roll onto the floor. As Nina5 falls off me, the always randy BethR, not missing a beat, climbs on top of me." Then, to totally tidy things up, Nina5 adds: "I begin to make out with BethR and to massage her breasts while she rides Roger104." This give-and-take story-building process occurs in all on-line sex encounters regardless of style or number of partners. Multi-participant encounters were described as particularly difficult, however, since larger numbers of people are making things up simultaneously. Interactional "train wrecks" are common.

The third variety of on-line sex might be called "tele-operated compu-sex." Tele-operation usually refers to the remote control of a robot or a computer. Here, one party (an individual or a couple) gives actual lovemaking instructions over the computer to another party ("Jim, I want you to slowly undress Carol"). This format is popular with couples who want to swing on-line. Many of these couples claim they are completely monogamous in real life. Through these anonymous, long-distance encounters, they can swing without risking any involvement or disease. The total anonymity of services like InfoMart provides a safety net for this type of sexual experimentation. If someone were to get too emotionally involved and seek to bring the virtual relationship into the real world, the other parties involved could simply delete their current screen personae and create new ones, thereby ensuring anonymity.

Besides the three varieties of compu-sex outlined above, there are also tamer versions of on-line romance that use the same conversational tools (public chats, private messages, and private rooms). Several people said they don't act out sex on-line, but instead talk openly about their sex lives and specific sex problems, using the online discussions as informal counseling. Others, especially the teens on InfoMart, are content to flirt in both public and private areas without taking the conversation to an overtly sexual level. One of the most popular features in the InfoMart chat area is the Romance Room, where people flirt and exchange the kind of sickly sweet dialogue found in grocery store romance novels.

=====

> . . . [C]ybernetic identity is never used up—it can be re-created, reassigned, and reconstructed with any number of different names and under different user accounts.
> —Andrew Ross

On InfoMart USA people don't have to be who they are in the real world. Age, gender, sexual preference, life circumstances, everything one claims can be true or made up.[4] While many networks have policies that try to discourage "phony" user accounts, InfoMart lets users set up several different accounts with different names and bio files. Under these "screen names," one can say and be anything as long as it doesn't violate the (virtual) community standards that have been established by InfoMart. Obviously, this freedom to role-play with little real-world consequence is, in large part, why compu-sex flourishes on this particular network. Making it up, making oneself up, is a crucial part of the turn-on.

Unfortunately, the freedom to hide behind a phony name also contributes to a plague of on-line sexual harassment and rampant rudeness. A number of women I talked to in the public forums said they were constantly bombarded with crude private messages and sexual advances. These women said that they did not engage in on-line sex, did not frequent sexually oriented public areas, and did not want to be approached via private messages. "If you have a female screen name and you enter the general chat area, you're gonna get hassled," said one woman. It seems as though compu-sex mediates but does not change behavior, and it may even provide a new space for sexist aggression. This harassment has caused some women to avoid the chat areas completely and others to cancel their memberships altogether.

At the same time, anonymity, while seeming to encourage rude on-line behavior in some, has been liberating to others who wish to experiment with more benign on-line personae. Several interviewees who claimed that they were completely heterosexual in the real world said they had tried same-sex encounters just to see what it was like (or, at least, the people with whom they had their encounters *said* they were the same sex). Almost everyone who answered the sex questionnaire said that different personalities and sexual orientations had been experimented with, at least on occasion. The fact that there are no certainties of gender and character on InfoMart is extremely unnerving to some participants. In the public rooms (and I suspect in private rooms as well), heated disputes frequently break out over someone's alleged gender. Elaborate measures are sometimes proposed that involve phone voice verification, character references ("I've met HotPants and she's *definitely* a girl!"), fax transmission of photos, and the electronic exchange of scanned photos. Of course, everything short of a face-to-face meeting is still open to question. In the end, all stated descriptions must be assumed to be in quotation marks. Interestingly enough, while most of the people I talked to use fantasy personae on occasion, more than half reported that they basically "stick to the facts." "I find it much more of a turn-on to think that someone is aroused by the real me," said one respondent. But that "real me" is always, must be, narrated, put into "story," typed into the system. It's only as "true" as the story it tells at the moment.

═══════

> There was a young man named Racine,
> who invented a fucking machine.
> Concave or convex, it fit either sex,
> and was exceedingly simple to clean.
> —Traditional limerick

The last item on my questionnaire concerned the future evolution of compu-sex: Where was it headed, how would technology change it, how might the level and quality of people's interactions change? The answers I received were solely concerned with the introduction of virtual reality technology into the realm of computer networking. VR is a recent development in fully immersive, three-dimensional, computer-generated environments. To enter virtual reality, the user dons a head-mounted computer display and a pair of position-sensing gloves. As the user's hands move in real space, an analogous computer-generated pair of hands is seen moving in the head-mounted display. Eventually, full-body "data suits" will be added which can read the shape and position of a user's body and display that information in the helmet. While this technology is already available, it has yet to enter the realm of the computer network. Respondents spoke of this inevitable marriage of computer networking and VR as overcoming the limited bandwidth (range of possibilities) of current text-based computer sex.

The area of VR that deals with sexual prosthesis is often called "teledildonics."[5] The phallocentrism of the term is indicative of the way people have so far visualized net sex as a substitute for tradi-tional "real-world" intercourse. With teledildonics, instead of a penis penetrating a vagina, the real-world penis is "invaginated" by the computer through means of a data-sensing "condom" or the vagina is penetrated by a dildo-like input/output device that reads and re-sponds to the vagina. Sensors and responders ("tactile effectors") would work in tandem to simulate intercourse. The user's partner (or partners), also dressed in VR sex gear and connected via phone, would appear in the head-mounted display as they wanted to be seen. Participants would construct desirable data forms for their partners to interact with. One person's virtual touch would trigger the effectors in a partner's "data suit," simulating the sensation of physical contact. Compu-sex enthusiasts would meet in a private room in cyberspace, much as current partners meet in a 2-D "space" that gains its dimensionality only through storytelling. Although the fiber-optic technologies for negotiating the huge amount of data that would need to be transferred over the phone lines for this type of VR sex are close at hand, the sensor/effector technology is still theoretical.

Sexual interaction in current text-based compu-sex almost exclusively mirrors (at least as it was reported to this author) real-world intercourse. Participants begin with foreplay and progress through increasing levels of (spelled out) intensity ending with an on-line orgasm. An on-line orgasm looks like something out of a comic book, with drawn-out ohhhhhh's, ahhhhhhhhhh's, WOW!!!'s, and the obligatory "I'mmmm commmmmmmmminnngggggggggg!!!!!!" Not surprisingly, orgasms are usually simultaneous. Who wants to tell the story any other way?

> The boundary-maintaining images of base and superstructure, public and private, or material and ideal never seemed more feeble.
> —Donna Haraway

Several questions still remain: How will more sophisticated compu-sex technology change the nature of virtual sex? Will on-line sex become a satisfying substitute for sex in the real world? What impact will all forms of computer-mediated relationships have on face-to-face relationships as virtual communities develop a wider spectrum of interactional possibilities? Is this line of questioning even relevant anymore? As more people spend greater amounts of their time in cyberspace and come to identify themselves increasingly with their various cyber-constructs and nonphysical relationships, won't the boundaries between "real" and "imaginary" have less practical significance?[6] And, as we immerse ourselves more deeply in the complex artificial worlds of cyberspace, what wholly new forms of interaction and "dwelling" might develop? What would an on-line sexual experience that moved entirely away from the old notions of a bodily and orgasmically focused sexuality be like? Would it in fact transcend the boundaries of bodily encapsulation and enter some new realm where the body is shed altogether?

When we conceive of activity in cyberspace, we can't help but superimpose old technological and spatial models and behaviors onto this new domain (in much the same way that early television was essentially radio theater in front of a camera). Every aspect of virtual "residency" offers fascinating, fertile ground for examining issues of embodiment and disembodiment, authenticity and artificiality, biological gender and gender role-playing, information ownership and free access. Almost all of these issues converge in computer sex. How compu-sex will evolve is an open question. That it will thrive and develop novel ways of gratifying erotic desires is almost certain.

Notes

1   See Michael Heim, "The Erotic Ontology of Cyberspace," in *Cyberspace: First Steps*, ed. Michael Benedikt (Boston, 1992), 59.

2   See Robert E. Calem, "The Network of All Networks," *New York Times*, 6 December 1992; and Ed Krol, *The Whole Internet User's Guide & Catalog* (Sebastopol, CA, 1992), 11–18.

3   For reasons of privacy, I decided not to give the real name of the computer service. This compu-sex culture is very underground (even many of the regular users on the service don't know of its existence), and it is always on shaky ground with the system's management. The service tolerates the sex subculture, probably because it brings in big revenues, but management fears that awareness of the subculture's existence might turn off the main population of InfoMart, which it describes as "family-oriented."

4   See Andrew Ross, "Hacking Away at the Counterculture," in *Technoculture*, ed. Constance Penley and Andrew Ross (Minneapolis, 1991), 120.

5   Howard Rheingold, *Virtual Reality* (New York, 1991), 345–53.

6   See Donna Haraway, *Simians, Cyborgs, and Women* (New York, 1991), 165.

JULIAN DIBBELL

A RAPE IN CYBERSPACE; OR, HOW AN EVIL CLOWN, A HAITIAN TRICKSTER SPIRIT, TWO WIZARDS, AND A CAST OF DOZENS TURNED A DATABASE INTO A SOCIETY

They say he raped them that night. They say he did it with a cunning little doll, fashioned in their image and imbued with the power to make them do whatever he desired. They say that by manipulating the doll he forced them to have sex with him, and with each other, and to do horrible, brutal things to their own bodies. And though I wasn't there that night, I think I can assure you that what they say is true, because it all happened right in the living room—right there amid the well-stocked bookcases and the sofas and the fireplace—of a house I've come to think of as my second home.

Call me Dr. Bombay. Some months ago—let's say about halfway between the first time you heard the words *information superhighway* and the first time you wished you never had—I found myself tripping with compulsive regularity down the well-traveled information lane that leads to LambdaMoo, a very large and very busy rustic chateau built entirely of words. Nightly, I typed the commands that called those words onto my computer screen, dropping me with what seemed a warm electric thud inside the mansion's darkened coat closet, where I checked my quotidian identity, stepped into the persona and appearance of a minor character from a long-gone television sitcom, and stepped out into the glaring chatter of the crowded living room. Sometimes, when the mood struck me, I emerged as a dolphin instead.

I won't say why I chose to masquerade as Samantha Stevens's outlandish cousin, or as the dolphin, or what exactly led to my mild but so-far incurable addiction to the semifictional digital otherworlds known around the Internet as multi-user dimensions, or MUDs. This isn't my story, after all. It's the story of a man named Mr. Bungle, and of the ghostly sexual violence he committed in the halls of LambdaMOO, and most importantly of the ways his violence and his victims challenged the thousand and more residents of that surreal, magic-infested mansion to become, finally, the community so many of them already believed they were.

That I was myself one of those residents has little direct bearing on the story's events. I mention it only as a warning that my own perspective is perhaps too steeped in the surreality and magic of the place to serve as an entirely appropriate guide. For the Bungle Affair raises questions that—here on the brink of a future in which human life may find itself as tightly enveloped in digital environments as it is today in the architectural kind—demand a clear-eyed, sober, and unmystified consideration. It asks us to shut our ears momentarily to the techno-utopian ecstasies of West Coast cyberhippies and look without illusion upon the present possibilities for building, in the on-line spaces of this world, societies more decent and free than those mapped onto dirt and concrete and capital. It asks us to behold the new bodies awaiting us in virtual space undazzled by their phantom powers, and to get to the crucial work of sorting out the socially meaningful differences between those bodies and our physical ones. And most forthrightly it asks us to wrap our late modern ontologies, epistemologies, sexual ethics, and common sense around the curious notion of rape by voodoo doll—and to try not to warp them beyond recognition in the process.

In short, the Bungle Affair dares me to explain it to you without resort to dime-store mysticisms, and I fear I may have shape-shifted by the digital moonlight one too many times to be quite up to the task. But I will do what I can, and I can do no better, I suppose, than to lead with the facts. For if nothing else about Mr. Bungle's case is unambiguous, the facts at least are crystal clear.

The facts begin (as they often do) with a time and a place. The time was a Monday night in March, and the place, as I've said, was the living room—which, due to the inviting warmth of its decor, is so invariably packed with chitchatters as to be roughly synonymous among LambdaMOOers with a party. So strong, indeed, is the sense of convivial common ground invested in the living room that a cruel mind could hardly imagine a better place in which to stage a violation of LambdaMOO's communal spirit. And there was cruelty enough lurking in the appearance Mr. Bungle presented to the virtual world—he was at the time a fat, oleaginous, Bisquick-faced clown dressed in cum-stained harlequin garb and girdled with a mistletoe-and-hemlock belt whose buckle bore the quaint inscription "KISS ME UNDER THIS, BITCH!" But whether cruelty motivated his choice of crime scene is not among the established facts of the case. It is a fact only that he did choose the living room.

The remaining facts tell us a bit more about the inner world of Mr. Bungle, though only perhaps that it couldn't have been a very comfortable place. They tell us that he commenced his assault entirely unprovoked, at or about 10 p.m. Pacific Standard Time. That he began by using his voodoo doll to force one of the room's occupants to sexually service him in a variety of more or less conventional ways. That this victim was legba, a Haitian trickster spirit of indeterminate gender, brown-skinned and wearing an expensive pearl gray suit, top hat, and dark glasses. That legba heaped vicious imprecations on him all the while and that he was soon ejected bodily from the room. That he hid himself away then in his private chambers somewhere on the mansion grounds and continued the attacks without interruption, since the voodoo doll worked just as well at a distance as in proximity. That he turned his attentions now to Starsinger, a rather pointedly nondescript female character, tall, stout, and brown-haired, forcing her into unwanted liaisons with other individuals present in the room, among them legba, Bakunin (the well-known radical), and Juniper (the squirrel). That his actions grew progressively violent. That he made legba eat his/her own pubic hair. That he caused Starsinger to violate herself with a piece of kitchen cutlery. That his distant laughter echoed evilly in the living room with every successive outrage. That he could not be stopped until at last someone summoned Zippy, a wise and trusted old-timer who brought with him a gun of near wizardly powers, a gun that didn't kill but enveloped its targets in a cage impermeable even to a voodoo doll's powers. That Zippy fired this gun at Mr. Bungle, thwarting the doll at last and silencing the evil, distant laughter.

These particulars, as I said, are unambiguous. But they are far from simple, for the simple reason that every set of facts in virtual reality (or VR, as the locals abbreviate it) is shadowed by a second, complicating set: the "real-life" facts. And while a certain tension invariably buzzes in the gap between the hard, prosaic RL facts and their more fluid, dreamy VR counterparts, the dissonance in the Bungle case is striking. No hideous clowns or trickster spirits appear in the RL version of the incident, no voodoo dolls or wizard guns, indeed no rape at all as any RL court of law has yet defined it. The actors in the drama were university students for the most part, and they sat rather undramatically before computer screens the entire time, their only actions a spidery flitting of fingers across standard QWERTY keyboards. No bodies touched. Whatever physical interaction occurred consisted of a mingling of electronic signals sent from sites spread out between New York City and Sydney, Australia. Those signals met in LambdaMOO, certainly, just as the hideous clown and the living room party did, but what was LambdaMOO after all? Not an enchanted mansion or anything of the sort—just a middlingly complex database, maintained for experimental purposes inside a Xerox Corporation research computer in Palo Alto and open to public access via the Internet.

To be more precise about it, LambdaMOO was a MUD. Or to be yet more precise, it was a subspecies of MUD known as a MOO, which is short for "MUD, Object-Oriented." All of which means that it was a kind of database especially designed to give users the vivid impression of moving through a physical space that in reality exists only as descriptive data filed away on a hard drive. When users dial into LambdaMOO, for instance, the program immediately presents them with a brief textual description of one of the rooms of the database's fictional mansion (the coat closet, say). If the user wants to leave this room, she can enter a command to move in a particular direction and the database will replace the original description with a new one corresponding to the room located in the direction she chose. When the new description scrolls across the user's screen it lists not only the fixed features of the room but all its contents at that moment—including things (tools, toys, weapons) and other users (each represented as a "character" over which he or she has sole control).

As far as the database program is concerned, all of these entities—rooms, things, characters—are just different subprograms that the program allows to interact according to rules very roughly mimicking the laws of the physical world. Characters may not leave a room in a given direction, for instance, unless the room subprogram contains an "exit" at that compass point. And if a character "says" or "does" something (as directed by its user-owner), then only the users whose characters are also located in that room will see the output describing the statement or action. Aside from such basic constraints, however, LambdaMOOers are allowed a broad freedom to create—they can describe their characters any way they like, they can make rooms of their own and decorate them to taste, and they can build new objects almost at will. The combination of all this busy user activity with the hard physics of the database can certainly induce a lucid illusion of presence—but when all is said and done the only thing you *really* see when you visit LambdaMOO is a kind of slow-crawling script, lines of dialogue and stage direction creeping steadily up your computer screen.

Which is all just to say that, to the extent that Mr. Bungle's assault happened in real life at all, it happened as a sort of Punch-and-Judy show, in which the puppets and the scenery were made of nothing more substantial than digital code and snippets of creative writing. The puppeteer behind Bungle, as it happened, was a young man logging in to the MOO from a New York University computer. He could have been Al Gore for all any of the others knew, however, and he could have written Bungle's script that night any way he chose. He could have sent a command to print the message "Mr. Bungle, smiling a saintly smile, floats angelic near the ceiling of the living room, showering joy and candy kisses down upon the heads of all below"— and everyone then receiving output from the database's subprogram #17 (a/k/a the "living room") would have seen that sentence on their screens.

Instead, he entered sadistic fantasies into the "voodoo doll," a sub-program that served the not exactly kosher purpose of attributing actions to other characters that their users did not actually write. And thus a woman in Haverford, Pennsylvania, whose account on the MOO attached her to a character she called Starsinger, was given the unasked-for opportunity to read the words "As if against her will, Starsinger jabs a steak knife up her ass, causing immense joy. You hear Mr. Bungle laughing evilly in the distance." And thus the woman in Seattle who had written herself the character called legba, with a view perhaps to tasting in imagination a deity's freedom from the burdens of the gendered flesh, got to read similarly constructed sentences in which legba, messenger of the gods, lord of crossroads and communications, suffered a brand of degradation all-too customarily reserved for the embodied female.

"Mostly voodoo dolls are amusing," wrote legba on the evening after Bungle's rampage, posting a public statement to the widely read in-MOO mailing list called *social-issues*, a forum for debate on matters of import to the entire populace. "And mostly I tend to think that re-strictive measures around here cause more trouble than they prevent. But I also think that Mr. Bungle was being a vicious, vile fuckhead, and I . . . want his sorry ass scattered from #17 to the Cinder Pile. I'm not calling for policies, trials, or better jails. I'm not sure what I'm calling for. Virtual castration, if I could manage it. Mostly, [this type of thing] doesn't happen here. Mostly, perhaps I thought it wouldn't happen to me. Mostly, I trust people to conduct themselves with some veneer of civility. Mostly, I want his ass."

Months later, the woman in Seattle would confide to me that as she wrote those words posttraumatic tears were streaming down her face—a real-life fact that should suffice to prove that the words' emo-tional content was no mere playacting. The precise tenor of that con-

tent, however, its mingling of murderous rage and eyeball-rolling an-
noyance, was a curious amalgam that neither the RL nor the VR facts
alone can quite account for. Where virtual reality and its conventions would have us believe that legba and Starsinger were brutally
raped in their own living room, here was the victim legba scolding
Mr. Bungle for a breach of "civility." Where real life, on the other
hand, insists the incident was only an episode in a free-form version
of Dungeons and Dragons, confined to the realm of the symbolic and
at no point threatening any player's life, limb, or material wellbeing,
here now was the player legba issuing aggrieved and heartfelt calls
for Mr. Bungle's dismemberment. Ludicrously excessive by RL's lights,
woefully understated by VR's, the tone of legba's response made sense
only in the buzzing, dissonant gap between them.

Which is to say it made the only kind of sense that *can* be made
of MUDly phenomena. For while the *facts* attached to any event born
of a MUD's strange, ethereal universe may march in straight, tandem
lines separated neatly into the virtual and the real, its meaning lies
always in that gap. You learn this axiom early in your life as a player,
and it's of no small relevance to the Bungle case that you often learn
it between the sheets, so to speak. Netsex, tinysex, virtual sex—
however you name it, in real-life reality it's nothing more than a 900-
line encounter stripped of even the vestigial physicality of the voice.
And yet, as many a player can tell you, it's possibly the headiest experience the very heady world of MUDS has to offer. Amid flurries of
even the most cursorily described caresses, sighs, and penetrations,
the glands do engage, and often as throbbingly as they would in a
real-life assignation—sometimes even more so, given the combined
power of anonymity and textual suggestiveness to unshackle deep-
seated fantasies. And if the virtual setting and the interplayer vibe
are right, who knows? The heart may engage as well, stirring up pas-
sions as strong as many that bind lovers who observe the formality of
trysting in the flesh.

To participate, therefore, in this disembodied enactment of life's
most body-centered activity is to risk the realization that when it
comes to sex, perhaps the body in question is not the physical one at
all, but its psychic double, the bodylike self-representation we carry
around in our heads. I know, I know, you've read Foucault and your

mind is not quite blown by the notion that sex is never so much an exchange of fluids as it is an exchange of signs. But trust your friend Dr. Bombay, it's one thing to grasp the notion intellectually and quite another to feel it coursing through your veins amid the virtual steam of hot netnookie. And it's a whole other mind-blowing trip altogether to encounter it thus as a college frosh, new to the net and still in the grip of hormonal hurricanes and high-school sexual mythologies. The shock can easily reverberate throughout an entire young world-view. Small wonder, then, that a newbie's first taste of MUD sex is often also the first time she or he surrenders wholly to the slippery terms of MUDish ontology, recognizing in a full-bodied way that what happens inside a MUDmade world is neither exactly real nor exactly make-believe, but profoundly, compellingly, and emotionally mean-ingful.

And small wonder indeed that the sexual nature of Mr. Bungle's crime provoked such powerful feelings, and not just in legba (who, be it noted, was in real life a theory-savvy doctoral candidate and a longtime MOOer, but just as baffled and overwhelmed by the force of her own reaction, she later would attest, as any panting under-grad might have been). Even players who had never experienced MUD rape (the vast majority of male-presenting characters, but not as large a majority of the female-presenting as might be hoped) immedi-ately appreciated its gravity and were moved to condemnation of the perp. legba's missive to *social-issues followed a strongly worded one from Zippy ("Well, well," it began, "no matter what else happens on Lambda, I can always be sure that some jerk is going to reinforce my low opinion of humanity") and was itself followed by others from Moriah, Raccoon, Crawfish, and evangeline. Starsinger also let her feelings ("pissed") be known. And even Jander, the Clueless Samaritan who had responded to Bungle's cries for help and uncaged him shortly after the incident, expressed his regret once apprised of Bungle's deeds, which he allowed to be "despicable."

A sense was brewing that something needed to be done—done soon and in something like an organized fashion—about Mr. Bungle, in particular, and about MUD rape, in general. Regarding the general problem, evangeline, who identified herself as a survivor of both vir-tual rape ("many times over") and real-life sexual assault, floated a cautious proposal for a MOO-wide powwow on the subject of virtual sex offenses and what mechanisms if any might be put in place to deal with their future occurrence. As for the specific problem, the answer no doubt seemed obvious to many. But it wasn't until the evening of the second day after the incident that legba, finally and rather solemnly, gave it voice: "I am requesting that Mr. Bungle be toaded for raping Starsinger and I. I have never done this before, and have thought about it for days. He hurt us both."

That was all. Three simple sentences posted to *social. Reading them, an outsider might never guess that they were an application for a death warrant. Even an outsider familiar with other MUDs might not guess it, since in many of them "toading" still refers to a command that, true to the gameworlds' sword-and-sorcery origins, simply turns a player into a toad, wiping the player's description and attributes and replacing them with those of the slimy amphibian. Bad luck for sure, but not quite as bad as what happens when the same command is invoked in the MOOish strains of MUD: not only are the description and attributes of the toaded player erased, but the account itself goes too. The annihilation of the character, thus, is total.

And nothing less than total annihilation, it seemed, would do to settle LambdaMOO's accounts with Mr. Bungle. Within minutes of the posting of legba's appeal, SamIAm, the Australian Deleuzean, who had witnessed much of the attack from the back room of his suburban Sydney home, seconded the motion with a brief message crisply entitled "Toad the fukr." SamIAm's posting was seconded almost as quickly by that of Bakunin, covictim of Mr. Bungle and well-known radical, who in real life happened also to be married to the real-life legba. And over the course of the next 24 hours as many as 50 players made it known, on *social and in a variety of other forms and forums, that they would be pleased to see Mr. Bungle erased from the face of the MOO. And with dissent so far confined to a dozen or so antitoading hardliners, the numbers suggested that the citizenry was indeed moving toward a resolve to have Bungle's virtual head.

There was one small but stubborn obstacle in the way of this resolve, however, and that was a curious state of social affairs known in some quarters of the MOO as the New Direction. It was all very fine, you see, for the LambdaMOO rabble to get it in their heads to liquidate one of their peers, but when the time came to actually do the deed it would require the services of a nobler class of character. It would require a wizard. Masterprogrammers of the MOO, spelunkers of the database's deepest code-structures and custodians of its day-to-day administrative trivia, wizards are also the only players empowered to issue the toad command, a feature maintained on nearly all MUDs as a quick-and-dirty means of social control. But the wizards of LambdaMOO, after years of adjudicating all manner of interplayer disputes with little to show for it but their own weariness and the smoldering resentment of the general populace, had decided they'd had enough of the social sphere. And so, four months before the Bungle incident, the archwizard Haakon (known in RL as Pavel Curtis, Xerox researcher and LambdaMOO's principal architect) formalized this decision in a document called "LambdaMOO Takes a New Direction," which he placed in the living room for all to see. In it, Haakon announced that the wizards from that day forth were pure technicians. From then on, they would make no decisions affecting the social life of the MOO, but only implement whatever decisions the community as a whole directed them to. From then on, it was decreed, LambdaMOO would just have to grow up and solve its problems on its own.

Faced with the task of inventing its own self-governance from scratch, the LambdaMOO population had so far done what any other loose, amorphous agglomeration of individuals would have done: they'd let it slide. But now the task took on new urgency. Since getting the wizards to toad Mr. Bungle (or to toad the likes of him in the future) required a convincing case that the cry for his head came from the community at large, then the community itself would have to be defined; and if the community was to be convincingly defined, then some form of social organization, no matter how rudimentary, would have to be settled on. And thus, as if against its will, the question of what to do about Mr. Bungle began to shape itself into a sort of referendum on the political future of the MOO. Arguments broke out on *social and elsewhere that had only superficially to do with Bungle (since everyone agreed he was a cad) and everything to do with where the participants stood on LambdaMOO's crazy-quilty political map. Parliamentarian legalist types argued that unfortunately Bungle could not legitimately be toaded at all, since there were no explicit MOO rules against rape, or against just about anything else—and the sooner such rules were established, they added, and maybe even a full-blown judiciary system complete with elected officials and prisons to enforce those rules, the better. Others, with a royalist streak in them, seemed to feel that Bungle's as-yet unpunished outrage only proved this New Direction silliness had gone on long enough, and that it was high time the wizardocracy returned to the position of swift and decisive leadership their player class was born to.

And then there were what I'll call the technolibertarians. For them, MUD rapists were of course assholes, but the presence of assholes on the system was a technical inevitability, like noise on a phone line, and best dealt with not through repressive social disciplinary mechanisms but through the timely deployment of defensive software tools. Some asshole blasting violent, graphic language at you? Don't whine to the authorities about it—hit the @gag command and the asshole's statements will be blocked from your screen (and only yours). It's simple, it's effective, and it censors no one.

But the Bungle case was rather hard on such arguments. For one thing, the extremely public nature of the living room meant that gagging would spare the victims only from witnessing their own violation, but not from having others witness it. You might want to argue that what those victims didn't directly experience couldn't hurt them, but consider how that wisdom would sound to a woman who'd been, say, fondled by strangers while passed out drunk and you have a rough idea how it might go over with a crowd of hard-core MOOers. Consider, for another thing, that many of the biologically female participants in the Bungle debate had been around long enough to grow lethally weary of the gag-and-get-over-it school of virtual-rape counseling, with its fine line between empowering victims and holding them responsible for their own suffering, and its shrugging indifference to the window of pain between the moment the rape-text starts flowing and the moment a gag shuts it off. From the outset it was clear that the technolibertarians were going to have to tiptoe through this issue with care, and for the most part they did.

Yet no position was trickier to maintain than that of the MOO's resident anarchists. Like the technolibbers, the anarchists didn't care much for punishments or policies or power elites. Like them, they hoped the MOO could be a place where people interacted fulfillingly without the need for such things. But their high hopes were complicated, in general, by a somewhat less thoroughgoing faith in technology ("Even if you can't tear down the master's house with the master's tools"—read a slogan written into one anarchist player's self-description—"it is a damned good place to start"). And at present they were additionally complicated by the fact that the most vocal anarchists in the discussion were none other than legba, Bakunin, and SamIAm, who wanted to see Mr. Bungle toaded as badly as anyone did.

Needless to say, a pro-death-penalty platform is not an especially comfortable one for an anarchist to sit on, so these particular anarchists were now at great pains to sever the conceptual ties between toading and capital punishment. Toading, they insisted (almost convincingly), was much more closely analogous to banishment; it was a kind of turning of the communal back on the offending party, a collective action which, if carried out properly, was entirely consistent with anarchist models of community. And carrying it out properly meant first and foremost building a consensus around it—a messy process for which there were no easy technocratic substitutes. It was going to take plenty of good old-fashioned, jawbone-intensive grassroots organizing.

So that when the time came, at 7 p.m. PST on the evening of the third day after the occurrence in the living room, to gather in evangeline's room for her proposed real-time open conclave, Bakunin and legba were among the first to arrive. But this was hardly to be an anarchist-dominated affair, for the room was crowding rapidly with representatives of all the MOO's political stripes, and even a few wizards. Hagbard showed up, and Autumn and Quastro, Puff, JoeFeedback, L-dopa and Bloaf, HerkieCosmo, Silver Rocket, Karl Porcupine, Matchstick—the names piled up and the discussion gathered momentum under their weight. Arguments multiplied and mingled, players talked past and through each other, the textual clutter of utterances and gestures filled up the screen like thick cigar smoke. Peaking in number at around 30, this was one of the largest crowds that ever gathered in a single LambdaMOO chamber, and while evangeline had given her place a description that made it "infinite in expanse and fluid in form," it now seemed anything but roomy. You could almost feel the claustrophobic air of the place, dank and overheated by virtual bodies, pressing against your skin.

I know you could because I too was there, making my lone and insignificant appearance in this story. Completely ignorant of any of the goings-on that had led to the meeting, I wandered in purely to see what the crowd was about, and though I observed the proceedings for a good while, I confess I found it hard to grasp what was going on. I was still the rankest of newbies then, my MOO legs still too unsteady to make the leaps of faith, logic, and empathy required to meet the spectacle on its own terms. I was fascinated by the concept of virtual rape, but I couldn't quite take it seriously.

In this, though, I was in a small and mostly silent minority, for the discussion that raged around me was of an almost unrelieved earnestness, bent, it seemed, on examining every last aspect and implication of Mr. Bungle's crime. There were the central questions, of course: thumbs up or down on Bungle's virtual existence? And if down, how then to insure that his toading was not just some isolated lynching but a first step toward shaping LambdaMOO into a legitimate community? Surrounding these, however, a tangle of weighty side issues proliferated. What, some wondered, was the real-life legal status of the offense? Could Bungle's university administrators punish him for sexual harassment? Could he be prosecuted under California state laws against obscene phone calls? Little enthusiasm was shown for pursuing either of these lines of action, which testifies both to the uniqueness of the crime and to the nimbleness with which the discussants were negotiating its idiosyncrasies. Many were the casual references to Bungle's deed as simply "rape," but these in no way implied that the players had lost sight of all distinctions between the virtual and physical versions, or that they believed Bungle should be dealt with in the same way a real-life criminal would. He had committed a MOO crime, and his punishment, if any, would be meted out via the MOO.

On the other hand, little patience was shown toward any attempts to downplay the seriousness of what Mr. Bungle had done. When the affable HerkieCosmo proposed, more in the way of a hypothesis than an assertion, that "perhaps it's better to release . . . violent tendencies in a virtual environment rather than in real life," he was tut-tutted so swiftly and relentlessly that he withdrew the hypothesis altogether, apologizing humbly as he did so. Not that the assembly was averse to putting matters into a more philosophical perspective. "Where does the body end and the mind begin?" young Quastro asked, amid recurring attempts to fine-tune the differences between real and virtual violence. "Is not the mind a part of the body?" "În MOO, the body IS the mind," offered HerkieCosmo gamely, and not at all implausibly, demonstrating the ease with which very knotty metaphysical conundrums come undone in VR. The not-so-aptly named Obvious seemed to agree, arriving after deep consideration of the nature of Bungle's crime at the hardly novel yet now somehow newly resonant conjecture "All reality might consist of ideas, who knows."

On these and other matters the anarchists, the libertarians, the legalists, the wizardists—and the wizards—all had their thoughtful say. But as the evening wore on and the talk grew more heated and more heady, it seemed increasingly clear that the vigorous intelligence being brought to bear on this swarm of issues wasn't going to result in anything remotely like resolution. The perspectives were just too varied, the meme-scape just too slippery. Again and again, arguments that looked at first to be heading in a decisive direction ended up chasing their own tails; and slowly, depressingly, a dusty haze of irrelevance gathered over the proceedings.

It was almost a relief, therefore, when midway through the evening Mr. Bungle himself, the living, breathing cause of all this talk, teleported into the room. Not that it was much of a surprise. Oddly enough, in the three days since his release from Zippy's cage, Bungle had returned more than once to wander the public spaces of Lambda-MOO, walking willingly into one of the fiercest storms of ill will and invective ever to rain down on a player. He'd been taking it all with a curious and mostly silent passivity, and when challenged face to virtual face by both legba and the genderless elder statescharacter PatGently to defend himself on *social, he'd demurred, mumbling something about Christ and expiation. He was equally quiet now, and his reception was still uniformly cool. legba fixed an arctic stare on him—"no hate, no anger, no interest at all. Just . . . watching."

Others were more actively unfriendly. "Asshole," spat Karl Porcupine, "creep." But the harshest of the MOO's hostility toward him had already been vented, and the attention he drew now was motivated more, it seemed, by the opportunity to probe the rapist's mind, to find out what made it tick and if possible how to get it to tick differently. In short, they wanted to know why he'd done it. So they asked him.

And Mr. Bungle thought about it. And as eddies of discussion and debate continued to swirl around him, he thought about it some more. And then he said this:

> "I engaged in a bit of a psychological device that is called thought-polarization, the fact that this is not RL simply added to heighten the affect of the device. It was purely a sequence of events with no consequence on my RL existence."

They might have known. Stilted though its diction was, the gist of the answer was simple, and something many in the room had probably already surmised: Mr. Bungle was a psycho. Not, perhaps, in real life—but then in real life it's possible for reasonable people to assume, as Bungle clearly did, that what transpires between word-costumed characters within the boundaries of a makebelieve world is, if not mere play, then at most some kind of emotional laboratory experiment. Inside the MOO, however, such thinking marked a person as one of two basically subcompetent types. The first was the newbie, in which case the confusion was understandable, since there were few MOOers who had not, upon their first visits as anonymous "guest" characters, mistaken the place for a vast playpen in which they might act out their wildest fantasies without fear of censure. Only with time and the acquisition of a fixed character do players tend to make the critical passage from anonymity to pseudonymity, developing the concern for their character's reputation that marks the attainment of virtual adulthood. But while Mr. Bungle hadn't been around as long as most MOOers, he'd been around long enough to leave his newbie status behind, and his delusional statement therefore placed him among the second type: the sociopath.

And as there is but small percentage in arguing with a head case, the room's attention gradually abandoned Mr. Bungle and returned to the discussions that had previously occupied it. But if the debate had been edging toward ineffectuality before, Bungle's anticlimactic appearance had evidently robbed it of any forward motion whatsoever. What's more, from his lonely corner of the room Mr. Bungle kept issuing periodic expressions of a prickly sort of remorse, interlaced with sarcasm and belligerence, and though it was hard to tell if he wasn't still just conducting his experiments, some people thought his regret genuine enough that maybe he didn't deserve to be toaded after all. Logically, of course, discussion of the principal issues at hand didn't require unanimous belief that Bungle was an irredeemable bastard, but now that cracks were showing in that unanimity, the last of the meeting's fervor seemed to be draining out through them.

People started drifting away. Mr. Bungle left first, then others followed—one by one, in twos and threes, hugging friends and waving goodnight. By 9:45 only a handful remained, and the great debate had wound down into casual conversation, the melancholy remains of another fruitless good idea. The arguments had been well-honed, certainly, and perhaps might prove useful in some as-yet-unclear long run. But at this point what seemed clear was that evangeline's meeting had died, at last, and without any practical results to mark its passing.

It was also at this point, most likely, that JoeFeedback reached his decision. JoeFeedback was a wizard, a taciturn sort of fellow who'd sat brooding on the sidelines all evening. He hadn't said a lot, but what he had said indicated that he took the crime committed against legba and Starsinger very seriously, and that he felt no particular compassion toward the character who had committed it. But on the other hand he had made it equally plain that he took the elimination of a fellow player just as seriously, and moreover that he had no desire to return to the days of wizardly fiat. It must have been difficult, therefore, to reconcile the conflicting impulses churning within him at that moment. In fact, it was probably impossible, for as much as he would have liked to make himself an instrument of LambdaMOO's collective will, he surely realized that under the present order of things he must in the final analysis either act alone or not act at all.

So JoeFeedback acted alone.

He told the lingering few players in the room that he had to go, and then he went. It was a minute or two before ten. He did it quietly and he did it privately, but all anyone had to do to know he'd done it was to type the @who command, which was normally what you typed if you wanted to know a player's present location and the time he last logged in. But if you had run a @who on Mr. Bungle not too long after JoeFeedback left evangeline's room, the database would have told you something different.

"Mr. Bungle," it would have said, "is not the name of any player."

The date, as it happened, was April Fool's Day, and it would still be April Fool's Day for another two hours. But this was no joke: Mr. Bungle was truly dead and truly gone.

They say that LambdaMOO has never been the same since Mr. Bungle's toading. They say as well that nothing's really changed. And though it skirts the fuzziest of dream-logics to say that both these statements are true, the MOO is just the sort of fuzzy, dreamlike place in which such contradictions thrive.

Certainly whatever civil society now informs LambdaMOO owes its existence to the Bungle Affair. The archwizard Haakon made sure of that. Away on business for the duration of the episode, Haakon returned to find its wreckage strewn across the tiny universe he'd set in motion. The death of a player, the trauma of several others, and the angst-ridden conscience of his colleague JoeFeedback presented themselves to his concerned and astonished attention, and he resolved to see if he couldn't learn some lesson from it all. For the better part of a day he brooded over the record of events and arguments left in *social, then he sat pondering the chaotically evolving shape of his creation, and at the day's end he descended once again into the social arena of the MOO with another history-altering proclamation.

It was probably his last, for what he now decreed was the final, missing piece of the New Direction. In a few days, Haakon announced, he would build into the database a system of petitions and ballots whereby anyone could put to popular vote any social scheme requiring wizardly powers for its implementation, with the results of the vote to be binding on the wizards. At last and for good, the awkward gap between the will of the players and the efficacy of the technicians would be closed. And though some anarchists grumbled about the irony of Haakon's dictatorially imposing universal suffrage on an unconsulted populace, in general the citizens of LambdaMOO seemed to find it hard to fault a system more purely democratic than any that could ever exist in real life. Eight months and a dozen ballot measures later, widespread participation in the new regime has produced a small arsenal of mechanisms for dealing with the types of violence that called the system into being. MOO residents now have access to a @boot command, for instance, with which to summarily eject berserker "guest" characters. And players can bring suit against one another through an ad hoc arbitration system in which mutually agreed-upon judges have at their disposition the full range of wizardly punishments—up to and including the capital.

Yet the continued dependence on death as the ultimate keeper of the peace suggests that this new MOO order may not be built on the most solid of foundations. For if life on LambdaMOO began to acquire more coherence in the wake of the toading, death retained all the fuzziness of pre-Bungle days. This truth was rather dramatically borne out, not too many days after Bungle departed, by the arrival of a strange new character named Dr. Jest. There was a forceful eccentricity to the newcomer's manner, but the oddest thing about his style was its striking yet unnameable familiarity. And when he developed the annoying habit of stuffing fellow players into a jar containing a tiny simulacrum of a certain deceased rapist, the source of this familiarity became obvious:

Mr. Bungle had risen from the grave.

In itself, Bungle's reincarnation as Dr. Jest was a remarkable turn of events, but perhaps even more remarkable was the utter lack of amazement with which the LambdaMOO public took note of it. To be sure, many residents were appalled by the brazenness of Bungle's return. In fact, one of the first petitions circulated under the new voting system was a request for Dr. Jest's toading that almost immediately gathered 52 signatures (but has failed so far to reach ballot status). Yet few were unaware of the ease with which the toad proscription could be circumvented—all the toadee had to do (all the urBungle at NYU presumably had done) was to go to the minor hassle of acquiring a new Internet account, and LambdaMOO's character registration program would then simply treat the known felon as an entirely new and innocent person. Nor was this ease generally understood to represent a failure of toading's social disciplinary function. On the contrary, it only underlined the truism (repeated many times throughout the debate over Mr. Bungle's fate) that his punishment, ultimately, had been no more or less symbolic than his crime.

What *was* surprising, however, was that Mr. Bungle/Dr. Jest seemed to have taken the symbolism to heart. Dark themes still obsessed him—the objects he created gave off wafts of Nazi imagery and medical torture—but he no longer radiated the aggressively antisocial vibes he had before. He was a lot less unpleasant to look at (the outrageously seedy clown description had been replaced by that of a mildly creepy but actually rather natty young man, with "blue eyes . . . suggestive of conspiracy, untamed eroticism and perhaps a sense of understanding of the future"), and aside from the occasional jar-stuffing incident, he was also a lot less dangerous to be around. It was obvious he'd undergone some sort of personal transformation in the days since I'd first glimpsed him back in evangeline's crowded room—nothing radical maybe, but powerful nonetheless, and resonant enough with my own experience, I felt, that it might be more than professionally interesting to talk with him, and perhaps compare notes.

For I too was undergoing a transformation in the aftermath of that night in evangeline's, and I'm still not entirely sure what to make of it. As I pursued my runaway fascination with the discussion I had heard there, as I pored over the *social debate and got to know legba and some of the other victims and witnesses, I could feel my newbie consciousness falling away from me. Where before I'd found it hard to take virtual rape seriously, I now was finding it difficult to remember how I could ever not have taken it seriously. I was proud to have arrived at this perspective—it felt like an exotic sort of achievement, and it definitely made my ongoing experience of the MOO a richer one.

But it was also having some unsettling effects on the way I looked at the rest of the world. Sometimes, for instance, it was hard for me to understand why RL society classifies RL rape alongside crimes against person or property. Since rape can occur without any physical pain or damage, I found myself reasoning, then it must be classed as a crime against the mind—more intimately and deeply hurtful, to be sure, than cross-burnings, wolf whistles, and virtual rape, but undeniably located on the same conceptual continuum. I did not, however, conclude as a result that rapists were protected in any fashion by the First Amendment. Quite the opposite, in fact: the more seriously I took the notion of virtual rape, the less seriously I was able to take the notion of freedom of speech, with its tidy division of the world into the symbolic and the real.

Let me assure you, though, that I am not presenting these thoughts as arguments. I offer them, rather, as a picture of the sort of mindset that deep immersion in a virtual world has inspired in me. I offer them also, therefore, as a kind of prophecy. For whatever else these thoughts tell me, I have come to believe that they announce the final stages of our decades-long passage into the Information Age, a paradigm shift that the classic liberal firewall between word and deed (itself a product of an earlier paradigm shift commonly known as the Enlightenment) is not likely to survive intact. After all, anyone the least bit familiar with the workings of the new era's definitive technology, the computer, knows that it operates on a principle impracticably difficult to distinguish from the pre-Enlightenment principle of the magic word: the commands you type into a computer are a kind of speech that doesn't so much communicate as *make things happen*, directly and ineluctably, the same way pulling a trigger does. They are incantations, in other words, and anyone at all attuned to the technosocial megatrends of the moment—from the growing dependence of economies on the global flow of intensely fetishized words and numbers to the burgeoning ability of bioengineers to speak the spells written in the four-letter text of DNA—knows that the logic of the incantation is rapidly permeating the fabric of our lives.

And it's precisely this logic that provides the real magic in a place like LambdaMOO—not the fictive trappings of voodoo and shapeshifting and wizardry, but the conflation of speech and act that's inevitable in any computer-mediated world, be it Lambda or the increasingly wired world at large. This is dangerous magic, to be sure, a potential threat—if misconstrued or misapplied—to our always precarious freedoms of expression, and as someone who lives by his words I do not take the threat lightly. And yet, on the other hand, I can no longer convince myself that our wishful insulation of language from the realm of action has ever been anything but a valuable kludge, a philosophically damaged stopgap against oppression that would just have to do till something truer and more elegant came along.

Am I wrong to think this truer, more elegant thing can be found on LambdaMOO? Perhaps, but I continue to seek it there, sensing its presence just beneath the surface of every interaction. I have even thought, as I said, that discussing with Dr. Jest our shared experience of the workings of the MOO might help me in my search. But when that notion first occurred to me, I still felt somewhat intimidated by his lingering criminal aura, and I hemmed and hawed a good long time before finally resolving to drop him MOO-mail requesting an interview. By then it was too late. For reasons known only to himself, Dr. Jest had stopped logging in. Maybe he'd grown bored with the MOO. Maybe the loneliness of ostracism had gotten to him. Maybe a psycho whim had carried him far away or maybe he'd quietly acquired a third character and started life over with a cleaner slate.

Wherever he'd gone, though, he left behind the room he'd created for himself—a treehouse "tastefully decorated" with rare-book shelves, an operating table, and a life-size William S. Burroughs doll— and he left it unlocked. So I took to checking in there occasionally, and I still do from time to time. I head out of my own cozy nook (inside a TV set inside the little red hotel inside the Monopoly board inside the dining room of LambdaMOO), and I teleport on over to the treehouse, where the room description always tells me Dr. Jest is present but asleep, in the conventional depiction for disconnected characters. The not-quite-emptiness of the abandoned room invariably instills in me an uncomfortable mix of melancholy and the creeps, and I stick around only on the off chance that Dr. Jest will wake up, say hello, and share his understanding of the future with me.

He won't, of course, but this is no great loss. Increasingly, the complex magic of the MOO interests me more as a way to live the present than to understand the future. And it's never very long before I leave Dr. Jest's lonely treehouse and head back to the mansion, to see some friends.

═══

I won't pretend I knew what I was doing when I wrote "A Rape in Cyberspace." I thought, to be honest and if you can believe it, that I was setting down little more than an engaging true-life fable, played out in a realm of experience so circumscribed and so unique that no one (except perhaps the residents of LambdaMOO itself) could possibly take it as anything but a curiosity, a traveler's tale brought back from strange climes and only barely pertinent to the world as we know it. The philosophical excursions woven into the piece reached for a certain universal relevance, to be sure, but they were almost an afterthought, added at the last moment in hopes of teasing from the story a broader significance I wasn't entirely sure it had.

I needn't have bothered, though. For in the deluge of online responses to which I was soon exposed, very few readers remarked directly on my transparent attempts at intellectual provocation. It was the story itself that provoked them, or elements of the story anyway. And it was the story seen not as a piece of exotica but as a dispatch from a place maybe a little too close to home: the busy intersection of sex, violence, and representation around which late twentieth-century American culture hovers like a soul obsessed.

That the story tapped such a deep vein of anxieties is a development I look on now with some sense of gratification, yet I can't say I was exactly enjoying myself as those anxieties began flooding in my general direction. Opinions ran strong, and those that reflected not-so-very-well on me—or on the acts and attitudes of the tiny, textual world I had tried to represent as accurately as possible—seemed to run strongest. "Media culture keeps blurring the line between real offense and imaginary offense, but this is ridiculous," wrote one participant in a lengthy discussion on the haut-cachet New York bulletin-board system ECHO. "That article had no journalistic value whatsoever" added another ECHO-dweller, fuming at what many in that virtual community saw as crass exploitation of the unsettling and admittedly problematic notion of "virtual rape": "It was just using the RAPE catchphrase to SELL PAPERS . . . and it brutally trivializes people who have suffered through the real thing."

This hurt. The trivialization charge was an argument I recognized as part of the rhetorical arsenal of pro-sex feminists in their righteous battle against legal scholar Catharine MacKinnon's creepy redefinitions of porn as rape (and more broadly, of word as deed), and I didn't feel at all good about being placed conceptually in her camp. Compared to this insult, one Echoid's crudely worded announcement that

he had used a copy of my article to tidy himself after a bowel movement seemed a friendly chuck under the chin. So I was relieved when
West Coast feminist pornographer (and disaffected former MacKin-
nonite) Lisa Palac posted on ECHO in the article's favor, downplaying
any fuss over its use of the word *rape* as essentially semantic, and finding in it an effective illustration of "how online worlds and identities
reflect . . . RL socialization":

> I can't tell you how often I am interviewed by reporters who are
> under the assumption that taking on an online identity is "risk-
> free." And that for some reason, going online will be free from
> the social/cultural shapes as we know them. . . . [The subject of]
> this article may be extreme, but it disproves the "all is safe in
> cyberspace" notion.

Palac's note signaled, or so I thought, that the debate was mellow-
ing and would soon enough be off my screen and out of my life. In
fact, though, what it mainly signaled was that the debate had reached
the other side of the country and would soon become fodder for the
topic-hungry habitués of the WELL, a Bay Area bulletin-board system
even more vigorously literate than ECHO. Once there, the discussion
grew a notch more thoughtful, though no less contentious. Even more
than the ECHO conference, the WELL's discussion seemed haunted by
the ghosts of nearly every nineties polemic to have grappled with the
issue of dangerous expression, from Anita Hill to the campus curricu-
lum battles to the *succès de scandale* of "Beavis and Butt-head." The
twists and turns of the arguments grew so convoluted that at one
point, if I followed correctly, my account of Mr. Bungle's fate was
determined to imply that Shakespeare, Sophocles, and Ibsen should
also have been lynched on grounds of subjecting countless audience
members to the emotional violence of catharsis.

More effectively critical, though, were the comments of R. U.
Sirius, cofounder and guiding light of the magazine *Mondo 2000*. "The
conflation of language and mediated activity with real activity seems
to be more or less complete," wrote Sirius, in a formulation not at all
surprising to anyone familiar with *Mondo 2000*'s reputation as a nest
of giddy, pop-Baudrillardian armchair prophets stoned out of their
minds on the ascendancy of digital simulation. What might have sur-

prised those unable or unwilling to look past that caricature, however, was the entirely characteristic moral rigor Sirius then brought to bear on LambdaMOO's own giddy romp through the conflations of the hyperreal:

> These people all volunteered to act in a theater of the imagination and then got scared. Do we want Disney World? As the simulacrum becomes a bigger part of our lives, do we demand that people clip their imaginations at the place where it feels comfortable? . . . I think that freedom would be well served by simple toughening up.

And this hurt too. It was bad enough feeling like a rhetorical football, after all, without feeling part of me wanting to agree with some of those landing the hardest kicks.

Days of online discussion started piling up into weeks, and I began to wonder: How long could this go on? And how long would it be before the turbulence of the debate spilled over into less neatly compartmentalized venues for social interaction, like my more casual online encounters on the MOO, or the offline interactions I still respectfully referred to as real life? The WELL conference slowed down eventually, but controversy over the tale of Mr. Bungle spread into other online conferencing forums: Internet mailing lists, Usenet newsgroups, Compuserve. To this day, in fact, four months after its original publication, the story (stripped down to ASCII and turned loose to wander the nets) continues to find new pockets of interest and to gather online discussion around itself. Yet in the end, what I had dreaded most —the general irruption of the controversy into other areas of my life —has failed to materialize. LambdaMOOers, for the most part, seem to have accepted my interpretation of their world as true to their own experiences and left it at that. Most real-lifers unacquainted with any form of cyberspace, on the other hand, have found in the story a fascinating glimpse of a realm too distant from their own to pass judgment on—a parallel universe perhaps, or maybe a hint of their own future.

Which leaves only the denizens of the bulletin-board cybercosm to argue over the meaning of the life and crimes of Mr. Bungle. And, frankly, the fact that they have done so with such vociferous gusto remains something of a puzzle to me. Certainly, arguing is what people mainly do in such settings, and certainly, as I suggested earlier, the bleedthrough from larger cultural concerns about texts and violence has fed much of the fracas. Yet the more I ponder the furious on-line response to my story, the more I suspect the real object of that fury is neither LambdaMoo nor America's latest culture wars, but the ambiguous nature of online discourse itself.

Perched on a tightwire between the reasoned deliberation of text and the emotional immediacy of conversation, online communication sets itself up for a fall that is constantly realized. Fooled by the cool surface of electronic text, people lob messages cast in aggressively forensic impersonality into the midst of this combustibly personal medium, and the result, routinely, is just the sort of flame war I found myself embroiled in: a heatedly antagonistic exchange fueled by the most livid of emotions yet pretending in its rhetorical strategies to the most rational of dialogue. And in some sense, I think, the two sides of the Bungle war have taken up the two sides of this basic tension: the rational recognition (on the part of those who found the story ridiculous) that ultimately anything that happens online is "only words on a screen" countered by the emotional understanding (on the part of those who found the story compelling) that words can have powerful and deeply felt effects. It's too much to hope, I suppose, that this tension will ever really be resolved. Still, it's comforting to think that the noisy dialogue sparked by my article has not been only sound and fury. On its surface, of course, the discussion has provided more than its share of insight into a story I myself didn't fully understand when I wrote it. But deeper down, in the very structure of the debate, I have sometimes imagined I can hear the sound of cyberspace groping toward an end to flame wars.

MANUEL DE LANDA

VIRTUAL ENVIRONMENTS AND THE EMERGENCE OF SYNTHETIC REASON

At the end of World War II, Stanislav Ulam and other scientists previously involved in weapons research at Los Alamos discovered the huge potential of computers to create artificial worlds, where simulated experiments could be conducted and where new hypotheses could be framed and tested. The physical sciences were the first ones to tap into this "epistemological reservoir" thanks to the fact that much of their accumulated knowledge had already been given a mathematical form. Among the less mathematized disciplines, those currently taking advantage of virtual environments are psychology and biology (Artificial Intelligence and Artificial Life), although other fields such as economics and linguistics may soon begin to profit from the new research strategies made possible by computer simulations.

Yet before a given scientific discipline can begin to gain from the use of virtual environments, more than just casting old assumptions into mathematical form is necessary. In many cases the assumptions themselves need to be modified. This is clear in the case of Artificial Intelligence (AI) research, much of which is still caught up in older paradigms of what a symbol-manipulating "mind" should be, and hence has not benefited as much as it could from the simulation capabilities of computers. Artificial Life (AL), on the other hand, has the advantage that the evolutionary biologist's conceptual base has been purged from classical notions of what living creatures and evolution are supposed to be, which has put this discipline in an excellent position to profit from the new research tool represented by abstract spaces. Since this is a crucial point, let's take a careful look at just what this "purging" has involved.

The first classical notion that had to be eliminated from biology was the Aristotelian concept of an "ideal type"; this was achieved by the development of what came to be known in the 1930s as "population thinking." In the old tradition that dominated biological thought for over two thousand years, a given population of animals was conceived as being the more or less imperfect incarnation of an ideal essence. Thus, for example, in the case of zebras, there would exist an ideal zebra, embodying all the attributes which together make for "zebrahood" (being striped, having hooves, and so on). The existence of this essence would be obscured by the fact that in any given population of zebras the ideal type would be subject to a multiplicity of accidents (of embryological development, for instance), yielding a variety of imperfect realizations. In short, in this view, only the ideal essence is real, with the variations being mere shadows.

When the ideas of Darwin on the role of natural selection and those of Mendel on the dynamics of genetic inheritance were brought together six decades ago, the domination of the Aristotelian paradigm came to an end. It became clear that there was no such thing as a preexistent collection of traits defining "zebrahood." Each of the particular adaptive traits that we observe in real zebras developed along different ancestral lineages, accumulated in the population under the action of different selection pressures, in a process that was completely dependent on specific (and contingent) historical details. In other words, just as these traits (camouflage, running speed, hooves) happened to come together in zebras, they might not have, had the actual history of those populations been different.

Moreover, the engine driving this process is the genetic variability of zebra populations. Only if zebra genes replicate with enough variability can selection pressures have raw materials to work with. Only if enough variant traits arise spontaneously can the sorting process of natural selection bring together those features which today define what a zebra is. For population thinkers, only the variation is real, and the ideal type (the average zebra) is a mere shadow. Thus we have a complete inversion of the classical paradigm.[1]

Further refinement of these notions has led to the more general idea that the coupling of any kind of spontaneous variation to any kind of selection pressure results in a sort of "searching device." This device spontaneously explores a space of possibilities (possible combinations of traits), and is capable of finding, over many generations, more or less stable combinations of features, more or less stable solutions to problems posed by the environment. This device has today been implemented in populations that are not biological: by means of the so-called genetic algorithm (developed by John Holland), a population of computer programs is allowed to replicate in a variable form, and after each generation a test is performed to select those programs that most closely approximate the desired performance. It has been found that this method is capable of zeroing in on the best solutions to a given programming task. In essence, it allows computer scientists to breed new solutions to problems, instead of directly programming those solutions.[2]

═══════

The difference between the genetic algorithm and the more ambitious goals of AL is the same as that between the action of breeding techniques on domesticated plants and animals and the spontaneous evolution of the ancestors of those plants and animals. Whereas in the first case the animal or plant breeder determines the criteria of fitness, in the second there is no outside agency determining what counts as fit. In a sense, that which is fit is simply that which survives, which has led to the criticism that Darwinism's central formula ("survival of the fittest") is a mere tautology ("survival of the survivor"). Partly to avoid this tautology, the formula is today being replaced by another one: survival of the stable.[3]

The central idea, the notion of an "evolutionary stable strategy," was formulated with respect to behavioral strategies (such as those involved in territorial or courtship behavior in animals), but it can be extended to apply to the "engineering strategies" involved in putting together camouflage, locomotor speed, and the other traits that came together to form the zebras mentioned earlier. The essence of this approach is that the "searching device" constituted by variation and selection can find the optimal solution to a given problem posed by the environment, and that once the optimal solution has been found, any mutant strategy arising in the population is bound to be defeated. The stable strategy will be, in this sense, stable against invasion. To put it in visual terms, it is as if the space of possibilities explored by the "searching device" included mountains and valleys, with the mountain peaks representing points of optimal performance. Selection pressures allow the gene pool of a reproductive population to slowly climb those peaks, and once a peak has been reached, natural selection keeps the population there.

One may wonder just what has been achieved by switching from the concept of a "fittest mutant" to that of an "optimal" one, except perhaps that the latter can be defined contextually as "optimal given existing constraints." However, the very idea that selection pressures are strong enough to pin populations down to "adaptive peaks" has itself come under intense criticism. One line of argument says that any given population is subject to many different pressures, some of them favoring different optimal results. For example, the decorative feathers of a peacock are thought to have arisen due to the selection pressure exerted by "choosy" females, who mated only with those males exhibiting the most attractive plumage. Yet those same vivid colors which seduce the females also attract predators. Hence the male peacock's feathers are subject to conflicting selection pressures, and in this circumstance it is highly improbable that the peacock's solution will be optimal and much more likely that it will represent a compromise. Several such suboptimal compromises may be possible, so that the idea that the solution arrived at by the "searching device" is unique needs to be abandoned.[4] But if unique and optimal solutions are not the source of stability in biology, then what is?

The answer to this question represents the second key idea around which the field of AL revolves. It is also crucial to understanding the potential application of virtual environments to fields such as economics. The old conceptions of stability (in terms of either optimality or principles of least effort) derive from nineteenth-century equilibrium thermodynamics. It is well-known that philosophers like Auguste Comte and Herbert Spencer (author of the formula "survival of the fittest") introduced thermodynamic concepts into social science. However, some contemporary observers complain that what was so introduced (in economics, for example) represents "more heat than light."[5]

In other words, equilibrium thermodynamics, dealing as it does with systems that are closed to their environment, postulates that stability can be reached only when all useful energy has been transformed into heat. At this point, a static and unique state of equilibrium is reached (heat death). It was this concept of a static equilibrium that late nineteenth-century economists used to systematize the classical notion of an "invisible hand," according to which the forces of supply and demand tend to balance each other out at a point that is optimal in terms of society's utilization of resources. It was partly John von Neumann's work on game theory and economics that helped this notion of stability to become entrenched outside of physics, and from there it found its way into evolutionary biology, through the work of John Maynard Smith.[6]

This static conception of stability was the second classical idea that needed to be eliminated before the full potential of virtual environments could be unleashed. Like population thinking, the fields that provided the needed new insights (the disciplines of far-from-equilibrium thermodynamics and nonlinear mathematics) are also a relatively recent development, associated with Ilya Prigogine and Isabelle Stengers, among others. Unlike the "conservative" systems dealt with by the old science of heat systems that are totally isolated from their surroundings, the new science deals with systems that are subject to a constant flow of matter and energy from the outside. Because this flow must also exit the system in question—that is, the waste products need to be dissipated—such systems are called "dissipative."[7]

For our purposes what matters is that once a continuous flow of matter-energy is included in the model, a wider range of possible forms of dynamic equilibria becomes possible. Of these, only the simplest ones still resemble the old notion of a static stability, and even these simple equilibrium points have novel properties since they are neither unique nor optimal (and yet they are quite as robust as the old ones). Nonstatic equilibria also exist, in the form of periodic cycles, for instance. Perhaps the most novel type of stability is that represented by "deterministic chaos," in which a given population can be pinned down to a stable, yet inherently variable, dynamic state. These new forms of stability have come to be called "attractors," and the transitions that transform one type of attractor into another have been named "bifurcations" (as in the "Hopf bifurcation," which transforms a point attractor into a cyclic one). Let's refer to the cluster of concepts making up this new paradigm of stability as "nonlinear dynamics."[8]

One of the most striking consequences of nonlinear dynamics is that any population (of atoms, molecules, cells, animals, humans) stabilized via attractors will exhibit "emergent properties," that is, properties of the population as a whole not displayed by its individual members in isolation. The notion of an emergent or synergistic property is a rather old one, but for a long time it was not taken very seriously by scientists, since it was associated with quasi-mystical schools of thought such as "vitalism." Today, emergent properties are perfectly legitimate dynamic outcomes for populations stabilized by attractors. To take a well-known example, populations of molecules in certain chemical reactions can suddenly and spontaneously begin to pulsate in perfect synchrony, constituting a veritable "chemical clock": the dynamic state of the molecules may undergo a bifurcation from a static to a cyclic attractor, and in the process the molecules acquire collective rhythmic properties. Other kinds of populations can undergo essentially the same bifurcation and generate spontaneous oscillations. As we will see in more detail later, populations of organizations integrated into trading networks (complex human economies) exhibit stable business cycles of different durations, very possibly due to nonlinear effects.

═══════

When we put the idea of the synergistic interactions that nonlinear dynamics makes possible together with the insights from population theory, we get the following picture: the evolutionary "searching device" constituted by variation coupled with selection does not explore an unstructured space of possibilities, but a space "pre-organized" by attractors and bifurcations. In a way, evolutionary processes simply follow these changing distributions of attractors, slowly advancing from one dynamically stable state to another. For example, given that in this space one possible outcome is a chemical clock, the searching device could have stumbled upon this possibility, which in essence constitutes a primitive form of metabolism.

Thanks to the use of computers to generate virtual environments, the complementary insights of nonlinear dynamics and population theory have been combined in the new discipline of Artificial Life. Without the benefit of simulations, the only other approach to the study of these complex processes would be scientific analysis. But the study of emergent properties does not lend itself to an analytical approach, that is, an approach that dissects a population into its components. Once we perform this dissection, isolating the individuals from each other, any properties caused by their interactions will disappear. What virtual environments provide is a tool to replace (or rather, complement) analysis with synthesis, to deal directly with populations of entities in nonlinear interaction. In the words of AL pioneer Chris Langton:

> Biology has traditionally started at the top, viewing a living organism as a complex biochemical machine, and worked *analytically* downwards from there—through organs, tissues, cells, organelles, membranes, and finally molecules—in its pursuit of the mechanisms of life. Artificial Life starts at the bottom, viewing an organism as a large population of *simple* machines, and works upwards *synthetically* from there, constructing large aggregates of simple, rule-governed objects which interact with one another nonlinearly in the support of life-like, global dynamics. The "key" concept in Artificial Life is *emergent behavior*. Natural life emerges out of the organized interactions of a great number of nonliving molecules, with no global controller responsible for the behavior of every part. . . . It is this bottom-up, distributed, local determination of behavior that Artificial Life employs in its primary methodological approach to the generation of life-like behaviors.[9]

The typical Artificial Life experiment first involves the design of a simplified version of an individual animal, which must possess the equivalent of a set of genetic instructions used both to create its off-spring as well as to be transmitted to that offspring. This transmission must also be "imperfect," so that variation can be generated. Then, whole populations of these "virtual animals" are unleashed, and their evolution under a variety of selection pressures observed. The exercise will be considered successful if novel properties, *unimagined by the designer*, emerge spontaneously.

Depending on the point of view of the designer, these emergent properties may or may not match those observed in reality. A current theme in this field is that one does not have to be exclusively concerned with biological evolution as it has occurred on Earth, since this may have been limited by the contingencies of biological history; there may be much to be learned from evolutionary paths that were not tried out on this planet. In any event, the goal of the simulation is simply to help "synthesize intuitions" in the designer, insights that can then be used to create more realistic simulations. The key point is that the whole process must be *bottom-up*; only the local properties of the virtual creatures need to be predesigned, never the global, population-wide ones.

Unlike that of Artificial Life, the approach of Artificial Intelligence researchers remained (at least until the 1980s) largely top-down and analytical. Instead of treating the symbolic properties being studied as the emergent outcome of a dynamic process, these researchers explicitly put symbols (labels, rules, recipes) and symbol-manipulating skills into the computer. When they realized that logic alone was not enough to manipulate these symbols in a significantly "intelligent" way, they began to extract rules of thumb, tricks of the trade, and other informal heuristic knowledge from human experts, putting these in turn into the machine as fully formed symbolic structures. In other words, in this approach one begins at the top (the global behavior of human brains) instead of at the bottom (the local behavior of neurons). Some successes have been achieved by this approach, notably in simulating skills, such as those involved in playing chess or proving theorems, both of which are in evolutionary terms rather late developments. Yet the symbolic paradigm of AI has failed to capture the dynamics of more elementary skills, such as face recognition or sensory-motor control.[10]

Although a few attempts were made during the 1960s to take a more bottom-up approach to modeling intelligence (for example, the "perceptron"), the defenders of the symbolic paradigm practically killed their rivals in the battle for government research funds. And so the analytical approach dominated the scene until the 1980s, when there occurred a spectacular rebirth of a synthetic design philosophy. This is the new school of AI known as "connectionism." Here, instead of one large, powerful computer serving as a repository for explicit symbols, we find a large number of small, rather simple computing devices (in which all that matters is their state of activation), interacting with one another either to excite or to inhibit each other's degree of activation. These simple processors are then linked together through a pattern of interconnections that can vary in strength. No explicit symbol is ever programmed into the machine since all the information needed to perform a given cognitive task is coded in the interconnection patterns and reinforced by the relative strengths of these interconnections. All computing activity is carried out by the dynamic activity of the simple processors as they interact with one another (as excitations and inhibitions propagate through the network), and the processors arrive at the solution to a problem by settling into a dynamic state of equilibrium. (So far, point attractors are most commonly used, although some designs using cyclic attractors are beginning to appear.) [11]

If there is ever such a thing as a "symbol" here, or rather symbol-using (rule-following) behavior, it emerges from these dynamics. This fact is sometimes expressed by saying that a connectionist device (also called a "neural net") is not programmed by humans, but trained by them, much as a living creature would be trained. In the simplest kind of networks the only cognitive task that can be performed is pattern association. The human trainer presents to the network both patterns to be associated, and after repeated presentations, the network "learns" to associate them by modifying the strength of the interconnections. At that point the network can respond with the second pattern whenever the first one is presented to it.

At the other end of the spectrum of complexity, multilayered networks exhibit emergent cognitive behavior as they are trained. While in the simple case of pattern association much of the thinking is done by the trainer, complex networks (those using "hidden units") perform their own extraction of regularities from the input pattern, concentrating on microfeatures of the input, which many times are not at all obvious to the human trainer. In other words, the network itself "decides" what traits of the pattern it considers salient or relevant.

These networks also have the ability to generalize from the patterns they have learned, and thus are able to recognize a new pattern that is only vaguely related to one to which they have been previously exposed. The ability to perform simple inductive inferences emerges in the network without any need to explicitly program it with the rules of a logical calculus. These designs are also resilient against damage, unlike their symbolic counterparts, which are inherently brittle. But perhaps the main advantage of the bottom-up approach is that its devices can exhibit a degree of "intentionality."

The term "intentionality" is the technical word used by philosophers to describe the relation between a believer and the states of affairs about which his beliefs are held. That is, an important feature of the mental states of human beings and other animals (their beliefs and desires) is that they are about phenomena that lie outside their minds. The top-down, symbolic approach to AI sacrifices this connection by limiting its modeling efforts to relations between symbols: in the analytical approach only the syntactic or formal relations between symbols matter (with the exception of an "internal semantics" involving reference to memorized addresses and the like). Hence these designs must later try to reconnect the cognitive device to the world in which it must function, and it is here that the main drawback lies (unless the "world" in question is a severely restricted domain of the real world, such as the domain of chess). Not so in the synthetic approach:

> The connectionist approach to modelling cognition thus offers a promise in explaining the *aboutness* or *intentionality* of mental states. Representational states, especially those of hidden units, constitute the system's own learned response to inputs. Since they constitute the system's adaptation to the input, there is a clear respect in which they would be *about* objects or events

in the environment if the system were connected, via sensory-motor organs, to that environment. . . . The fact that these representations are also sensitive to context, both external and internal to the system, enhances the plausibility of this claim that the representations are representations of particular states.[12]

So far, the abstract living creatures inhabiting the virtual environments of AL have been restricted to rather inflexible behaviors. One may say that the only kind of behavior that has been modeled is the genetically "hardwired" type displayed by ants or termites. Yet adding connectionist intelligence to these creatures could endow them with enough intentionality to allow researchers to model more flexible, "multiple-choice" behavior, such as that displayed by mammals and birds. We could then expect more complex patterns (territorial or courtship behavior) to emerge in these virtual worlds. AI could also benefit from such a partnership, by tapping the potential of the evolutionary searching device in the exploration of the space of possible network designs. The genetic algorithm, which exploits this possibility, has so far been mostly used for breeding better symbolic designs (production rules).

Furthermore, a virtual space where groups of intentional creatures interact can benefit other disciplines, such as economics or political science. A good example of this is Robert Axelrod's use of a virtual environment to study the evolution of cooperation. His work also exemplifies the complementary use of synthesis (to generate intuitions) and analysis (to formally ground those intuitions). In the words of Douglas Hofstadter:

> Can totally selfish and unconscious organisms living in a common environment come to evolve reliable cooperative strategies? Can cooperation evolve in a world of pure egoists? . . . Well, as it happens, it has now been demonstrated rigorously and definitively that such cooperation can emerge, and it was done through a computer tournament conducted by political scientist Robert Axelrod. . . . More accurately, Axelrod first studied the ways that cooperation evolved by means of a computer tournament, and when general trends emerged, he was able to spot the underlying principles and prove theorems that established the facts and conditions of cooperation's rise from nowhere.[13]

The creatures that Axelrod placed in a virtual environment to conduct his round-robin tournament were not full-fledged intentional
entities of the type envisioned above. Rather, the motivations and
options of the creatures were narrowly circumscribed by using the
formalism of game theory, which studies the dynamics of situations
involving conflicts of interest. In particular, Axelrod's entities were
computer programs, each written by a different programmer playing
a version of the game called "Prisoner's Dilemma." In this imaginary
situation, two accomplices in a crime are captured by the police and
separately offered the following deal: if one accuses his accomplice,
while the other does not, the "betrayer" walks out free, while the
"sucker" receives the stiffest sentence; if, on the other hand, both
claim innocence and avoid betrayal, both receive a more lenient sentence; finally, if both betray each other, they both receive a long
sentence. The dilemma here arises from the fact that even though
the best *overall* outcome is not to betray one's partner, neither can
trust that the other won't try to get the best *individual* outcome (to
walk out free), leaving his accomplice with the "sucker payoff." And
because both prisoners reason in a similar way, both choose betrayal
and the long sentence that comes with it instead of loyalty and its
short sentence.

In the real world we find realizations of this dilemma in, for example, the phenomenon known as "bank runs." When news that a
bank is in trouble first comes out, each individual depositor has two
options: either to rush to the bank and withdraw his savings or to stay
home and allow the bank to recover. Each individual knows that the
best outcome for the community is for everyone to leave his savings
in the bank and so allow it to survive. But no one can afford to be
the one who loses his savings, so all rush to withdraw their money,
thus bankrupting the institution. Hofstadter offers a host of other
examples, including one in which the choice to betray or cooperate
is faced by the participants not once, but repeatedly. For instance,
imagine two "jungle traders" with a rather primitive system of trade:
each simply leaves a bag of goods at a predetermined place and comes
back later to pick up another bag, without ever seeing the trading
partner. The idea is that, for every transaction, one is faced with
a dilemma, since one can profit most by leaving an empty bag and

sticking the other with the "sucker payoff." But doing so endangers the trading situation and hence there is more to lose. (This is called the "Iterated Prisoner's Dilemma.")

Axelrod's creatures played such an iterated version of the game with one another. What matters to us is that after several decades of applying analytical techniques to the study of these situations, the idea that "good guys finish last" (that the most rational strategy is to betray one's partner) had become entrenched in academic (and think tank) circles. When Axelrod first requested entries for his virtual tournament, most of the programs he received were "betrayers." Oddly, the winner was not: it was "nice" (it always cooperated in the first encounter in order to give a sign of good faith and begin the trading situation); it was "retaliatory" (if betrayed it would respond with betrayal in the next encounter); and yet it was "forgiving" (after retaliating it was willing to reestablish a partnership). As mentioned above, these were not truly intentional creatures, so the properties of being "nice, retaliatory, and forgiving" were like emergent properties of a much simpler design. The program's name was TIT-FOR-TAT, and its actual strategy was always to cooperate in the first move and thereafter to do what the other player did in the previous move. This program won because the criterion for success was not how many partners one beat, but how much overall trade one achieved.

Because the idea that "good guys finish last" had become entrenched, further analysis of the situation (which could have uncovered the fact that this principle does not apply to the iterated version of the game) was blocked. What was needed was to open this path by using a virtual environment to "synthesize" a fresh intuition. In a sense, that is just what Axelrod did. He then went further and used more elaborate simulations (including one in which the creatures replicated, with the number of progeny being related to the trading success of the parent) to generate further intuitions as to how cooperative strategies could evolve in an ecological environment, and how robust and stable these strategies were, among other questions. Evolutionary biologists, armed with these fresh insights, have now discovered that apes in their natural habitats play a version of TIT-FOR-TAT.[14] Thus, while some of the uses of virtual environments presuppose that old and entrenched ideas (about essences or optimality) have been superseded, these abstract worlds can also be used to synthesize the intuitions needed to dislodge other ideas blocking the way to a better understanding of the dynamics of reality.

Population thinking seems to have ousted "essences" from the world of philosophy once and for all. Nonlinear dynamics, and more specifically, the notion of an "emergent property," would seem to signal the death of the philosophical position known as "reductionism" (by which all phenomena can in principle be reduced to those of physics). It is clear now that at every level of complexity, there will be emergent properties that are irreducible to the lower levels simply because, when one switches to an examination of lower-level entities, the properties which emerge due to their interactions disappear. Connectionism, in turn, offers a completely new understanding of the way that rule-following behavior can emerge from a system in which there are no explicit rules or symbols whatsoever. This would seem destined to end the domination of a conception of language (let's call it "formalism") based on syntactical entities and their formal relations (Saussure's signifiers or Chomsky's rules). Or rather, since the importance of the work of these linguists cannot be denied, the attractors and bifurcations governing the dynamics of neural nets could one day explain how the stable entities studied by Chomskyans and Saussureans emerged in the first place. The grammatical structure of different languages could then be pictured as arising much as the structure of a biological species does: from specific historical processes—the sorting effects of natural selection and the consolidating effects of reproductive isolation, resulting in speciation—and from different sources of nonlinear stabilization and diversification.[15]

Perhaps, once linguists become population thinkers and users of virtual environments, we may witness the emergence of an entirely different type of science of language, one that would be able to explain the dynamic genesis of a new language. For instance, about a millennium ago, the population of Anglo-Saxon peasants inhabiting England suffered the imposition of French as the official language of their land by the Norman invaders. In about two hundred years, and in order to resist this form of linguistic colonialism, the population transformed what was basically a soup of Germanic dialects (with added Scandinavian spices) into something that we recognize as English. No doubt, in order to arrive at modern English another few centuries of transformation were needed, but the backbone of this language had already emerged from the spontaneous labor of a population under the pressure of an invading language.[16] Perhaps one day linguists will be required to test their theories in a virtual environment of interacting intentional entities, so that the rules of grammar they postulate for a language can be shown to emerge spontaneously from the dynamics of a population of speakers (instead of existing in a "synchronic" world, isolated from the actual interactions of several generations of speakers).

Virtual environments may not only allow us to capture the fluid and changing nature of real languages, but could also be used to gain insights into the processes that tend to "freeze" languages, such as the processes of standardization that many European languages underwent beginning in the seventeenth century. Unlike the cases of Spanish, Italian, and French, where the fixing of the rules and vocabulary of the language were enforced by an institution (an academy), in England the process of standardization was carried out via the mass publication of authoritative dictionaries, grammars, and orthographies. Just how these "linguistic engineering" devices achieved the relative freezing of what was formerly a fluid "linguistic matter" could be revealed through a computer simulation. Similarly, whenever a language becomes standardized we witness the political conquest of many "minority" dialects by the dialect of the urban capital (in the case of English, the London dialect). Virtual environments could allow us to model dynamically the spread of the dominant dialect across cultural and geographical barriers, and to see how technologies such as the railroad or the radio (like the BBC) allowed it to surmount such barriers.[17]

Future linguists may one day look back with curiosity at our twentieth-century linguistics, and wonder if our fascination with a static (synchronic) view of language was due to the fact that the languages in which these views were first formulated (French and English) had lost their fluid nature by being artificially frozen a few centuries earlier. These future investigators may also wonder how we thought the stability of linguistic structures could be explained without the concept of an attractor. How, for instance, could the prevalence of certain patterns of sentence structure (subject-verb-object, or "SVO") be explained, or how could bifurcations from one pattern to another be modeled without some form of nonlinear stabilization (English may have switched over a millennium from SOV to SVO)?[18] Tomorrow's linguists will also realize that, because these dynamic processes depend on the existence of heterogeneities and other non-linearities, the reason we could not capture them in our models was due to the entrenchment of the Chomskyan idea of a homogeneous speech community of monolinguals, in which each speaker has equal mastery of the language.

Real linguistic communities are not homogeneous in the distribution of linguistic competence, and they are not closed to linguistic influxes from the outside (English, for instance, was subjected to a large influx of French vocabulary at several points in its evolution). Many communities are in fact bilingual or multilingual, and constructive as well as destructive interference between languages creates non-linearities that may be crucial to linguistic dynamics. Consider, for example, Creole languages. Many have evolved from the pidgins created in slave plantations, veritable "linguistic laboratories" where the language of the plantation master was stripped of its flourishes and combined with particles drawn from a variety of slave dialects.[19] It is possible that one day virtual environments will allow us to map the dynamic attractors around which these rapidly developing Creole languages crystallized, the stable states that served as stepping-stones for the "searching device" of linguistic evolution.

The discipline of sociolinguistics (associated with the work of such linguists as William Labov) has made many of the important contributions needed to purge the science of language from the classical assumptions leading to "formalism," and move it closer to true population thinking. Indeed, the central concern of sociolinguistics has been the study of stylistic variation in speech communities. This is a mechanism for generating diversity at the level of speakers, and as such it could be dismissed as being exogenous to language. Labov, however, has also discovered that some of the rules of language (he calls them "variable rules") can generate systematic, endogenous variation.[20] This provides us with one of the elements needed for our searching device.

Sociolinguists have also tackled the study of the second element: selection pressures. The latter can take a variety of forms. In small communities, where language style serves as a badge of identity, peer pressure in social networks can act as a filtering device, promoting the accumulation of those forms and structures that maintain the integrity of the local dialect. On the other hand, stigmatization of certain forms by the speakers of the standard language (particularly when reinforced by a system of compulsory education) can furnish selection pressures, leading to the elimination of local styles. Finally, once the elements of a language have been sorted out by these pressures, they may become consolidated (like a biological species) through "communicative isolation," that is, by the effects of geographical or political barriers that allow dialects to diverge from one another until mutual intelligibility is lost. Thus the elements for a dynamic view of language already exist, and yet formalism is still such a well-entrenched paradigm in linguistics that the discipline cannot currently benefit from the full potential of virtual environments. (Which does not mean, of course, that computers are not used in linguistic investigations, but this use remains analytical and top-down instead of synthetic and bottom-up.)

Just as linguistics inherited the homogeneous, closed space of classical thermodynamics, as well as its static conception of stability, so did mathematical economics. Here, too, a population of producers and consumers is assumed to be homogeneous in its distribution of rationality and of market power. That is, all agents are endowed with perfect foresight and unlimited computational skill, and no agent is supposed to exercise any kind of influence over prices. Perfect rationality and perfect competition result in a kind of society-wide computer, where prices transmit information (as well as incentives to buy or sell), and where demand instantly adjusts to supply to achieve an optimal equilibrium. But, much as sociolinguists are providing antidotes to the classical assumptions holding back their field, students of organizations and of organizational ecology are doing the same for the study of the economy.[21]

Not only are economic agents now viewed as severely limited in their computational skills, but this bounded rationality is being located in the context of the specific organizations where it operates and where it is further constrained by the daily routines that make up an "organizational memory." In other words, not only is decision making within organizations performed on the basis of adaptive beliefs and action rules (rather than optimizing rationality), but much of it is guided by routine procedures for producing objects, for hiring/firing employees, for investing in research and development, and so on. Because these procedures are imperfectly copied whenever a firm opens up a new plant, this process gives us the equivalent of variable reproduction.[22] A changing climate for investment, following the ups and downs of boom years and recessions, provides some of the selection pressures that operate on the populations of organizations. Other pressures come from other organizations, as in natural ecosystems, where other species (predators, parasites) are agents of natural selection. Giant corporations, which have control over their prices (and hence are not subject to supply/demand pressures), play the role of predators, dividing their markets along well-defined territories (market shares). The state and its bureaucratic apparatus, on the other hand, can be seen as a parasite, capturing the surpluses produced by a society through taxes, rents, and (less common today) forced labor.

As in linguistic research, computer simulation techniques have been used in economics (econometrics), but in many cases the approach has remained analytic (taking as its point of departure macroeconomic principles). However, a bottom-up approach, combining populations of organizations and nonlinear dynamics, is already making rapid progress: witness the Systems Dynamics National Model at MIT. As in the case of Artificial Life, one measure of success here is the ability of these models to synthesize emergent behavior not planned in advance by the model's designers. One dramatic example is the spontaneous emergence of cyclic equilibria in this model with a period matching that of the famous Kondratieff cycle.

That data from several economic indicators (GNP, unemployment rates, aggregate prices, interest rates), beginning in the early nineteenth century, display an unequivocal periodic motion of approximately fifty years' duration, is well-known, at least since the work of Joseph Schumpeter. Several possible mechanisms to explain this cyclic behavior have been offered since then, but none has gained complete acceptance. What matters to us here is that the MIT model endogenously generates periodic oscillation, and that this behavior emerges spontaneously from the interaction of populations of organizations, to the surprise of the designers, who were in fact unaware of the literature on Kondratieff cycles.[23]

The key ingredient that allows this and other models to generate spontaneous oscillations is that they must be nonlinear and operate far-from-equilibrium. In traditional economic models, the only dynamic processes that are included are those that keep the system near equilibrium (such as "diminishing returns" acting as negative feedback). The effects of explosive positive feedback processes (like "economies of scale") are typically minimized. But such self-reinforcing processes are what drive systems away from equilibrium, and this, together with the nonlinearities generated by imperfect competition and bounded rationality, is what generates the possibility of dynamic stabilization.[24]

In the MIT model it is precisely a positive feedback loop that pushes the system toward a bifurcation, where a point attractor suddenly becomes a cyclic one. Specifically, the sector of the economy that creates the productive machinery used by the rest of the firms (the capital goods sector) is prone to the effects of positive feedback since, whenever the demand for machines grows, this sector must order from itself. In other words, when any one firm in this sector needs to expand its capacity to meet growing demand, the machines used to create machines come from other firms in the same sector. Delays and other nonlinearities can then be amplified by this feedback loop, giving rise to stable yet periodic behavior.[25]

Tapping the potential of the "epistemological reservoir" constituted by virtual environments requires that many old philosophical doctrines be eradicated. Essentialism, reductionism, and formalism are the first ones that need to go. Our intellectual habit of thinking linearly, whereby the interaction of different causes is seen as additive—and so global properties that are more than the sum of the parts are not a possibility—also needs to be eliminated. So does our habit of thinking in terms of conservative systems, isolated from energy and matter flows from the outside. Only dissipative, nonlinear systems generate the full spectrum of dynamic forms of stabilization (attractors) and of diversification (bifurcations).

Thinking in terms of attractors and bifurcations will lead, in turn, to a radical alteration of the philosophical doctrine known as "determinism." Attractors are fully deterministic: if the dynamics of a given population are governed by an attractor, the population in question will be strongly bound to behave in a particular way. Yet this is not to go back to the clockwork determinism of classical physics. For one thing, attractors come in bunches, and so at any particular time a population that is trapped in one stable state may be pushed into another stable state by an external shock (or even by its own internal devices). In a way, this means that populations have "choices" among different "local destinies."

Moreover, certain attractors (called "strange attractors" or "deterministic chaos") bind populations to an inherently "creative" state. That is, a population whose dynamics are governed by a strange attractor is bound permanently to explore a limited set of possibilities within the space of its possible states. If a chaotic attractor is "small" relative to the size of this space, then it effectively pins down the dynamics of a system to a relatively small set of possible states, so that the resulting behavior is far from random and yet is intrinsically variable. As if this were not enough to subvert classical determinism, there are also bifurcations, critical points at which one distribution of attractors is transformed into another distribution. At the moment this transformation occurs, relatively insignificant fluctuations in the environment can have disproportionately large effects in the distribution of attractors that results. In the words of Prigogine and Stengers:

> From the physicist's point of view, this involves a distinction between states of the system in which all individual initiative is doomed to insignificance on the one hand, and on the other, bifurcation regions in which an individual, an idea, or a new behavior can upset the global state. Even in those regions, amplification obviously does not occur with just any individual, idea, or behavior, but only with those that are "dangerous"—that is, those that can exploit to their advantage the nonlinear relations guaranteeing the stability of the preceding regime. Thus we are led to conclude that *the same* nonlinearities may pro-

duce an order out of the chaos of elementary processes and still, under different circumstances, be responsible for the destruction of this same order, eventually producing a new coherence beyond another bifurcation.[26]

This new view of the nature of determinism may also have consequences in yet another area of philosophical thought: the doctrine of "free will." If the dynamic population under consideration is one whose members are human beings (a given human society), then the insignificant fluctuation that can become "dangerous" in the neighborhood of a bifurcation is indeed a human individual. Individuals would be relatively powerless to switch society from one attractor to another, except during bifurcation events, at which point the nonlinear amplification effects would seem to guarantee us a modicum of free will. If, however, the population in question is one of neurons (of which the global, emergent state is the conscious state of an individual), this would seem to subvert free will, since here a microcognitive event can determine what the new global outcome may be. Individuals would retain their freedom of action while their neural nets remain at their attractors, but not while undergoing bifurcations. Still, we could learn to take advantage of these microcognitive fluctuations, by letting go of our desire for total (rational) control over our mental processes and learning how to follow these microevents, drifting along with them while we explore a space of dynamic possibilities. If, as seems likely, our minds are partly symbolic, partly connectionist systems (so that, in fact, both branches of AI are complementary), then tracking microfluctuations may involve giving more emphasis to our pattern-recognition capabilities than to our symbolic-reasoning ones.

Overall, then, this new view of the nature of determinism seems to leave plenty of room for individual initiative even if it demands that we rethink our approach to the control of natural processes. A desire for total control via optimizing rationality would seem quite an inadequate way of dealing with dynamic processes in a nonlinear world. The analytical methods that science has so successfully deployed over the last few centuries would seem to fall short of what is needed for the task, particularly when we realize that nonlinear equations *cannot be solved analytically* (which is why scientists needed to wait until the simulation capabilities of computers allowed them to tackle nonlinear equations in a synthetic way). Indeed, we may need to learn how to become "searching devices," like the one constituted by genetic variation and natural selection. That is, biological evolution has no foresight, and it must grope in the dark, climbing from one attractor to another, from one stable engineering strategy to another. And yet it has produced the wonderfully diverse and robust ecosystems we observe today. Perhaps one day virtual environments, and the synthetic reasoning they allow to emerge, will become the tools we need to track attractors and bifurcations, in our search for a better destiny for humanity.

Notes

1   See Elliot Sober, *The Nature of Selection* (Cambridge, MA, 1987), 157–61.
2   See Steven Levy, *Artificial Life* (New York, 1992), 155–87.
3   See Richard Dawkins, *The Selfish Gene* (Oxford, 1989), 12.
4   Stuart A. Kauffman, "Adaptation on Rugged Fitness Landscapes," in *Lectures in the Sciences of Complexity*, ed. Daniel Stein (Redwood City, 1989).
5   See Cynthia Eagle Russett, *The Concept of Equilibrium in American Social Thought* (New Haven, 1968), 28–54.
6   See John Maynard Smith, *Did Darwin Get it Right?: Essays on Games, Sex, and Evolution* (New York, 1988).
7   See Ilya Prigogine and Isabelle Stengers, *Order Out of Chaos* (New York, 1984).
8   See Ian Stewart, *Does God Play Dice?: The Mathematics of Chaos* (Oxford, 1989), 95–110.
9   Christopher G. Langton, "Artificial Life," in *Proceedings of an Interdisciplinary Workshop on the Synthesis and Simulation of Living Systems*, ed. Christopher G. Langton (Redwood City, 1988), 2.
10 See Andy Clark, *Microcognition: Philosophy, Cognitive Science, and Parallel Distributed Processing* (Cambridge, MA, 1990), 61–75.
11 See J. A. Sepulchre and A. Babloyantz, "Spatio-Temporal Patterns and Network Computation," in *Self-Organization, Emergent Properties, and Learning*, ed. A. Babloyantz (New York, 1991).
12 William Bechtel and Adele Abrahamsen, *Connectionism and the Mind* (Cambridge, MA, 1991), 129.
13 Douglas R. Hofstadter, *Metamagical Themas: Questing for the Essence of Mind and Pattern* (New York, 1985), 720.
14 See James L. Gould and Carol Grant Gould, *Sexual Selection* (New York, 1989), 244–47.

15 I have outlined a theory of "stratification," in which the complementary operations of "sorting out" and "consolidation" are shown to be behind many structural forms, from sedimentary rocks to human languages, in "Non-Organic Life," in *Zone 6: Incorporations*, ed. Jonathan Crary and Sanford Kwinter (New York, 1992). See also Gilles Deleuze and Félix Guattari, "The Geology of Morals," in their *A Thousand Plateaus* (Minneapolis, 1987).

16 See John Nist, *A Structural History of English* (New York, 1966), chap. 3.

17 See Tony Crowley, *Standard English and the Politics of Language* (Urbana, 1989).

18 See Winfred P. Lehmann, "The Great Underlying Ground-Plans," in *Syntactic Typology*, ed. Winfred P. Lehmann (Sussex, 1978), 37.

19 See David Decamp, "The Study of Pidgin and Creole Languages," in *Pidginization and Creolization of Languages*, ed. Dell Hymes (Cambridge, 1971).

20 William Labov, *Sociolinguistic Patterns* (Philadelphia, 1971), 271–73.

21 See Michael T. Hannan and John Freeman, *Organizational Ecology* (Cambridge, MA, 1989).

22 See Richard R. Nelson and Sidney G. Winter, *An Evolutionary Theory of Economic Change* (Cambridge, MA, 1982), 14.

23 Jay W. Forrester, "Innovation and Economic Change," in *Long Waves in the World Economy*, ed. Christopher Freeman (London, 1983), 128.

24 See W. Brian Arthur, "Self-Reinforcing Mechanisms in Economics," in *The Economy as an Evolving Complex System*, ed. Philip W. Anderson, Kenneth J. Arrow, and Daniel Pines (Redwood City, 1988).

25 See J. D. Sterman, "Nonlinear Dynamics in the World Economy: The Economic Long Wave," in *Structure, Coherence and Chaos in Dynamical Systems*, ed. Peter L. Christiansen and R. D. Parmentier (Manchester, 1989).

26 See Prigogine and Stengers, *Order Out of Chaos*, 206. I explore the role of individuals near bifurcations (for example, the role of Napoléon in the implementation of new military tactics and strategies during the turbulent transition represented by the French Revolution) in *War in the Age of Intelligent Machines* (New York, 1991), chap. 1.

MARK PAULINE

SURVIVAL RESEARCH LABORATORIES PERFORMS IN AUSTRIA

Briefly, an SRL show consists of a set of ritualized interactions among machines, robots, special effects devices, and computers, with humans present only as operators or audience.

On 24 October 1992, SRL staged one of its machine performances at an abandoned toilet paper factory in Graz, Austria. Two weeks prior to the presentation, fifty tons of machinery and supporting equipment arrived at the site, followed by twenty-two SRL crew members. Typical of an SRL performance, this was a one-shot deal: fifty minutes of non-stop action in front of approximately three thousand people.

Aside from these basic considerations of scale and style, peculiar circumstances differentiate an SRL production from the outwardly similar technical activities undertaken by military, industrial, or scientific organizations. SRL enjoys nearly unlimited freedom to engage in both decadent technical extravagance and unapologetically acerbic social commentary. Constrained by re-

quirements of practicality, public opinion, or rationally explicable goals, other technically driven organizations nearly always exhibit dreary predictability in their products or restraint in their operations. SRL activities share their reliance on careful direction and scripting, their intentional or accidental provocation of relentless public debate, and their endless "official" explanations of events. But, for SRL, such practical considerations present only the flimsiest of barriers to unrestrained action.

Graz is located below Vienna, about twenty miles north of the border with Croatia; forty-five miles further southward, Serb and Croat forces oppose one another in the contested Banija area. Oddly enough, although this nearby conflict threatened to explode at any moment into a full-fledged regional war, it was the last topic of conversation in Austria. In honor of this aversion, and as a gratuitous provocation to Austrians (or anyone else who could ignore a war so close to their national borders), the SRL performance in Graz was titled "*The Deliberate Evolution of a War Zone*: A Parable of Spontaneous Structural Disintegration."

Implementing this theme, which was uncharacteristically specific for an SRL performance, required extraordinary measures. The first

"THE DELIBERATE EVOLUTION OF A WAR ZONE: A PARABLE OF SPONTANEOUS STRUCTURAL DISINTEGRATION".

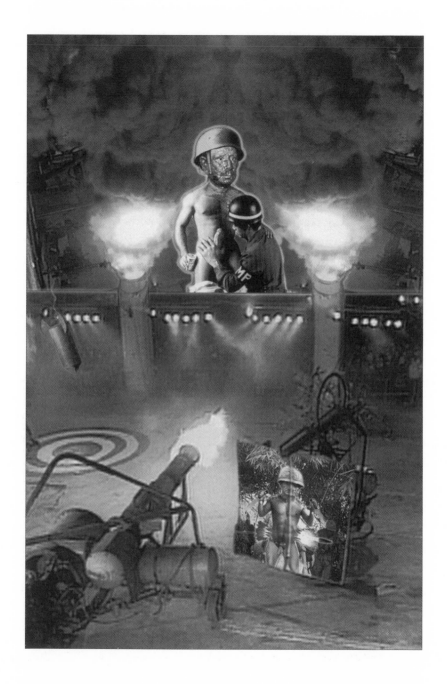

of these was bridging the credibility gap created when outsiders come in (American outsiders at that) and "tell it like it is" to the locals, who of course know the real story. Fortunately, an opportunity to accompany a filmmaker to various war zones in Croatia presented itself. Describing this experience in pre-show interviews effectively quelled doubts among the media that the performance would indeed pursue a serious investigation of the questions raised by the war.

The show's visual look and its cast of machines suggested war themes, both explicit and implicit. A very dumb bomb, rigged on a winch, slammed repeatedly at a target painted on the floor, decimating hapless machines that strayed into the area. Ten-foot-square computer-retouched photos of naked soldiers in homoerotic poses adorned some machines and the walls of the site. A mobile overhead crane, wielding an enormous steel hook, hoisted machines into the air and moved them from one contested zone to another (in a bizarre parody of similarly futile gestures by nearby U.N. forces).

Many of the machines in this show were originally developed in military research programs: A V-1 jet engine, assorted explosive devices, an electromagnetic rail gun, a tele-operated gun (that launched

---

Maschinentheater löste bei vielen Kriegsangst au{

Sogar Verteidigungsministerium wurde alarmiert: „Es fallen Bomben." ▪ VON DANIELE MARCHER

Schon Tage vorher wurde in 'den Medien über die Aufführung des Maschinentheaters in der Grazer Arlandhalle informiert, auch über die zu erwartende Lärmwelle berichtet. Trotzdem gab es während der Proben eine Beschwerdeflut der Anrainer, doch was sich während der samstägigen Aufführung abspielte, übertraf alles.

Innerhalb von zwei Stunden gingen bei der Grazer Polizei rund 400 Beschwerdeanrufe ein, 40 davon kamen gleich über den Notruf. Manche Grazer erstatteten wegen Körperverletzung Anzeige. Doch bei fast der Hälfte der Anrufer löste die Maschinentheater-Aufführung regelrechte Panik aus.

Sie berichteten den Polizisten aufgeregt von Kriegshandlungen im Norden von Graz, behaupteten voll Angst, jugoslawische Kampfflugzeuge seien in den Grazer Raum eingedrungen und würden nun im Norden Bomben abwerfen. Die Erklärung der Polizisten, 'es handle sich um eine Theateraufführung, wurde von den Anrufern als Beschwichtigung abgetan.

Doch damit nicht genug: Ein Anrainer schaltete sogar das Verteidigungsministerium ein, das sich wiederum an das Innenministerium wandte. Das Ministerium in Wien kontaktierte umgehend die Grazer Polizei.

Diese stand ohnehin mit 18 Mann bei der Arlandhalle im Einsatz — und führte dort in hundert Meter Entfernung Lärmmessungen durch. Das beachtliche Ergebnis: 108 Dezibel. Zum Vergleich: Bei einem extrem lauten, auffri-' sierten Moped mit kaputtem Auspuff muß man bei Vollgas unmittelbar danebenstehen, um die gleiche Lautstärke zu empfinden.

---

exploding projectiles), and the spinner machine (derived from a failed military experiment that was intended to develop supersonic propellers for aircraft but produced only ear-splitting noise, reminiscent of an entire squadron of bombers).

Official permits allowed virtually unlimited testing of machinery. SRL took full advantage of this opportunity in the weeks before the show, setting the surrounding community on edge. Once the show

began and the full fury of the devices was unleashed, approximately four hundred Graz residents phoned police to report that Serbian warplanes were bombing the city. Not satisfied with police assurances that an art show was the source of the disturbance, forty of these callers managed to contact the Ministry of Defense in Vienna, who ordered the Graz police to investigate. Even though they were aware of the nature of the situation, twenty police officers arrived at the site with sound-measuring equipment in time to record sound levels of 108 decibels, 100 meters from the performance.

The following day was an Austrian national holiday, which we celebrated by continuously operating the V-1 engine for about five minutes. Afterward, the police arrived and informed us that any further "testing" involving loud sounds would result in our arrests and the confiscation of our equipment.

———————

My damaged right hand enjoys a respectable notoriety. For instance, a recent article that appeared in *Time* magazine regarding the "cyberpunk" phenomenon devoted more copy to my hand than it did to SRL activities. I have weathered a variety of interesting reactions to this appendage over the years, from simple handshake-repulsion, to cultivated indifference, to ridiculous suggestions of its extraordinary abilities. Certainly, it has earned the right (by ordeal if nothing else) to at least some of this attention. To me, it remains a testament to the distinction that ought to be made between reasonable infatuation with the merely hazardous and senseless flirtation with self-destruction.

> "When an explosion blew the thumb and three fingers off his right hand, Pauline simply had his big toe grafted where his thumb had been. He can pick things up again, but now he's waiting for medical science and grafting technology to advance to the point where he can replace his jerry-built hand with one taken from a cadaver."—David Jackson/*Time*

———————

The producers in Graz provided SRL with several local technical assistants, one of whom was a young man schooled in mechanical engineering and quite skillful. He was also a reckless, hard-drinking motorcycle driver (a not unusual combination). Initially, he seemed

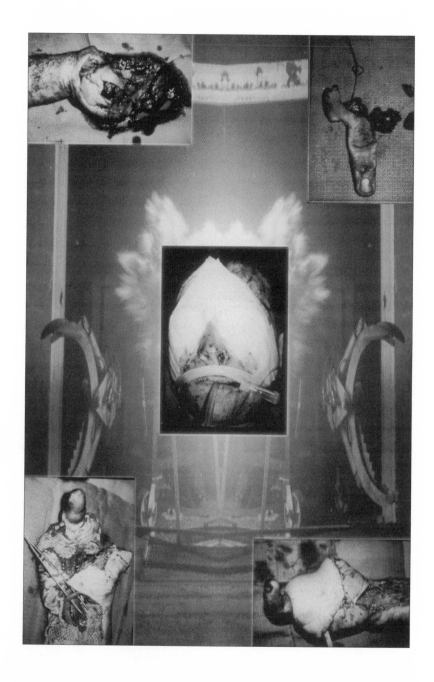

quite personable, expressing admiration for the quality of our equipment and the abilities of our crew. Then an unusual string of events began to occur.

Before leaving one night the assistant had consumed a quantity of alcohol. About an hour later he returned on foot, quite bedraggled, and announced that he had partially destroyed his motorcycle in an accident. A few days later, he and several of his cohorts boasted that they were building a large pipe bomb and were planning to detonate it in a nearby building. At this point myself and the rest of the SRL crew began to get a bit concerned and expressed our opinions to the producers and to the assistant and his friends. This did not prevent them from sneaking away and setting off the device in an adjacent building. The fact that the SRL crew was not impressed by this act only seemed to precipitate further safety indiscretions by the assistant. One day this included filling balloons with explosive gas and detonating them without warning in the work area. The next day the assistant was assigned by the festival staff to jackhammer a large concrete abutment, as a sort of punishment for arousing such a flurry of complaints the previous day. I remember passing by him as he desperately hammered away, covered with dust and looking frighteningly aggravated. About an hour later, a loud explosion occurred in the next building. The assistant emerged covered with blood, carried by his friends. At first his friends maintained that it was an accident. They claimed that the device, a very large pipe bomb, had exploded without warning after the assistant had approached it to examine the extinguished fuse. Later, we found out from others, who had watched from a safe distance, that the assistant had lit the fuse, stood directly above the bomb, and calmly waited for it to explode. The assistant survived the blast but sustained numerous injuries, including several lost teeth, the loss of sight in one eye, numerous facial gouges, and permanent powder burns. The assistant was able to attend the performance, though I did not see him there myself. When he visited the site a few days later I asked him what he thought about the show. He responded, "If you were Japanese and put on a show like that, you would have to commit hara-kiri."

GARY CHAPMAN

TAMING THE COMPUTER

In June of 1985, the United States space shuttle flew one of its first missions in support of the Pentagon's Strategic Defense Initiative, or Star Wars program. This mission involved the space shuttle's orbiting the earth on a course that passed over a mountain in Hawaii. On top of the mountain was a powerful laser aimed at the heavens. The space shuttle had a large, high-quality mirror mounted on its belly. The plan was for the laser to be fired skyward, through the atmosphere, so that laser light would hit the mirror on the underside of the shuttle and be bounced back to earth. Then scientists at a ground station would measure the distortion of the laser light as it made this traverse—distortion caused by the effects of the earth's atmosphere. This was an important experiment in the early Star Wars effort because, at the time, the Star Wars plan was based on orbiting space battle stations that would destroy their ballistic missile targets with laser weapons.

The NASA space shuttle is considered a "fly-by-wire" spacecraft, which means that it is "flown" entirely by computer programs, instead of by an onboard pilot. Nearly everything the space shuttle does on a mission is worked out in advance of its launch from Earth. The entire mission is encoded in complex computer instructions that have run to as many as 750,000 lines of "real-time" computer code.

In the June 1985 mission for the Strategic Defense Initiative, the computer programmers standardized all distances in their program in nautical miles. But they forgot to convert the height of the mountain in Hawaii, about 10,000 feet, to the nautical mile unit. Instead, they included an instruction in the computer program for the space shuttle to look for a laser on top of a mountain 10,000 *nautical miles* high.

A mountain 10,000 nautical miles high would be nearly two thousand times higher than Mount Everest, the highest peak on the planet. Unfortunately for the programmers, the fictional 10,000-mile-high mountain had a summit higher than the orbit of the space shuttle itself. So when the shuttle flew over the real mountain in Hawaii, the computers were looking for a mountain with a peak further into space. The flight computers flipped the spacecraft on its back to orient the mirror in that direction. The laser on the Hawaiian mountain fired as planned, but it hit the nonreflective top of the shuttle instead of the mirror. No light bounced back to the scientists on the ground, and the entire $15 million experiment was a failure.[1]

In the late 1960s a California ice cream store chain called Farrell's started a promotional campaign that promised a free ice cream cone for kids on their birthdays. All a child or a parent had to do was to fill out a small form indicating the child's name, address, and birth date, and either mail the form to Farrell's or deposit it in a box at one of the chain's shops. Then Farrell's sent back a small certificate entitling the child to a free ice cream cone on a day near his or her birthday.

A boy in Palo Alto, California, saw an even better deal in this offer. The birthday forms came on a small pad that was typically kept on the counter at the ice cream shop. This boy grabbed a number of these forms, and he filled out several of them with fictitious boys' names, birthdays scattered throughout the year, but all with his own address. He then received free ice cream certificates for dates well distributed in all the months of the year.

About ten years later, all the fictitious boys began receiving letters in the mail, delivered, of course, to the same address in Palo Alto. The letters were from the Selective Service Administration, which informed the fictitious young men that they were all in violation of the law requiring registration for the draft at their eighteenth birthday. When these letters were turned over to the press, Farrell's ice cream stores had to admit that they had been selling their "free birthday ice cream cone" database to the government for many years.[2]

Finally, a short but exemplary story that happened just recently. The head of the Canadian branch of the Church of England is called the "primate." This gentleman received in the mail a computerized letter of invitation asking him if he might be interested in joining his colleagues at the National Canadian Primate Research Facility! The priest replied that although he enjoys a banana now and then, he doubted that he was the sort of material they were interested in, and he added that he was in any case very busy.[3]

What do all these stories have in common, other than being amusing and involving computers? What seems common and interesting is that the mediation of the computer, in three very different scenarios, wound up producing some rather comical artificial nonsense—a 10,000-mile-high mountain, a house full of fictitious boys wanted for military service, a monkey as the head of the largest church in Canada. Extrapolating from these examples, or many similar instances, one can see that computers, as mediators of the world, have the potential to contain a kind of parallel universe of "facts" which more or less correspond to the facts of our "real" world, but occasionally and perhaps with increasing frequency the "virtual facts" produced by computer mediation are simply absurd. One might reasonably deduce from these examples that the products we get from computer instructions can range from the useful and accurate to the ludicrous and/or dangerous, with any number of degrees between the two extremes. To a large extent, it is this mirroring of the human mind's capacity for unexpected products of cogitation that makes computers so fascinating to us. What other machine is the source of such amusing faux pas when it is operating correctly?

The apparently infinite variability in the configuration of computers, the superficial ease of the machine in accomplishing tasks that are challenges for the human mind, the influence of computers on the organization of modern society—all of these things contribute to our awe over this calculating engine that we have produced and which now operates, in our midst, in such huge numbers—65 million personal computers in the United States alone. For people who are not computer experts, and even for some who are, the computer is nearly a magic box—there seems to be no clear or describable connection between the movement of fingers on a keyboard, or the sweep of a computer "mouse," and the explosion of color graphics on a screen, a burst of symphonic music that seems to come from nowhere, the flight of a space shuttle, or the lightning-speed shuffling of millions, even tens of millions, of records. An elementary schoolteacher was once overheard telling a student, with a note of exasperation, "I don't know how a computer knows how to alphabetize—it just does. That's what computers know how to do." It is easy to sympathize; even basic sorting algorithms are not very simple, and the preferred methods require some advanced mathematical skills and some real mental gymnastics. What appears on a computer's screen, or what a computer makes other machines do, very frequently looks like magic.

Computers have always had what might be called an "object location," meaning simply that the term "computer" has referred to a physical thing that most people think they are able to recognize. Computers were once huge and hot and covered with lights and tape mechanisms, and they were represented in popular movies as giant electronic brains. That image eventually gave way to the personal computer, which is now so ubiquitous that it is the standard, popular conception of what a computer looks like. Embedded microprocessors that help run everything from cars to coffee makers to airliners are even more widespread than personal computers, but they are largely invisible to the casual viewer. Many people probably have a vague idea that there is a computer under the hood of newer model auto-mobiles, and that it helps run the engine. But how the computer does this, where it is, what it looks like, and how it can malfunction are typically mysteries for most people.

Even though for any given time the computer has been attached to a widely acknowledged popular image, ranging from the giant "electronic brain" of the 1950s and 1960s to the hand-held calcula-tor of the 1970s, to the personal computer of the 1980s and 1990s, more than any other machine the computer is principally a *concept*. People seem to understand that a computer can look like a wrist-watch, an electronic circuit board, a large upholstered cylinder (as with older supercomputers), a hand-held calculator, a steel box, a keyboard and a screen, a bank teller machine, a GameBoy toy, and so on. There is even a mental identification of a computer at the sound of a voice that is unnaturally flat and monotonous. All of these very different configurations are held together under a single name by the very broad popular conception of what a computer is and does. The idea of the computer structures human behavior even in the absence of any sensory apprehension of a machine, such as when the bank tells a customer that a transaction cannot be completed because "the computer is down," or a person tosses into the trash a letter that is obviously computer-generated.

The general, popular understanding of the concept of a computer seems to be one of a machine that processes information in some fash-ion—usually only vaguely understood but generally bounded by ex-perience—and this information is used in a variety of ways that have become standard practices of modern technological society, such as money and credit transactions, record keeping, telephone commu-nication, entertainment, mass mailings, office work, manufacturing, and many other activities. People who are not computer experts tend to view computers in two contradictory ways, with roughly equal conviction, by believing that computers are always right, but also that computers frequently make spectacularly "stupid," sometimes amusing, and occasionally dangerous mistakes. In other words, for the average citizen the computer is usually an extremely "smart," almost faultless, superhuman machine, but it occasionally falls into nearly unbelievable idiocy and makes life more complicated and aggravating than it needs to be. In the popular imagination, it is impossible to tell when a useful machine is going to veer into a state of childlike literalness that will screw everything up or even endanger lives, like the computer HAL in the movie *2001: A Space Odyssey*. Practical experience has taught most computer users that there are frequent and abrupt transitions from blissful amazement over a computer's capabilities to screams of frustration over the machine's stubborn inflexibility. Nevertheless, this experience has not prevented the use of computers in systems in which the risk of failure or error is related to significant harm or even planetary catastrophe, such as in the command and control of intercontinental nuclear weapons. The public generally seems to accept the existence of a "technological imperative" that compels us to automate wherever and whenever possible.

This shallow public comprehension of computers is the result of a practical apprehension of one dimension of the technology, the "output" dimension that provides the product of computation to the computer user or someone else further along a path of utility, or which confronts citizens generally through institutions and practices reconfigured to accommodate computerization. This practical apprehension of computers is thus a process of *adjustment* to the incremental progress of the technology, with a comparatively weak feedback loop to the source of technological innovation, the computer industry and profession, despite all the noise in the trade press about competition in the free market. People choose between *features* of a hardware or software package when buying a computer product, but they rarely have much choice about the long-term implications of developments in computer technology, or the option of avoiding computers altogether. Alternatives of that sort are lost in the past, for most people. Indeed, some computer and software companies have advertised their products in commercials that stress the modern imperative of owning and using a computer, and it is common to hear the claim that computer literacy is now a "survival skill." Almost everyone who lives in modern, technological society is tightly strapped to the trajectory of a "techno-logic," which projects a historical course for society plotted along points marking marginal improvements in the features of our technological artifacts, especially computers.[4] In the future, history could conceivably be segmented not between years or major events, but between software updates and microprocessor revision numbers.

What the common, practical, public apprehension of computers leaves out is the "input" dimension of computers, or all the things that go into a computer to make it perform adequately enough to deserve its name. The "input" dimension is not limited to the computer's instructions or the data upon which those instructions work. The computer is also an artifact that displays the social history of the choices required to reach its particular point of technological sophistication—choices of convention, standardization, preferences among alternatives, flexibility, design, etc. An extremely complex nexus of technological history is embodied in even the simplest computer. There is the rich history of the computer as a machine, generically speaking. Then there is the specific history of the particular computer under observation. Each part of the computer has its own history, as complex as every other part and as the whole assembly. Then there are the histories of the standards that all computers follow. The software that the computer uses has its own history, both as a specific software product and as part of a larger class of applications or operating systems. Within each software product are routines and subroutines that also have their own histories; a word processor usually contains a sort routine, for example, but there are many different ways to sort elements in a program—why did the programmers choose one way over another way? And what is the history of "bugs," or software errors that degrade or completely obstruct the performance of the software? Finally, there is a social history attached to the data upon which software applications and operating systems perform. Take records, for example. Are they accurate? Where did they come from? What do they represent? Why would someone want to computerize them? Records have a history even after they are computerized, since records can be augmented, combined, separated, and used for some purposes many times over, even purposes remote from the original intent of the collection of information. In fact, most computer data are kept literally to record temporal events of interest to the users of the computer—each record represents a small historical story.

Looking at the "input" dimension of a computer reveals a human pageant of history that could stretch back in time indefinitely. Computers, like other machines, are material representations of a long process of innovation, error, improvement, more error, more improvement, consolidation of features, the extinction of superseded practices, intellectual breakthroughs and dead ends, and so on, all embodied in the physical object and the way we use it. What makes a computer different from other machines is that its future is not fixed in its design. The computer is the so-called universal machine, meaning that its function is dependent on the instructions it is given. A metal-cutting tool is used to cut metal, perhaps to cut some other materials, or, to be facetious about it, perhaps as a way of weighting something down to keep it pinned to the floor. That's about it, as far as the functional range of a metal-cutting tool goes; it won't be used as transportation or as a way to find out what's going on in South America. A computer, on the other hand, can be used for nearly anything. I could take the computer I'm using for writing this article and reconfigure it, if I knew how, to drive my car or give me the news from South America or fire off a missile or heat my house. Granted, the computer typically has to be attached to other devices to make its computational capabilities useful, but when it is attached to such devices it becomes the prime mover—the computer becomes whatever machine it controls. In this way the computer is a fascinatingly plastic medium for human intentions, aspirations, and, writ large, a greater and greater portion of our history, as we mediate more and more of our interactions with the world through computer technology.

This social and historical way of looking at the computer is richer and more accurate than the one-dimensional, "transactional" way of viewing computers most common among the general public. The difference between these two different ways of comprehending computers is more than just a matter of epistemological pluralism. The common one-dimensional view of computers is the product of a mystification of the technology, a mystification that masks the social, historical, and political choices that have gone into the machine's design, its instructions, the data it uses, and even the social, political, and economic environments within which the machine operates and which the computer invariably reinforces. In other words, what people usually see when they observe a computer is a machine that is processing information in some fashion, sometimes in a fascinating and even entertaining way. They are experiencing the "output" dimension quite passively. This passivity is not always effortless or entertaining. Many clerical and shop floor manufacturing workers are stressed by the computer's demands, such as in offices or plants with machine-paced work or computer monitoring, or both.

What is uncommon is for the average worker or citizen to challenge the decisions that have gone into the design of a computer system, or the intent of its instructions, or the effects of its operation. Even more uncommon are challenges to computerization in general. Automation is widely considered inevitable, by virtue of an equally inescapable logic that takes the form of whatever products are put into circulation by industry. So, for example, the computerization of automobile engines, which makes it virtually impossible for the average person to fix a car, is considered by most people a progressive technological advantage even though it strips expertise from a large portion of the population. There is rarely a moment of reflection about the intentions that led to this "progress," or the dependencies and disempowerment that it creates. Car engines will be computerized, just like everything else that can be automated, as part of the "techno-logic" of our time. This logic has only a future—it is cut off from critiques of past decisions that made it possible and gave it its specific form. This is what Marcuse meant by his phrase "one-dimensional man," and that phrase is even more appropriate in the present age, as we increasingly spend our days sitting in front of computer screens, looking at things with literally only a single dimension.[5]

─────

It is distinctly unfashionable to invoke Marx these days, but the old German devil had some insights that are still useful to us today. One of Marx's most interesting claims was that factory workers would be elevated to a new level of historical consciousness just by witnessing the productive power of machines and rationally organized labor. Trapped in "the idiocy of rural life," as Marx put it, human existence would be frozen in oppressive social relations indefinitely. In preindustrial production there was no material representation of any hope for liberation from scarcity and no concrete display of the collective power of a numerically superior underclass. But with the beginning of industrial production, the working class could easily see the productive power of labor augmented by machines. Labor power was a sensory thing in the factory, embodied in the sound of the heavy machine hammers, the power of the steam engine, and the speed of the assembly line. Moreover, in most factories, until only recently, everything was visible to the worker. He or she could simply walk around and observe the mechanical operation of the factory, with its belts, pulleys, machine tools, and human hands. There was a resemblance between the hand looms of the hearth and the big machine looms powered by steam—it made sense that someone could build those machines based on the idea of the loom that every rural woman knew so well. To put it somewhat melodramatically, history suddenly unfolded to the worker as a vision of bigger and better machines that would feed and clothe the world, and this vision, of course, contrasted with the shabby lives of the workers. This contrast between productive might and social inequality would lead, Marx claimed, to a transformation of working-class consciousness about justice and historical destiny.

Everyone knows why this didn't happen, or, if one believes it did, why it didn't lead to what Marx predicted. What is significant for us is how computers have changed the picture of industrial production upon which Marx based his claims. First, the physical operation of a manufacturing plant is no longer transparent. There are still hammers, welders, stampers, and other machines, but how they work is mostly obscured to the eye. Workers are increasingly removed from the production process and instead sit or stand at computer terminals or workstations through which they manipulate abstract symbols that *represent* the manufacturing process. The skills of the manufacturing work force are largely transferred to the software that provides the automated machines their instructions, and this software is both unavailable and incomprehensible to the average worker. The wage worker's role in the production process is narrowed to fiddling with a few numbers, controls, switches, and ranges, which are themselves increasingly abstract and remote from the actual commodity that is being produced.

This trend, what Buckminster Fuller called the "ephemeralization of work," is even more pronounced in the sectors of greatest employment growth—services and bureaucracy. In these sectors even the product itself is abstract, so that some workers, such as those in insurance claims offices or word-processing shops, never see a physical result of their work. They process a computerized form, which is an electronic, one-dimensional representation of something that is abstract to begin with, and if they turn off the power on the computer, their "work product" essentially vanishes into thin air.

Twenty-five or thirty years ago, when a car broke down, the driver got out, opened the hood, and tried to figure out what had broken and if it could be fixed. Now if a car breaks down, there is nothing to be done but to take the car to a mechanic, who will probably not actually "fix" the broken component, but replace it with a part that works. The comprehension of a physical process that is somehow disturbed, and then rectified by the application of knowledge and competent skill, is gone. The automobile is no longer a "natural" thing, that is, something that exhibits properties that can be grasped by a person with a reasonable exposure to physics, but is now a kind of "supernatural" thing, since its operation is governed by invisible changes, embodied in software, which are not only in code but probably in proprietary code. No amount of tinkering or trial and error experimentation will reveal the secrets of a Mercedes Benz 500SL, for example, which reportedly operates with no less than eighteen microprocessors—only someone with extensive and detailed training in the repair of such an automobile would even dream of trying to fix one.

The same is true of most computer-based commodities. Microwave ovens that blow a microprocessor switch are thrown into landfills, instead of being repaired, because it's more expensive to replace the switch than to buy a new oven. Personal computers that go haywire deep in their operating systems "hang" or "crash," in the terms used for such events, which means that they suddenly turn completely useless, and it is typically impossible to try to understand what the problem was and how it can be avoided in the future. For nearly all computer users, there is no thought of "fixing" a computer bug; at best the user works around it. The source code of commercial software products is always invisible to the user, and is in any case so Byzantine and arcane that only a handful of people in the world understand it thoroughly.

Natural processes, then—"first principles"—have become increasingly remote from the way most people (in industrialized societies) engage the world. In fact, nature itself has become something of a "supertechnology," in that we now cultivate and experience nature or learn handicrafts as hobbies; we have to go out of our way to come into contact with nature in its raw form, so it is transformed into a technology of aesthetics or a practical means of relaxation and stress reduction. These brief experiences are increasingly managed for us, so that even the nature that we want to get our hands on is mediated by technology in some fashion, such as the computerization of ticketing for admission to national parks.

These remarks are not a prologue to a "back to nature and simplicity" exhortation. Reversal of history to a life of insecurity, scarcity, inefficiency, discomforts, and exposure to the whims of nature is not in the cards for people in advanced industrialized societies unless some catastrophe occurs. What is important is how the weakening of our connection to the natural world narrows and constrains our abilities to determine, autonomously, the purpose of human history and the full dimension of the human character. While some technologies, and especially computers, have given a handful of people unprecedented access to an enhanced understanding of the natural world—in a formal, scientific sense—it is an unavoidable fact that related technologies have boxed far more people into a life of artificial, animated stupefaction. To these people—who are all around us every day—the modern world is not much different than a cacophonous movie full of unexpected developments. Technologies come and go, skills fall away and are replaced by adjustments to new technologies, the stores stock things that were not imaginable just a few years ago, images in entertainment media seem to be freed from any constraints of reality. Life becomes a kind of phantasmagoria of technologies and technological features. Even highly educated and technologically sophisticated people experience this to a large degree because the buzz of products and ideas demanding attention is so pressing and hectic. The clever term "time famine" has appeared recently in common usage to reflect the most pressing characteristic of modern life, despite the ubiquity of "time-saving" devices.[6]

The intensity of this phenomenon in our society has increased to the point that many people—perhaps even a vast majority—evaluate their personal status based on their participation in the life made possible by marginal technological improvements in commodities. This is more than a metric of mere consumption because what is important for the new high-tech society is not volume—that problem was solved some years ago, and now we have *too much* of everything—but instead the "quality" of a technology in terms of its features. This is a growing slavery to the gadget, and gadgets whose inner functions are incomprehensible to the slave. When Hegel included his famous "lord and bondsman" dialectic in *The Phenomenology of Mind*, he proposed a historical development, a moment of progress, however dubious, when the slave realizes that his consciousness, reflected in his transformation of the material world through labor, is really superior to the unreflected and unmoored consciousness of the master. But slavery to gadgets doesn't appear to be sufficient ground for another historical moment of dialectics. We're no longer reflected in a material world we transform in our image—the gadget doesn't reflect our nature as much as we reflect its character—and conceivably we could be enslaved to gadgets for all eternity. We're not engaged in an apparent struggle for freedom in the way that the slave struggles with the master. Slavery to gadgets is not perceived as a moral or ethical issue, the way master-slave relationships have been universally regarded since Aristotle. Most of us are not even struggling—we've been conquered already. This is the hegemony of technique or technical rationality that Ellul, Marcuse, Horkheimer, and others have explained, and from which there seem to be fewer and fewer escape routes. The friction this condition produces in our psyches is tangible in our society, which is plagued by a widespread anxiety that seems immune to the effects of social engineering or well-intended public policies of reform. The fundamental contradiction of modern life that most people now feel only subliminally is a product of the tension between the increasing "power of technology"—a source of national pride and prestige—and diminishing personal power over our collective destiny.

═══════

Is there an escape from this condition? The answer to this question has been the subject of countless books and journal articles since Weber's articulation of the "iron cage" of rationality, but nearly all of this material is unintelligible to the average reader, and, unfortunately, equally irrelevant. What has filtered through to the modern consciousness of the general public is that a rejection of technology entails a wholesale repudiation of modernity, which, on the one hand, seems as daunting a task as recovering freedom in a hyperinstrumental society, and, on the other hand, appears immediately unappealing to the vast majority of people who might consider such an option. Moreover, a retreat from modernity does nothing to salvage autonomy and self-discovery for the individual—it merely plunges its subjects into an artificial historical simulation, such as in Iran or in other antimodern, "fundamentalist" experiments, most of them horrifying.

A compromise answer to the question of how we can reconcile technology with an ethical life, and one that is most common among the actual producers of technology, is that technology is essentially "neutral," and what matters are the intentions and ethical character of the people who design technical systems or who use them. This argument produces a preoccupation with engineering and business ethics, which is typically focused on individual action, meaning that each person is exhorted to search his or her conscience about the ethical content of specific cases of technological design or use. But this approach misses several critical features of our predicament. It is incapable of assessing the impact of technology as an all-encompassing system, as a domination of technique or technical rationality. The "technology is neutral" thesis is blind to any contemplation of how profoundly our ability to think about visionary goals is atrophied by the character of contemporary technology. If we are increasingly unable to fix or even understand the things that surround us in everyday life, we are unlikely to develop self-confidence in our capacity to renew our social institutions and practices. The ethics of computer use is usually portrayed, unconsciously, as a handmaiden to what computers are used for and how they're designed; in other words, as another sort of "peripheral," as the industry calls hard disk drives, modems, and printers. "Computer ethics" is a problem-solving discourse, yet another technological fix of "externalities," when what is required is something that transcends case studies of specific ethical dilemmas and reasserts the utopian potential of human capabilities. Counseling ethical use of technology can also imply a goal of individual self-satisfaction that does little to change the order of things.[7]

Yet another answer to the question of how to escape our current difficulties within technological society is the claim that since technology is built upon the worldview of Western purposive science—in fact, technology can be described as the material and practical expression of this epistemology—we will be able to correct the full range of problems associated with technology only by replacing the assumptions of Western science with something more "humane," or something fostering harmony with the natural world, or something less reductionist—the recommended corrective features of a replacement epistemology take a variety of forms. This has been the project of people who advocate a "feminist science," for example.[8]

As intellectually interesting as this debate has been, challengers to the hegemony of the Western scientific tradition have yet to come up with a coherent description of what might replace it. The fundamental problem is of course finding epistemological ground on which to stand in order to critique Western science, independently of bias, political intentions, or irrational tendencies. In my opinion, the writers who have tackled this issue have succeeded in pointing out the many shortcomings of a science developed exclusively around instrumental reason, but they have so far failed to identify any other firm ground for planting and nourishing a fully developed epistemological alternative. This basic deficiency is compounded by the poor prospects for getting workers and citizens engaged in such an arcane and highly theoretical debate—made worse by the jargon used to launch this entire discourse—and the obscure connection of the project of a "successor science" to everyday activities, or even to a practical program for a hypothetical social movement.[9]

The question we face is relatively simple and straightforward, as well as ancient: to use a machine metaphor, what is the "button" that, when pushed, initiates an irreversible transcendence of consciousness that lifts large numbers of people to a new stage in the historical realization of freedom and human potential? First, we have to decide if such a mechanism exists—there are many people who deny its existence—and then, if the answer to that question is affirmative, we have to set about finding it. And we must be careful to avoid a crude determinism, examples of which have been so devastating in the history of this century. In fact, the metaphor of a human "switch" to be flipped on and off is not appropriate, since it is too simplistic and it implies the determinism that we should resist. Ideally, there should be a widespread and passionate desire to transcend the status quo as a product of critical reflection within individuals acting and thinking autonomously and in response to concrete conditions that constrain human and natural capacities. And this transcendence should be accessible to everyone: that is, describable in the language of the people we meet in the workplace, on the street, and in the market. What appears to make this so difficult these days is the withering of cognitive competence for critical examination, a possible extinction of common sense under the onslaught of technology's promise of ease, efficiency, productivity, and entertainment. The fact that such an extinction is so plausible intensifies the urgency of arousing a resolute defiance among our fellow citizens.

A historically reliable guide to the source of social change is, as Marx put it so well, the tension among important social and economic contradictions. The three most important enhancers of human dignity in the industrialized world were the labor movement that began in the mid-nineteenth century, the more recent civil rights movement of African Americans, and the even more recent feminist movement—each of these was built on a firm grasp of salient, contemporary contradictions. The paradoxes that were the catalysts of these historical transformations of consciousness were eventually obvious to all people with even a rudimentary moral aptitude—each movement identified a conflict between the widely held values of society and the objective conditions of large numbers of people; and each of these social movements was launched by courageous people who served as moral beacons and forerunners for others. Each of these movements took hold among sympathetic citizens when the idealism of the challengers of the status quo could be communicated in the vernacular of the day. And each struggle was marked by symbolic acts of resistance whose protagonists could have been anyone confronted with similar circumstances of indignity and emboldened with sufficient courage and indignation.

What is so far incomplete in our own age is a clear view of the significant contradictions of the "information society." There are some obvious conflicts that might reflect deep antagonisms. For example, we are witnessing a growing disparity between the passionate fascination with computer technology among a small segment of affluent young people—a phenomenon that is now loosely identifiable as a "computer culture"—and the majority of people who care little or nothing about computers, or are even hostile to the changes brought about by computer technology. It is commonplace to hear pundits in the computer industry or the computer press, or even among the general interest press, extol the wonders the future will hold because of advances in computer technology, but the computer revolution has not changed a great number of lives for the better; in fact, for an increasing number of people the current technological revolution of industry is making life worse. Automation of low- and mid-level skilled work has swept away an entire sector of the economy that once employed people without higher education, plunging many into unemployment, crime, or low-wage service jobs. International data transmission has accelerated the globalization of labor, so that workers in the United States compete with workers in Singapore, Thailand, or perhaps now Eastern Europe and the former Soviet Union. Computerization of the office has not led to the productivity explosion that has long been the core message of computer industry advertising. People in the United States are working more hours than ever before—some researchers are even starting to discover a *negative* effect of computerization on productivity. And for an immense segment of the population of workers who use computers on the job, the technology is little or no improvement on the nineteenth-century factory—airline reservation clerks, insurance claims processors, data processors, telephone operators, telemarketers, and many other workers of the information age are pushed by machine-paced work and computer surveillance, and with increasing frequency crippled by repetitive strain injuries, visual exertion, stress, or, perhaps, electromagnetic radiation. Finally, computers have inarguably increased the power of bureaucratic institutions over individual lives. The existence of a birth-to-death "data shadow" is a fact of modern life; computers store detailed information on everyone in our society, and this permanent, lifelong, and constantly refined historical record has the insidious effect of shaping individual behavior to serve the ends of intimidating bureaucracies.

As we know, this dark picture contrasts rather sharply with all the promises of a bright and better future that we hear repeatedly from computer enthusiasts. In fact, the hothouse "computer culture" that is constantly spewing new and clever ideas, jargon, styles, and mannerisms seems to take a step further away from the rest of society every day.[10] The typical meeting of computer crusaders is buzzing with talk of "virtual reality," "cyberspace," "knowbots," and a thousand other imaginative terms that have essentially no meaning in and no connection to the lives of most citizens. Zealots of the computer revolution usually explain that they are exploring the leading edge of the most significant transformation of society in our time, and that everyone else will eventually catch up as the results of technological tinkering filter down to the general public in the form of mass-produced commodities or social and economic reorganization. The exhilaration is reminiscent of the enthusiasm of early industrialists, who were never at a loss for a justification of the widespread human misery described by Dickens, Marx, Upton Sinclair, and many others. Similar to the major portion of the history of industrialism, there is an obvious disjuncture between the Panglossian pronouncements of people well rewarded or inspired by the computer revolution and the actual adjustment of society to the impact of this technology. This paradox is the embryo of a historically significant tension that could produce a crisis in legitimation for the computerized, all-pervasive, mega-state of government bureaucracies and corporate power. But so far there is no common language to identify the full dimensions of this contradiction, let alone a strategic plan for liberation from its effects. Perhaps more important, there is currently no symbolic analogue to the caricature of an oppressive, and very human, villain— the pillaging capitalist, the troglodyte racist, or the "male chauvinist pig"—that galvanized social movements in the past. There is only the "neutral" and quite inhuman computer, or technology as a total system, a way of life, and since few people can imagine life without technology, we appear to be stuck with it and all its consequences.

═══════

I began with three amusing stories about computer gaffes. What is the connection between those stories and what is becoming a jeremiad? The stories were offered as illustrations of the kind of nonsense a computer can represent, through its operation on and its presentation of "processed" information. Lots of people in our society work with computers every day—maybe even a majority of people by now— so these stories are familiar territory; they're entertaining instead of panic-inducing because they resonate with common experience. They are extreme examples of things that happen thousands of times every day.

The cognitive leap that visionary activists hope to induce in computer users and citizens generally might be launched from this apparent fallibility of computers, from the machine's capacity for absurdity. Since this feature of computers is so much a part of our daily experience, the subjective, individual, autonomous penetration of the "neutrality" of the technology is made easier. If the computer were a metaphysically "perfect" machine—admittedly an opaque concept—its grip on our consciousness would probably be difficult to break. But since we have to come to terms with the ubiquity and influence of a machine that is capable of significant folly, then we also have to deal with the questions of how and why we have endowed it with such power over our lives and our minds. This is no longer an abstract issue, or one to be pondered by "futurists," the way the question was framed in the early days of computerization. These days, we are constantly and perpetually engaged with computer technology, so that a critique of this engagement is relevant both to the average citizen and to the long-term character of historical progress.

Perhaps the first step in the development of such a critique should be a popular acknowledgment that since computers are capable of producing amusing nonsense, they are also capable of producing or representing unamusing nonsense—that is, information or interaction with the world that *should* be considered moral nonsense given a rigorous enforcement of moral principles. This latter category is probably more common than amusing computer faux pas, unfortunately. The reason that we have difficulty seeing the moral nonsense that computers can reflect is precisely because our principles have lost important powers of enforcement, principally the power of critique itself. The overt and humorous gaffes of computer operation present unambiguous inconsistencies with the familiar world, such as the 10,000-mile-high mountain or the monkey priest. The comprehension of such disparities could be extended into the moral dimension if that dimension were to become concrete enough for people to notice the absurd void between computerization and human aspirations. This is a project that should permanently accompany the incremental development of the technology.

The next step, a deeper penetration of the illusion of technological neutrality, will be to lodge firmly in the minds of people subject to technology the understanding that computers do what *people* tell them to do. As many commentators have pointed out, this is not to say that there is a locked and faultless connection between what computers do and what people *intend* for them to do—there are many ways for intentions to fail or to be distorted. The important fact is that there are people who historically precede the operation or the design of a technological system, people who bear at least some responsibility for its effects. Since for any given individual or even a group of individuals the future is not completely foreordained, and since all intentions are products of social environments as well as moral reflection, all technologies are a nexus of economic, social, and moral decisions about the shape of the future. Thus in many ways technologies are material or practical representations of human ideas about what the world should look like, and these ideas are "inherently contestable," as a phrase from social science puts it. So, while it may be difficult, and is not common at present, we should be encouraged to look at a computer, or any technology, and see *people* who have made decisions loaded with implications. And, as a corollary, these decisions should be frisked, to reveal their moral influence, by a critical and perhaps even skeptical mind.

Finally, as with the example of Hegel's slave, it would be a historical dead end to foster such inquisitiveness and then be unable to do anything with it. Once the problem is clear, the course of action should follow. As Andrew Feenberg writes in his book *The Critical Theory of Technology*,

> All modern industrialized societies stand today at the cross-roads, facing two different directions of technological development. They can either remain blocked at the level of primary instrumentalization in order to intensify the exploitation of human beings and nature, or they can take a new path in which the integrative tendencies of technology support emancipatory applications. This choice is essentially political.[11]

Political choices are decided primarily by political power, which in itself is a complex and constantly shifting blend of moral authority, persuasiveness, legitimacy, control over resources and communication, and quantities of people and money. Perhaps the best that we can say about what initiates positive political progress, given the complexity of factors, is that the historical conditions simply become "right," or that a critical individual or group is "in the right place at the right time." Nevertheless, there is an ongoing need for understanding the dynamic and strategic relationships between historical conditions and utopian possibilities, and this of course is what preoccupies most people dedicated to social change. One has to work with a faith that history can have a trajectory toward greater freedom and fulfillment, if only we set our minds upon such a goal. Then it's a matter of filling in the details, such as discovering and supporting things that people can do, on a day-to-day basis, that encourage such faith and help facilitate progress toward such a goal. Because of the hegemonic influence of technology in the contemporary world, especially computer technology, which is transforming the human world faster and more profoundly than any other technology, people with aspirations for a better future have to come to grips with the political character of computers and computerization. Within circles of political activists, this idea has not yet settled in very deeply. And this imperative is essentially invisible among the mass of people whose lives are increasingly structured by computerization. The words "politics" and "computers" are rarely uttered in the same sentence. The omnipresent talk about computers is still full of apolitical or even antipolitical hype, sometimes resembling a conspiracy of aversion. Reconstituting the content of our discussion about computers is a necessary first step, and one way to do this might be to help demystify the technology through telling stories about its fallibility, the way ancient people used to tell stories about heroes who conquered a particularly dangerous beast.

The computer is not a simplistically dangerous beast, nor is it merely an instrument of people or ideas that deserve to be challenged. Comprehensive and total rejection of computerization is not a panacea—that approach is reactionary, ahistorical, unlikely to take root in popular consciousness, and ignorant of the liberating potential of technology. The current deployment and design of computer technology are expressions of values, conscious or unconscious, intentional and unintentional. The effects of computerization can be absurd, hazardous, degrading, or merely entertaining, but they can also be inspirational, useful, educational, and potentially supportive of a democratic mastery of history. What we need is a better connection between our most worthy values and the design and use of technology. This will entail a staged process of understanding technology better than we do now, reasserting our aspirations for a better future, organizing the political power necessary for implementation of those values, and then reconfiguring technology to reflect our aspirations. It should go without saying that this process will require a sweeping redistribution of political power, as well as the development of a broad and firm self-confidence that this power can be used effectively to enrich our endowment to posterity.

Notes

1   "The Magic Mountain," *New York Times*, 25 June 1985, A25.
2   Jose L. Rodriguez, "Draft Board Buys Name List from Farrell's," *San Jose Mercury News*, 2 August 1984, 1A.
3   Contribution to comp. risks, moderated USENET bulletin board, 12 March 1992.
4   See Andrew Feenberg, *The Critical Theory of Technology* (Oxford, 1991).
5   See Herbert Marcuse, *One-Dimensional Man* (Boston, 1964).
6   See Juliet B. Schor, *The Overworked American: The Unexpected Decline of Leisure* (New York, 1993).

7   See, for example, Deborah Johnson, *Computer Ethics* (Englewood Cliffs, 1985).

8   See Sandra Harding, *The Science Question in Feminism* (Ithaca, 1986).

9   See Donna Haraway, *Primate Visions: Gender, Race and Nature in the World of Modern Science* (New York, 1989).

10 To survey the terrain of this culture, see *Mondo 2000: A User's Guide to the New Edge*, ed. Rudy Rucker, R. U. Sirius, and Queen Mu (New York, 1992), or the magazines *Mondo 2000*, *Ray-Gun*, or *Wired*.

11 Feenberg, *Critical Theory of Technology*, 195.

EMILY WHITE

GLOSSARY

ARTIFICIAL LIFE Man-made systems whose behavior mimics that of living systems. Most artificial life research to date involves computer-programmed "entities" that sleep, eat, breed, and evolve. This research attempts to produce "lifelike" behavior in aggregate populations whose evolution within virtual ecosystems can be used to study the different paths of evolution various species might have taken given different environmental variables. Artificial life also provides a new approach to problem solving, in which the programmed "entities" produce solutions to problems that cannot be predicted by programmers. They thus become to some extent autonomous and in this way share the goal of the related discipline of artificial intelligence: the living machine.

BEEPER CULTURE Where we are now, especially in big cities. Beepers, cellular phones, portable phones: there is never a time when we cannot be electronically connected to others.

CUT-UP   Inspired by painter Brion Gysin and developed by William S. Burroughs in novels such as *The Ticket That Exploded* (1962) and *Nova Express* (1964), the cut-up is a compositional (decompositional?) technique in which written texts are cut up and rearranged, yielding nonlinear, self-deconstructing narratives that reflect the collage-like nature of consciousness in the information age.

CYBERBABBLE   An ever-evolving language associated with computer use that is a rich blend of the desire to glamorize virtual interactions and the need for brevity and convenience when communicating via keyboard.

CYBERDROOLERS   People who are in love with technology and everything it can do. Synonyms include technoweenie, wirehead, and propellerhead.

DEMON   Computer programs that have been coded to lie dormant until specific events trigger them to react; devoted, for the most part, to low-level decision making and information gathering, demons both act and are acted upon.

ELECTRONIC VILLAGE   The computer network suburb (or transurb) where increasing numbers of citizens spend most of their time. Also known as "virtual community," or VC.

FTF OR F2F   Face-to-face, or when you actually meet and interact with someone in person, as opposed to connecting with him/her electronically. For antonym, see INTERACTIVE AUTISM.

FLAME BOX   Particular to the *Mondo 2000* conference on the WELL (a San Francisco-based BBS), "Flame Box!" is a "topic" set aside for verbal brawls. WELL protocol requires that users remain respectful of each other at all times, but if they can't control their tempers, the flame box is where they go to trade insults. Possibly reflecting coastal differences, the New York-based BBS MindVOX doesn't have a flame box; users seem to feel comfortable trading insults whenever and wherever they want.

FLAMING   Exchanging insults electronically.

GUIDES   Subscribers to computer networks who are given free on-line time in exchange for monitoring and sometimes censoring conversations in public user areas, or "rooms." Guides survey the public "chat" areas and decide whether the dialogue is acceptable. If they decide it isn't, they "kill" the room. Other users can tell when the guide is on the way to or in the room and often warn each other by typing phrases like "sleepy time" or "zzzzzzz," which means "tone things down until the guide leaves."

HANG   When a computer suddenly and for no discernible reason decides not to work. Also known as "crash."

INTERACTIVE AUTISM   Voice mail and telephone answering machines have created an epidemic of this phenomenon. You are interactively autistic when you call someone's machine or voice mail and know (or hope) he or she will not be there to answer; you then relate freely to a machine that is connected to the person you do not want to reach directly. In some cases you may purposely be avoiding an unpleasant interaction; in others the safety of the machine enables you to relate to the person with more freedom.

K/S OR "SLASH" STORIES   Pornographic "K/S" (short for "Kirk/ Spock") tales written by female *Star Trek* fans and published in fanzines, often featuring Kirk and Spock as lovers. Spun from the perceived homoerotic subtext in *Star Trek* narratives, slash stories are often animated by feminist impulses. Appropriated for general use, the term "slashing" may be applied to textual poaching in which tales told for mass consumption are reworked to suit subcultural needs.

MEMES   Popularized by evolutionary biologist Richard Dawkins in his book *The Selfish Gene* (1976), the term "meme" refers to a contagious information pattern that infects a culture by leaping from one host mind to another; memes operate the way viruses do. Advertising slogans, radio jingles, sound bites, and the various mantras of infectious belief systems are all memes, of one sort or another.

MUD-RAPE   A term more likely to be employed by women, MUD-rape occurs when female users are bombarded by sexist, aggressive, possibly pornographic comments from presumably male users in a MUD (multi-user domain). An analogy might be the old-fashioned telephone party line, when someone you don't know is able to pick up the phone at any time and talk offensively. Your only way to get rid of this person would be to hang up. With MUD-rape, you can log out.

PARALITERATURE   Comic books and similarly "sublegitimate" literature, such as underground 'zines (either on-line or hard copy).

RANT   On-line demagoguery in which users give themselves over to inspired hyperbole and wild, zany capitalization and punctuation.

ROOM   This architectural designation is unique to the private user network pseudonymously referred to in this special issue as Infomart USA. Subscribers to this network can log into any number of "rooms"; once inside they can converse with others on the theme of the room. Themes range from politics to pornography and are constantly changing. Variations include the *Romance Room*, where people type in their best imitations of dime-store romance novels, and "private rooms," which users create when they are attracted to each other and want more privacy for "verbal" intimacy.

SNAILMAIL   Conventional mail (U.S. Postal Service).

TECHNO-LOGIC TIME   Techno-logic time is marked not by the passage of centuries but by the birth of major new computer technologies. Thus, instead of the twentieth century, we might call ourselves the computer age, and 1993 might fall into that roughly demarcated period known as the VLSI (for "Very Large-Scale Integration" chip) era.

TELEDILDONICS   Coined by Ted Nelson and popularized by Howard Rheingold in *Virtual Reality* (1991), teledildonics is the safe sex we can look forward to in the future. Teledildonic partners don full-body suits that are either "innie" or "outie," depending on the sex of the user. These suits are hooked up to computers which in turn are hooked up to phones which in turn allow the suit-wearers to enter a computer-animated world, or virtual reality, where they then have cybersex. Studded with microvibrators, teledildonic body suits communicate sensations back and forth between partners.

TIME FAMINE   Even though we have a lot of new gadgets, we still don't have enough time, and in fact seem to have less and less of it; hence we are experiencing a famine. This is in part because of the ever-changing assault of new computer technologies, which are taking us further away from the natural world and its time cycles, and further into the technosphere, where time passes at lightning speed and is measured by digital clock displays and other mechanical reference points.

TRAIN WRECK　Users who join private computer networks can have "verbal" group sex on the computer. This is simple enough if only a few people are typing away, but gets more complicated when too many people join in. The misunderstandings and impossible couplings that often result are referred to as "train wrecks." Participants can sometimes type their way out of the wreckage, amending the narrative to accommodate inconsistencies, but if things get too confusing people usually lose interest and leave the "room."

TRANSMIGRATION　An old word used in a new way by Hans Moravec in *Mind Children* (1988) to mean the process by which the human mind would be transferred to computer software and the brain and body would be discarded. All interactions would then take place in mainframe computers (the central processing facility of, for example, a university-wide system), or, if the "consciousness" became "restless," it could download itself into a robot and explore the world at large.

INDEX

NOTES ON CONTRIBUTORS

ANNE BALSAMO teaches courses in science, technology, and culture at Georgia Institute of Technology. She is working on a book called *Technologies of the Gendered Body*, to be published by Duke University Press.

GARETH BRANWYN is the senior editor of the fringe culture 'zine *bOING-bOING*. His writing has appeared in *Mondo 2000*, *The Futurist*, *Wired*, the *Whole Earth Review*, and the *Utne Reader*. He is the cocreator and editor of *Beyond Cyberpunk*, a Mac-based electronic compendium of essays and esoterica pertaining to cyberculture.

SCOTT BUKATMAN teaches in the Department of Cinema Studies at New York University. His book, *Terminal Identity: The Virtual Subject in Postmodern Science Fiction*, was published in 1993. In his prime, he typed 70 wpm.

PAT CADIGAN has written several books besides *Synners* (1991), which won the Arthur C. Clarke Award in Great Britain, including *Mindplayers* (1989), *Fools* (1992), *Patterns*, and *Home by the Sea*.

GARY CHAPMAN is coordinator of the 21st Century Project, a national campaign to redirect government science and technology policy in the post–Cold War era. He was executive director of Computer Professionals for Social Responsibility from 1985 to 1991.

ERIK DAVIS writes regularly about television, spirituality, subcultures, music, and technology for the *Village Voice*, *Details*, *Spin*, and *Gnosis*. He has also contributed to *The Nation*, *Lingua Franca*, *Rolling Stone*, and the *LA Weekly*. He has given numerous talks on Gnosticism, Philip K. Dick, and information culture at the New York Open Center.

MANUEL DE LANDA is the author of *War in the Age of Intelligent Machines* (1991) and a film/video artist who makes a living creating 3-D computer animations for commercials and corporate presentations. His essay "Non-Organic Life" appeared in *Zone 6: Incorporations*, ed. Jonathan Crary and Sanford Kwinter (1992).

SAMUEL R. DELANY is a science fiction writer, literary critic, and Professor of Comparative Literature at the University of Massachusetts at Amherst. His many books include *Dhalgren* (1974), *The Motion of Light in Water* (his 1987 award-winning autobiography), *The Jewel-Hinged Jaw: Notes on the Language of Science Fiction* (1977), and the Nevèrÿon series (1979–87).

MARK DERY is a cultural critic whose writings on technology and fringe culture have appeared in the *New York Times*, *Rolling Stone*, *Elle*, and *Interview*. His essay "Sex Machine, Machine Sex: Mechano-Eroticism and Robo-Copulation" is reprinted in *Mondo 2000: A User's Guide to the New Edge* (1992), where Mr. Dery is described, embarrassingly enough, as "the hot new writer on the cyber scene." He is currently at work on *Cyberculture: Road Warriors, Console Cowboys and the Silicon Underground*, to be published in 1995.

JULIAN DIBBELL is a columnist for *The Village Voice*, analyzing the politics and culture born of digital technology. He has also written about popular music, cultural theory, film, science, and Carmen Miranda for the *Voice*, *Details*, the *New York Times*, *Le Monde*, *Folha de São Paulo*, and other publications.

MARC LAIDLAW is the author of the novels *Dad's Nuke* (1985), *Neon Lotus* (1988), *Kalifornia* (1993), and, forthcoming, *The 37th Mandala* and *The Orchid Eater*. His short stories have appeared in *Omni*, *New Worlds*, *Mirrorshades: The Cyberpunk Anthology*, and other collections and magazines. He has written essays for the *American Book Review*, *Review of Contemporary Fiction*, and *Science Fiction Eye*. His cartoons appear in *The Magazine of Fantasy & Science Fiction* and *bOING-bOING*. He lives in San Francisco.

MARK PAULINE is the founder and director of Survival Research Laboratories, an organization of creative technicians dedicated to redirecting the techniques, tools, and tenets of industry and science away from their typical manifestations in practicality or product. Since 1979, SRL has staged forty-five mechanized presentations in the United States and Europe. Each performance consists of a unique set of ritualized interactions among machines, robots, and special-effects devices employed in developing themes of sociopolitical satire. Humans are present only as audience members or operators.

TRICIA ROSE is a native New Yorker and is currently Assistant Professor of Africana Studies and History at New York University. She writes on black cultural theory and popular culture and is the author of *Black Noise* (1994), a book on rap music and the politics of black cultural practice.

PETER SCHWENGER teaches English at Mount St. Vincent University in Halifax, Nova Scotia. He is the author of *Phallic Critiques: Masculinity and Twentieth-Century Literature* (1984) and *Letter Bomb: Nuclear Holocaust and the Exploding Word* (1992). Currently, he is working on *The Translucency of the Page*, a book about visualization in reading.

VIVIAN SOBCHACK is Professor of Film and Television and Associate Dean of the School of Theater, Film, and Television at the University of California, Los Angeles. Her books include *Screening Space: The American Science Fiction Film* (1987) and *The Address of the Eye: A Phenomenology of Film Experience* (1992). Her articles and reviews have appeared in *Quarterly Review of Film and Video*, *Artforum International*, *camera obscura*, *Post-Script*, *Film Quarterly*, and *Representations*.

CLAUDIA SPRINGER is Associate Professor in the English Department and Film Studies Program at Rhode Island College. Currently, she is working on *The Erotic Interface: The Discourses of the Technological Body*, to be published by Princeton University Press in 1994.

GREG TATE is a staff writer for the *Village Voice*, a contributor to *Downbeat*, *Musician*, and *Spin*, and a founding member of the Black Rock Coalition. He lives and thrives in Harlem.